Margaret Murray Washington

Margaret Murray Washington
The Life and Times of a Career Clubwoman

Sheena Harris

The University of Tennessee Press / Knoxville

All images are courtesy of the Tuskegee University Archives.

Copyright © 2021 by The University of Tennessee Press / Knoxville.
All Rights Reserved. Manufactured in the United States of America.
First Edition.

LIBRARY OF CONGRESS CATALOGING-IN-PUBLICATION DATA

Names: Harris, Sheena, author.

Title: Margaret Murray Washington : the life and times of a career clubwoman / Sheena Harris.

Other titles: Life and times of a career clubwoman

Description: First edition. | Knoxville : The University of Tennessee Press, [2021] | Includes bibliographical references and index. |

Summary: "In this book, Sheena Harris contends that individual black, female leadership continues to be a blind spot in much scholarly historical literature, and Margaret Murray Washington, the third wife of Booker T. Washington, and her accomplishments have been overshadowed by the success of her husband. Harris discusses M. M. Washington's importance as an active clubwoman, educational reformer, and integralpartner to her husband and his success with the Tuskegee Institute. Harris's biography of M. M. Washington lays the groundwork for understanding the rising educated class of black women and the early civil rights movement"— Provided by publisher.

Identifiers: LCCN 2020032185 (print) | LCCN 2020032186 (ebook) | ISBN 9781621906193 (hardcover) | ISBN 9781621906209 (adobe pdf)

Subjects: LCSH: Washington, Margaret James Murray, 1865–1925. | African American women social reformers—Alabama—Tuskegee—Biography. | African American women—Societies and clubs—History—19th century. | Tuskegee Woman's Club—History. | Women—Societies and clubs—History—19th century. | Women social reformers—Alabama—Tuskegee—Biography. | African American women educators—Alabama—Tuskegee—Biography. | Women educators—Alabama—Tuskegee—Biography. | Tuskegee Institute. | Washington, Booker T., 1856–1915. | Alabama—Social conditions—19th century.

Classification: LCC E185.97.W42 H37 2021 (print) | LCC E185.97.W42 (ebook) | DDC 370.92 [B]—dc23

LC record available at https://lccn.loc.gov/2020032185
LC ebook record available at https://lccn.loc.gov/2020032186

*To my grandmother, Lena Mae Anthony Harris,
and my aunt Leila Marie Harris Chapman.
I am because you were.
Your spirits and influence live on forever.*

Contents

Acknowledgments xi

Introduction 1

Chapter One.
   Margaret Murray's Early Life 11

Chapter Two.
   A Family That Prays Together Stays Together 29

Chapter Three.
   Building an Empire through Home Economics 53

Chapter Four.
   Tuskegee Women Unite 81

Chapter Five.
   The National Shall Rise 99

Chapter Six.
   Beyond City Limits 129

Conclusion 147

Notes 155

Bibliography 191

Illustrations

Following page 72

Fannie N. Smith, Booker T. Washington's First Wife

Olivia America Davidson, Booker T. Washington's Second Wife

Margaret Murray Washington with Friends in Jackson, Mississippi, circa 1906

The Booker T. Washington Monument

Margaret Murray Washington's Workstation

Dorothy Hall

A Younger Margaret Murray draped in an Embroidered Dress

Girls Industrial Building, Dorothy Hall

The Young Washington Family, circa 1899

Earnest, Baker, Margaret, Booker, and Portia Washington

Booker, Margaret, Portia, Earnest, Baker, and Laura Murray

The Executive Council of Tuskegee Institute, circa 1906

An Older, More Experienced Margaret Murray Washington

An Aged Portrait of Margaret Murray Washington

Acknowledgments

I owe immense debts of gratitude to the many people and institutions who offered me assistance throughout this project. What follows is a modest attempt to thank graduate school advisors, colleagues, friends and family who gave advice, revisions, support, and in those lonely hours, much needed encouragement for this project and my life. A special thanks is owed to my editor at the University of Tennessee Press, Thomas Wells. Thank you for your guidance and patience toward this monograph's completion.

This book would not be possible without the archival collections held at Tuskegee University, The Library of Congress, and Fisk University. Although the bulk of Margaret Murray Washington's correspondence could be found at Tuskegee University, extensive research was also carried out in Washington, D.C.; New York City; Macon, Mississippi; Montgomery, Alabama; Memphis and Nashville, Tennessee; and Accra, Ghana. Grants from Florida Agricultural & Mechanical University, the University of Memphis, and Penn State University, provided important travel and writing support to complete this book.

I owe huge debts of gratitude to colleagues who sent materials relevant to my research, assisted with my proposal, and forced me to ask tough questions of myself and the research. Special thanks go to Ula Yvette Taylor, Tanisha Ford, Tara White, Juanita Robinson, Caroline Gebhard, and Zanice Bond. I owe special thanks to the mentorship of the former First Lady of Tuskegee University Shemeka Barnes Johnson and to Tuskegee University's first female President Dr. Lily D. McNair. Thank you for sharing your professional wisdom and resources with me. To Dr. Barbara Oguntade and Phyllis Green, your encouragement helped me to better understand my place in academia and life. To my dissertation advisor, Beverly Bond, thank you for your mentorship and guidance throughout the years. I am also appreciative of the countless professors and colleagues who encouraged me along the way and taught me the importance of telling our stories.

I extend a special thanks to the students, staff, faculty, and administration of Tuskegee University. Without their support this book would not exist. Undergraduate assistants DesTenee Green, Egypt Muhammad and Andrea Stokes, thank you for your love of black women and your commitment to put in the work to ensure that their voices are heard.

I owe a special thanks to the countless black women who have experienced Margaret with me through the years. To the many women who have served with me on panels, read drafts, offered revisions, and those who have helped me unpack the complexities of a life lived. To my dear girlfriends, I thank and love you endlessly. The courage you display in your work gives me life. Le'Trice DanYell, (hey boo), thank you for always challenging me to see history through various lenses. Kenisha Nicole, thank you for your love of truth telling and reminders to remain unapologetic. To my girls, K.T. Ewing, Kimberly Brown Pellum, Courtney Griffin, Jervette Ward-Ellis, Shirletta Kinchen, Armanthia Duncan, Christina Davis, Daleah Goodwin, and Kenisha Burke, thank you for your support throughout the years. Your love and patience helped me to see this project to its completion. A special shout out to the Association of Black Women Historians and our writing group. Thank you for the sisterhood, consistency, and safe space.

I also wish to thank those women who could not be with me while I produced this monograph, but whose contributions are reflected throughout its pages. Throughout my life they taught me what it meant to be a woman, a sister, a caretaker, an educator, and a storyteller. They include my great aunts Adella, Josephine, Corrine, Cynthia, Debra, Vivian, Mattie Mae, Ossie (Pearl), Betty, Gloria, and Ida. They also include my aunts Gail, Helen, Angelena, Vanessa, Faith, Wallena, Nicole, Sherry Pearl, Veronica, Toni, Latasha, Cantrell, Sandra, and Shawn. I especially acknowledge the spirit of my grandmother Lena Mae Anthony Harris and my auntie Leila Marie Harris Chapmen. I miss you both to life. I feel your presence daily. I am better because you lived and loved me in such a special way. To my mother, Tunita Louise, thank you for being my first teacher. Thank you for giving me an appreciation for written word and critical inquiry. To my sister, Shonobe, my brother, Kelsey, my sister-in-law, Lucy, and my play sister, Courtney

Sharisse; you are the best parts of me. Thank you for holding me down and always supporting my work. I love you. To my nephews, Kelsey, Jr., Kaleb, and Kasun, you are my light, my future, and my greatest inspirations. I love you.

I have been fortunate to have had amazingly supportive and patient friends during this process. Though they have different professions, they breathed Margaret with me and allowed me to lean on their shoulders throughout the years. Thank you Marluy Andrade, Henrietta Brown, and Cameisha Smith for always making me laugh, for the cross-mental stimulation, and for reminding me that I am more than the sum of my profession. A special thanks to my partner Kamili. Thank you for being who you are and for loving me perfectly.

This monograph is in honor of Margaret "Maggie" James Murray Washington and the countless African American women who devoted their lives to "uplifting the race" and themselves. *A Luta Continua!*

INTRODUCTION

> I believe that there are women . . . who are going to stand
> courageously for this chance, for this deal to a group of
> women who have had less than you have had . . .
>
> —Margaret Murray Washington
> (*The Negro Home*, 1920)[1]

On the crisp autumn afternoon of October 4, 1972, the once short-statured, fair-skinned, Margaret Murray Washington (1861–1925) of Tuskegee, Alabama was inducted into the Alabama Women's Hall of Fame (AWHF).[2] At first glance, the turbulent 1970s appeared to mirror American society at the turn of the century when Washington led the Black Women's Club Movement. However, nearly forty-five years after her death, the state of Alabama recognized her lifelong commitment to social justice. The installation ceremony took place at the all-girl campus of Judson College in the spacious Herrick Chapel. Among the attendees were the AWHF board members, including Minnie L. Gaston (1909–2000), a graduate of Tuskegee Institute, and wife of black business magnate Arthur George Gaston (1892–1996). As the director and founder of the Booker T. Washington Business College in Birmingham, Alabama, Minnie Gaston initiated the petition that led to Margaret Washington's selection as the first-ever inductee of African descent. Also, as a charter member of the Birmingham chapter of the National Council of Negro Women, Gaston penned a petition that made clear her own remarkable journey as a race woman would not have been possible, had it not been for the foundational groundwork laid by Margaret Murray Washington. "Mrs. Washington was 100 years ahead of her time," proclaimed Gaston. "What a pity Alabama and the nation did not see the value of her work seventy-five years ago."³

To better understand the influence of Washington, one must consider the intersectionality of race, sex, segregation, second-class citizenship, disfranchisement, along with the changing composition and influence of intragroup class relationships on late nineteenth-century African Americans. Washington is remembered as a national reformer, but her roots were deeply ingrained in the South. Born in the midst of slavery, her steadfast determination to see first-class citizenship granted to blacks drove her to transform her circumstances of birth into a life and career of service and community activism. Washington's life provides an individual lens into the internal working of the Black Women's Club Movement and illuminates the experiences of a race woman who came of age during the Jim Crow South.⁴

* * *

I first came upon Margaret Washington's story through my research of nineteenth-century black clubwomen. As a black feminist and history graduate student at Florida Agricultural and Mechanical University (FAMU), I was drawn to the complex and often underrepresented lives of black female administrators at Historically Black Colleges and Universities (HBCUs). Washington not only served as the Lady Principal at Tuskegee Institute, but she also led the Black Women's Club Movement of the late nineteenth and early twentieth centuries. I was eager to learn of the larger movement through the optic of a Southern-born black woman who was educated and who labored in the South. Washington's marital status also heightened my interest. After marrying twice widowed race leader Booker T. Washington, she joined the ranks of the new and rising black middle-class.

Researching her life, I was curious to learn how she fit into this complex society and maintained her sense of personal identity, separate from the movement and her husband. I also wondered if she ever imagined her life apart from these public obligations. She often referred to herself as Mrs. Booker T. Washington, and exclusively used this title after her husband's death in 1915. A woman of her time, this practice allowed her entrance into spaces that the patriarchal system denied most women. She undoubtedly used this singular access to advance the race and move her black body throughout a nation that sought to destroy her humanity. Washington toiled in the trenches of Alabama, befriending such women as Cornelia Bowen, Mary Church Terrell, and Mary McLeod Bethune, who have been written about extensively by scholars such as Joan Quigley, Ashley Robertson, and Gwendolyn Boyd.⁵

This earlier generation of women lived in a world very different than the one we currently occupy. Yet, in their own right they were feminists, even if they did not call themselves as such. These circumstances piqued my interest in understanding the events of Washington's life, and her story of defeat and triumph.

I refer to Margaret Washington as Washington throughout the text, except in instances when it is unclear whether I am referring to Booker or Margaret. In those cases, I use Margaret Washington. During her early years I use Maggie, a name used by her family, close friends, and Booker. For her later years, primarily after the death of her husband, I use Mrs. Booker T. Washington and Washington interchangeably.

* * *

This is the first biography of Margaret Murray Washington. Outside of the occasional mentions when discussing club work or Booker T. Washington, there is not a single monograph on her life. More specifically, scholars Jacqueline Anne Rouse and Linda Rochell Lane have written brilliant works on Washington. In Rouse's 1996 article "Out of the Shadow of Tuskegee," she positioned Washington as a leader who stood independent of her husband Booker T. Washington. Historian Linda Rochell Lane in 2001 adds an invaluable compilation of Washington's primary documents in *A Documentary of Mrs. Booker T. Washington*. These studies help us to better understand the need for a complete biography on her legacy. To be sure, the life of Washington is an American saga and broadens our understanding of race in America, higher education, black organizations and the larger Civil Rights Movement.⁶

Drawing upon black feminist theoretical frameworks and performance theory this book analyzes Washington's transgressive behavior, particularly with regard to her public activism, which helped construct her personified, gendered identity. At first glance, Washington's public life consumed her private affairs. However, through a rereading of personal letters and diaries, her most intimate self is revealed. Washington

Introduction

led a rather conservative life, using the tools of positive propaganda to help reshape her own narrative, often sharing just enough to give the illusion of transparency. Similar to other race women, she carried the burden of leadership in silence, oftentimes in direct contradiction to her own needs and desires as a woman.[7]

Befitting the spouse of a race leader, most of Washington's social reforms fit into the Tuskegee model of industrial education and self-help. Yet, the public knows very little about the woman behind the man and Institute. For many black feminist historians, a lack of traditional resources has made it difficult to resurrect and retell the important histories of both familiar and obscure black women. In the case of prominent black male leaders, too often the historical impact their wives had on their philosophy of activism is diminished, as was the case with Amy Jacques Garvey. However, her story of black nationalism and Pan-Africanism was contextualized by historian Ula Yvette Taylor. Through a close reading of Amy Garvey's diaries and personal papers, Taylor told the broader story of Marcus Garvey and Garveyism.[8] What I find particularly engaging and which forms a crucial component of this work, are the ways in which Washington and other black women publicly engaged in this performance of secrecy, and yet worked publicly to broaden our understanding of the intersectionality of what it meant to be black, a woman, a southerner, a wife, a leader, and a caregiver, in an often violent and deadly society.[9]

In the midst of protecting her personal space, Margaret Washington used her platform of leadership to extend the efforts and agenda of Booker T. Washington onto females and children of the race. She expanded the Girls' curriculum at the Institute, organized Tuskegee's local women, introduced Mothers' Meetings into her community, and worked with clubwomen across the nation. Washington embodied service leadership and empowered generations of women to do the same.

Margaret "Maggie" James Murray was born at the onset of the American Civil War, on Saturday, March 9, 1861 in Macon, Mississippi. Her mother, Lucy Murray, was enslaved, and her white Irish father, James Murray, worked the railroads. Despite her mixed parentage, Maggie was born enslaved and her formative years were marked by extreme violence, poverty, and she used education as a means to escape these depredations.[10]

Macon, Mississippi and its imprint on her future philosophies of respectability cannot be underestimated. Throughout the South, many formerly enslaved blacks saw positive propaganda through literacy as proof to the progress the race had made. Education served as a public testament of their rights to citizenship. At the time of her birth, less than four years had passed since the Supreme Court decision in the Dred Scott case legalized the race's exclusion from first-class citizenship—an exclusion that became synonymous with blackness. It is no wonder that Washington became a stark proponent of creating a positive persona through the tenets of respectability politics. The legacy of the Dred Scott ruling seemed only to extend to the 1896 *Plessy v. Ferguson* decision, which deemed blacks separate and unequal.[11]

The consequences of this new social order proved dire for many African Americans. As a black woman living during the nadir, Lucy Murray understood the limitations that quasi-freedom placed on black bodies. In addition to the legal restrictions, Lucy Murray also had little power to exert her full humanity or femininity due to the racial hierarchy, toxic masculinity, and overt poverty, all of which in turn added to her declining health. Yet, her intuitive foresight laid an important foundation for Washington's activism, as she believed in her ability to exercise power through education. Immediately following emancipation, Lucy Murray ensured her daughters were educated. She used her limited power to provide a better future for her offspring, a privilege not afforded to her mother and countless other black mothers during slavery. However, despite her efforts, her children and other blacks of this generation faced numerous challenges to their freedom.

The burden of poverty in Mississippi during Reconstruction was debilitating. We learn that a Quaker brother and sister, the Saunders, informally adopted Maggie at the age of seven. While a resident in their home she practiced a strict moral code, strong work ethic, and upheld values of thrift. Her exposure to these principals influenced her move to Nashville, Tennessee, where she began her lifelong career as a journalist, orator, educator, and clubwoman.

In 1881 Washington enrolled as a part-time student in Fisk University's preparatory school. She commonly worked in the homes of faculty and staff, forming important relationships while also offsetting the cost of tuition. During her eight years at Fisk she befriended fellow classmate William Edward Burghardt Du Bois. The two worked together as investigative journalists and editors for the school's newspaper, the *Fisk Herald*. This experience helped to frame Washington's ideas about race politics and the myriad avenues of education. Working with the school paper thrust her into the community as she visited and reported on the progress of local black schools. In retrospect, her time at Fisk provided a more nuanced perspective of gender and class responsibilities to the race. It served as a crucial learning center for how she saw her role in race progress and influenced the campaigns she endorsed throughout her career.

Washington graduated from Fisk University in 1889 and joined the staff at Tuskegee Normal and Industrial Institute in Tuskegee, Alabama as an English Instructor. Her stature on campus soon mushroomed as she transitioned from teaching to the position of Lady Principal.

Margaret's rising influence impacted her personal life. Soon after arriving to the campus, she began a public relationship with Booker. As the founding Principal of Tuskegee Institute, it was well-known that he was a potential suitor, following the death of his second wife, Olivia America Davidson. Olivia died shortly after giving birth to their second son, Ernest. Booker's first wife Fannie Smith, also deceased, had given birth to their only daughter, Portia. In less than three years at the Institute, Margaret and Booker married. Their union was one of service to the greater community. In 1895 Booker gave his famous "cast down your bucket" speech at the Cotton States and International Exposition in Atlanta. He urged both races to work together towards a common good. Following the 1895 death of abolitionist Fredrick Douglass, Booker became the new leader of the race. This placed his marriage to Margaret at the forefront of the larger movement of racial equality. An investigation into their partnership helps to unravel who Margaret Washington became as a woman, a wife, a clubwoman, an educator, and a member of a new middle class. The new black elite helped to lay important foundations and perspectives within which Washington and other clubwomen of the nineteenth century saw themselves. Their membership allowed them to check the proverbial boxes of respectability and social acceptability. In essence, the class status afforded her the privilege of reflection.

As an adult, well into her thirties, Washington used lessons from her youth to guide her future aspirations. She often talked about her mother's insistence on education, her Quaker upbringing, her college education at Fisk University, and her early work in the community. In addition, her marriage to a recognized leader and involvement with black women leaders in the North and South helped to reinforce Washington's status within the nation and among the black elite. However, her social class did little to mute the violent society in which many blacks found themselves at the turn of the century.

The impact of racial uplift on black women's public and private lives cannot be overestimated. Race leaders lacked the social, political, and economic means to change the dominant ideologies of white America. This forced them to create alternative images in order to combat vicious attacks against their womanhood and humanity. The advancement of the race depended on it. This psychological form of protection has been documented by psychologists and historians alike. Black feminist historian Darlene Clarke Hine refers to this practice as dissemblance: "the behavior and attitudes of black women that created the appearance of openness and disclosure but actually shielded the truth of their inner lives and selves from the oppressors," and arguably the race.[12] Washington and other intellectual elites worked against the system that attempted to define them solely on their race and sex, in effect creating spaces that protected their womanhood.

Washington's activism in the pursuit of racial and economic uplift, and cutting-edge educational philosophies at HBCUs during the Progressive Era, were important to her identity. Historian Audrey Thomas McCluskey reminds us of the long history of black female educators laboring in the Jim Crow South to form HBCUs, such as Lucy Laney's Haines Institute, Mary McLeod Bethune and the Daytona Educational and Industrial Training School for Negro Girls, and Charlotte Hawkins Brown's Memorial Palmer Institute. These HBCU administrators were collectively committed to education as a means to full citizenship rights, similar to the efforts being carried out by Margaret Washington at Tuskegee Institute. Studies also highlight the transitions made by model schools, initially part of the normal school curriculum, in their evolution into HBCUs. Stressing the importance of experimental learning at these educational centers, Washington saw her work in the community as an extension of her work on campus.[13]

Thus, Washington's intellectual and professional work reveals the extent to which black women were deeply influential in the betterment of their community and education of the race. Her life provides a lens into the internal workings of the black elite, while also demonstrating the woman's sphere. This study broadens our understanding of race and education in America, revealing how far we have come in terms of race and gender while also challenging us to incorporate the experiences of marginalized groups in the narrative of American history.

Washington's social work also provides insight into her deep-seated belief that education started in the home. Due to poverty in her formative years and her mother's insistence that her daughters become educated, Washington better understood the significance of the professionalization of domesticity. She created advanced curricular programs to meet the needs of her students and community. She knew that in order to be useful citizens, the race needed to understand English and thrift, math and gardening, politics and good nutrition. The development of the nation depended on stable homes and the implementation of women's clubs. She challenged the ways in which curriculum was approached in the twentieth century, laboring in both the classroom and community. Whether she served as president or participated in other positions within the Black Women's Club Movement, her expertise and influence were often solicited and emulated.[14]

Her work with the local chapter of Mothers' Meetings in Tuskegee, Alabama, and the creation of the Tuskegee Woman's Club (TWC) are arguably the foundations of her professional career. She used her experience in Tuskegee to expand the Tuskegee Machine through local partnerships. With the collaboration of local Tuskegee women like Cornelia Bowen, Bess Bolden Walcott, and Josephine Washington, the clubwomen created the Mt. Meigs Reformatory for Boys, placed bibles in prisons, championed health awareness throughout the South, and established a Red Cross chapter in Tuskegee, among other initiatives. The TWC alone qualified Washington as an intellectual force and community builder. Deplorable conditions in Alabama made it essential for Washington to prioritize the black home. Waiting for the state to honor its post-Reconstruction promises proved all too daunting. Washington's instrumental role in the Tuskegee Machine fills a long-existing gap about her life, especially her work with the Tuskegee Woman's Club. Through her leadership we learn of the intersectionality of education and home life as measures blacks could implement to advance their own plight within a racist society.

By the turn of the century, the Tuskegee Machine had a lasting impact on women of the race. Washington worked on local, national, and international platforms to garner support for her educational campaigns, as well as to chastise the race for behaviors she deemed uncivilized, all the while promoting ideas of race progress. The TWC critically reshapes our understanding of Washington's achievements. She was a stern disciplinarian and a frequently called-upon mentor and organizer. She redefined club work and female activism through her influence on the campus of Tuskegee. Within the community, she ensured the women were themselves educated in all matters concerning the race.

There has not been extensive research on her life as it pertains to her presidency of the first national organization of black clubwomen, the National Federation of Colored Women's Clubs, which Washington co-founded in 1895. A number of sources have been written that include information about black Women's Clubs, particularly the NACW. However, none have placed Washington's work with this organization at the center of their research. Margaret Washington, like other clubwomen, had the obligation to create sustainable institutions in the midst of hostility and rejection from white society at large and black men who opposed female leadership. However, because of her astute political savvy, she was elected chairwoman, vice-president, and, eventually the fifth president of the NACW. Under that umbrella, Washington formed such groups as the Alabama Federation of Colored Women's Clubs in 1898 and the Southern Federation of Colored Women's Clubs in 1899. Her efforts within the NACW solidified her position as a national leader.

In reflecting on Washington's foresight, clubwoman Addie W. Hunton, in "The Southern Federation of Colored Women" published in the *Voice of the Negro* in 1905, stated that Washington had a wider opportunity to study the state of the black community and that people considered her "a pioneer in club work among colored women."[15] Washington used the platform of club work to help advance the position of the race.

Paying homage to her journalistic work with the *Fisk Herald*, Washington helped create the official publication of the NACW, *The National Notes*. As editor of the *Notes*, Washington encouraged women to create local clubs of their own. Despite her expertise, she still faced challenges from within. A few clubwomen found her oversight to be too overbearing and mirrored the control her husband had over the race. Washington also faced stiff opposition to the editing and printing of the *National Notes* at Tuskegee Institute. Numerous attempts were made by clubwomen such as Ida B. Wells-Barnett to relocate the *Notes*. Despite the protest, Washington managed to keep the organization's official organ until 1922.

Washington's international influence and her ideas of Pan-Africanism were only heightened after the 1915 death of her husband.

Introduction

With the onset of America's involvement in World War I, black soldiers were in direct contact with cultures from around the world. Fully aware of these changes taking place among military men, Washington believed female students were equally deserving of a global education as well. She wanted girls to be informed in all matters of society. She promoted ideas of a New Negro woman: a race woman who may not have had the experience of physical travel, but who was well versed in world affairs and in her responsibility to uplift the race. This mission became further realized through her club work. Washington created the International Council of Women of the Darker Races (ICWDR) in 1922, to continue her efforts of community improvement. The organization laid an important context to international partnerships, and the development of Washington's perspective on issues of race and racism across the globe. Through the ICWDR, she established an agenda that promoted the education of African Americans the world over.

* * *

This political and intellectual biography of Margaret "Maggie" James Murray Washington not only restores her to the history of HBCU administrators and club women, but also illuminates the interconnections among movements that stood against racial and gender opposition. Rereading her life and work reminds us of the possibilities for alliances that remain implicit in resistance to all forms of oppression, and of the centrality of the Black Women's Club Movement's intersectional praxis to effect social and political change. Washington was an intellectual force, and although overlooked as the wife of a race leader, her life and reform work undoubtedly represent the efforts of one of the most influential clubwomen of the Progressive Era, through her husband and in her own right.

Chapter One

Margaret Murray's Early Life

> In every home there must be a father and a mother, and the children in that home must be taught respect . . .
>
> —Margaret Murray Washington
> (*The Negro Home*, 1920)[1]

Margaret Murray Washington's path to service leadership had an aura of predetermination. Born into the system of American slavery, her mother's intuitive foresight laid an essential foundation for her activism. As a black female, Margaret had very little identifiable power. Like most other blacks during the eras of Reconstruction and Jim Crow, she needed to believe in her ability to exercise power through education. Especially in an era where the perception of personal power was the only real privilege afforded to many black southerners. During her formative years the strong influence of her mother, her adoptive family ties, her southern schooling, and her education at Fisk University provided an important context to Margaret Washington's performance of respectability, experimental approaches to education, and her emphasis on collaborations as political organizing groups.

Washington was born Margaret "Maggie" James Murray on Saturday, March 9, 1861 in Macon, Mississippi, only four days after President Abraham Lincoln promised not to interfere with the system of American Slavery. She was the child of an enslaved domestic servant, Lucy Murray, and an Irish railroad worker father, James Murray. The Murray family had at least one other child at the time of Maggie's birth, despite the fact she recounted conflicting stories throughout her adult life.[2]

Both her parents were transplants to Mississippi prior to the start of the Civil War. They were not legally married, but her mother and father experienced much of the violence and discrimination that plagued residents. This trauma had a tremendous impact on her upbringing. The system of American slavery provided a significant context for Southerners, and the war only aided in spreading the flames of discontent and uncertainty. Maggie's family was more than likely uprooted and in serious doubt about how the chaos would impact their lives. While she was still very young, she found herself in the center of the Civil War and at the dawn of emancipation and Reconstruction.

Accounts from a formerly enslaved female, Dora Franks, on a Mississippi plantation, reveal how she overheard rumors of a pending Northern victory. "De firs' thing dat I 'member hearin' 'bout de war was when Marse [Master] George come in de house an' tell miss Emmaline . . . " recalled Dora. "He feared all de slaves 'ud be took away . . . from dat minute I started prayin' for freedom. All de res' o' de women done de same."[3] Claims of freedom also brought with them the fear of violence. In fact, by 1865 South Carolina and Mississippi had implemented numerous severe statutes known as black codes. In the absence of slavery, these codes sought to control blacks economically and socially. Emancipated blacks, notably children, would be at the center of the South's labor dilemma for generations. Maggie's mother, despite her limited power, would ensure that her children, her daughters in particular, escaped the postwar fate of millions of blacks who were forced into the system of sharecropping, as divisions of labor became tied directly to education.

During her youth, racial discrimination was so prevalent in Mississippi that Jim Crow legislation and black codes became completely unnecessary. Vigilante violence ran rampant. Although Mississippi claimed that it had some prominent African American political officials like John R. Lynch, Blanche K. Bruce and Hiram Revels, it was clear that black Mississippians knew just how far they could go before whites perceived them as a threat. Blacks and whites performed under specific racial codes. It is important to understand the political and social environment that Margaret Washington endured in order to fully grasp the stern educator she became. She lived under a system of segregation and inequality that saw many of the hopes and dreams of blacks shattered due to the state's denial of first-class citizenship rights and limited access to an education. As Margaret learned during Reconstruction, whites would stop at nothing to reestablish their positions. Along with separating the races, many whites resorted to a continued tradition of domestic terror.[4]

According to Maggie, her father, James Murray, immigrated to the United States from Ireland. Prior to her birth, scores of Irish men and women migrated from Ireland when they experienced the potato famine of 1845–49 that caused mass unemployment and claimed nearly a million lives. Based on the U.S. Census Bureau records it is possible that James Murray was a railroad worker, since the Murrays lived in close proximity to the "railroad yard workers' boardinghouse in Macon," and that he died while fighting in the Civil War.[5]

The relationship between Maggie's mother and father is unclear. All southern states had laws making interracial marriage a criminal offense. Although, it is possible that her parents lived together unwed. Still, they would have experienced a harsh backlash from whites arguing against the courtship, based on ideas of morality.[6] According to journalist Stephan Talty "There was a core of prejudice distinguished from one end of the country to the other: if laws varied, social sentiment was overwhelmingly negative. There was a feeling that the union was literally against nature, as God had made blacks a separate and unequal race."[7]

Furthermore, the relationship of the Irish towards blacks was not a positive one, since both groups had to prove their Americanness. During the 1840s Irish immigrants were not even considered white, therefore, a union with an African American did not directly challenge conventional notions of respectability. According to legal scholar Christian G. Amito, in many regards "these relationships were not [even] considered interracial."[8]

It is also important to mention that Lucy may have had little means to actually give consent or non-consent to their union, even after the period of legalized slavery. As a black woman, Lucy's body did not always belong to her. She would have had little power to exert her femininity due to the racial order, toxic masculinity, and overt poverty. These influences had a conscious and subconscious impact on Maggie's later views of power and respectability. Not only were interracial relationships confusing, but issues of class further complicated the matter. Following emancipation, poverty had debilitating consequences within the black community, which in turn affected their psyche, diets, living conditions and health. This destitution was exacerbated by an inadequate health care system. All of which impacted Washington, her career choices, and her later connection to residents in the Black Belt districts.

Little is known of Maggie's maternal family lineage. According to

Washington, "My grandmother had thirteen sons and daughters, every one of whom lived to rear large families." It is likely that most, if not all, of these children were born enslaved. Her mother, Lucy Murray was born enslaved in Georgia. She worked as a washerwoman when Maggie was a child. Margaret recounts her mother as resourceful and hardworking. It was common practice for black women, in the wake of emancipation, to work outside the household. A migrant to Chicago later told an interviewer that, in Mississippi:[9] "A [black] woman was not permitted to remain at home if she felt like it. If she was found at home some of the white people would come to ask why she was not in the field and tell her she had better get to the field or else abide by the consequences."[10]

The same migrant worker went on to say that "any of the white people could send for any Negro woman to come and do the family washing at .75 cents to $1.00."[11] Since Washington's mother was only twenty-six at her birth, as the mother of two toddlers, she more than likely took in laundry. Following emancipation, freedwomen, who did not work in the fields, frequently found work as washerwomen and maids, backbreaking labor that gave them more autonomy and leisure to rear their children. Yet, job availability in the urban south for a black woman was scarce.[12]

By 1870 Maggie had four other siblings, the eldest being ten-year-old Laura Murray. However, accounts from those closest to Washington at Tuskegee Institute varied. Jennie Moton, a friend and subsequent First Lady at Tuskegee Institute, wrote in the *Tuskegee Messenger*, after the death of Margaret Washington that "there were five children in the family of which she was the third." Another account from Booker T. Washington's private secretary, Emmett Scott, reveals "when she grew old enough to count she found herself one of a family of ten, and, like nearly all children of Negro parentage at that time, very poor."[13]

Margaret Washington herself claimed "my mother had ten [children], most of whom have lived long enough, but they have no children." Whether poverty caused high mortality rates in her family remains unclear. The 1880 Census records show that Maggie was the second child after Laura and seven-year old Willis was the third. These combined sources suggest that Maggie had a minimum of four other siblings. Family in the black community was not always nuclear. Concepts of family were even more complicated in the aftermath of slavery, as multiple families coalesced and formed one unit.[14]

The youngest sibling, Joseph, had the surname Cotton. By 1880 he would have been ten years old but was no longer listed as living in the household. There are many possible explanations as to why Joseph was not recorded. He could have been indentured or even have died from the effects of poverty and poor nutrition. There is no doubt that poverty affected Maggie and her family in many ways. The likelihood of her having a total of nine other siblings, several deceased in childhood, is credible, given the era's high infant mortality rates.[15]

The life expectancy of black men and women was thirty-three years. If a woman survived into her twenties, she could expect to see at least one of her children die before reaching their tenth birthday. Women who outlived their husbands or partners, as did Maggie's mother, had to deal with the combined effects of a poorly funded healthcare system and marginal survival on meager earnings, making it next to impossible to sustain a family without the financial support of a spouse. There is also a probability that Joseph Cotton was either informally adopted, a neighbor, distant relative, or orphan.[16]

The work and home-life of southern black women were equally unclear. By 1880, Maggie's mother had moved to District 31, nearly sixteen districts from the location of Margaret's birth, and married a black brick mason by the name of Henry Brown. Her occupational status changed as well. She no longer listed herself as a washerwoman, instead documenting her employment as "keepinghouse." This minor change in occupation that Lucy presumably gave to a white enumerator spoke volumes to the way she self-identified, signifying a rare form of autonomy afforded to poor black southern women: the ability to be ambiguous. There is much in a name. Similar to the ways formerly enslaved blacks renamed themselves after emancipation, many reclassified their trades. As with her neighbor Georgiana Clarke, the occupation of "housekeeping" entailed wage-earning duties as well as childrearing. This could include working in the homes of whites as maids, nannies, washerwomen, and garden laborers for meager wages. This context better explains the mental psyche of Washington and the possible presence of her mother in the home, as opposed to arduous labor under the heat of a blazing sun. Housekeeping may have provided Lucy with a greater exposure to access for her children and their education.[17]

We can only speculate about details surrounding the informal adoption of Maggie. In 1858 at the age of seven, Maggie moved in with the Saunderses, a Quaker family who lived in close proximity to her home.[18] Emmett J. Scott gave a brief history of the Saunders. He claimed they came to the South in 1864 and were more than eager to help the freedmen get an education after the war. According to Scott, Maggie's first documented memories as a child were of her father's death, which prompted her to move with the Saunders at the age of seven, never to live at home again. The 1880 Census, however, lists Murray as still living within the home of her mother, Lucy, which is unlikely. By 1880 she was nineteen years old, living in Nashville, Tennessee and only a year away from entering Fisk University. She moved to Nashville with the help of the Saunders. Quakers were a religious body that formed private communities. They regularly debated effective ways to abolish persistent injustices—including, prior to the Civil War, slavery. The religious Society of Friends, as Quakers were frequently called, also formed or joined manumission and colonization societies before the Civil War, petitioned Congress on behalf of enslaved blacks, and opened schools for African Americans. Quakers routinely adopted black children and taught them their religious doctrines.[19] There are no documents to explain if Murray and her older sister were the only siblings to live with the Quakers, whether she actually lived in their household, or in a facility resembling a foster home or shelter.[20]

Much of what Murray learned to appreciate about her youth came directly from her mother's sacrifices towards her family's survival.[21] Despite her limited resources, Maggie's mother was steadfast in ensuring her children received an education. Perhaps her mother approached education in a way similar to that of other southern mothers. For example, Civil Rights leader Fannie Lou Hamer remembered her mother's insistence on learning to read because "when you read, you know—and you can help yourself and others."[22] In her adult years, Murray recalled that her younger brother, Tommy, was also sent away to school, despite the fact that her mother continued to include him on her 1880 census as living in the household. It is highly probable that all of her siblings had some form of schooling that included expenses for room and boarding at young ages.[23]

Early accounts of Margaret Murray's home structure somewhat contradict where dates and events are concerned. However, they help to establish a more in-depth picture of how she formalized concepts of family and home life. And while she was born into a world she did not choose, her path to community-building through the black home and education was formed by her mother and the Saunders, at a very crucial juncture in her overall development.

The privilege of memory is often forgotten. As an adult, Murray gave conflicting accounts of her youth. This was not uncommon The traumatic psychological pain of slavery impacted the daily lives of freedmen. Many former bondsmen either erased or rewrote their past due to the pain involved in remembering—both their own and that of their ancestors. Fear and trauma were often passed down from generation to generation, never resolved. Her turbulent beginnings socialized Maggie into the culture of black southern womanhood. They contained invaluable lessons and a painful truth that she, nor her mother could afford to forget: the freedom of the race would not be given—they would have to fight for it. Margaret Washington came to view education as the great equalizer for her race and her gender.[24]

As Murray would discover, freedom was both political and performative. The pursuit of an education became an important crossroad throughout Maggie's youth. Surrounded by the constant reminders of sharecropping and exploitation of black bodies, she became cognizant of the restricted freedom associated with emancipation. From an early age, she understood that blacks were forced to prove their humanity to an unrelenting class of whites. Like most blacks during this time, she labored under ideas of respectability and the belief that equality would be granted, once the race proved they were ready for freedom and first-class citizenship rights through the performance of respectability.

The Saunders helped to shape Maggie's character, providing an escape, albeit temporary, from the forces of overt poverty and terrorism by whites. Despite opposition from white demagogues, such as the burning of schools and unwillingness to fund education, black and white teachers from the North and South, missionary organizations, churches, and schools worked to provide educational opportunities for blacks. While the diligence of northern missionaries was honorable in the climate of the times, scholars such as Mary Frances Berry caution against giving total praise to northern reformers who, in many instances, came to the south with their own racial prejudices. Although they opposed slavery, freedom was not synonymous with equality. Berry goes on to note, "the education they [blacks] received was also problematic because of the skepticism of some northern teachers about the ability of their charges and the cultural differences between teachers and students." Despite these challenges, blacks who received lessons from northern white missionaries fared better than those who, due to rigorous working conditions, were unable to attend school.[25]

Maggie's experience was unique among southern black children born into servitude, for it carried an air of privilege not afforded to many African Americans, especially black girls. Although born in a small shack, she did not have to work in the fields. Instead, she spent her days in her studies as she learned to read and write at an early age. This did not, however, shield her completely from the disparaged condition of her race. As a pre-teen, she bore witness to turmoil, apprehension and increased forms of violence, as many of the gains made by blacks during Reconstruction in Mississippi were reversed. The privilege of mobility provides another important context. In addition to her mother's direct influence on her ideas about family and community responsibility, her development as a leader was further formed after her move to Nashville, Tennessee.[26]

When Murray arrived in Nashville she saw the contrast from her hometown of Macon, Mississippi. Nashville in 1860, on the eve of the Civil War, had a population of 16,988, and of that number nearly 4,000 were African Americans. Nashville housed a substantial number of progressive blacks as well as a sizable Quaker community. Murray likely lived with or near Quakers. Since the Quakers were strong proponents of education, her assimilation into this community could have been a driving force for her later enrollment into the elite Fisk University.[27]

As in other southern states, blacks in Tennessee hungered for the opportunity to become literate. In 1860 nearly ninety percent of the South's adult population, and almost all of its black population, was illiterate. Many formerly enslaved African Americans felt that with education the racial stigma of inferiority would dissipate, and they could assert their equality.[28] Congress created the Freedmen's Bureau during Reconstruction, which sought to help newly freed black men and women as well as displaced whites. According to historian George Bentley "some of the proponents of the Freedmen's Bureau were motivated by an idealistic desire to help the newly freed slaves, while others thought of the Bureau primarily as a tool for exploiting that part of the country where the freedmen lived . . . both groups succeeded." Union General Oliver Otis Howard headed the Bureau from its beginning in 1865, and also co-founded Howard University in the nation's capital, Washington, D.C.[29]

Nashville was successful in its efforts to solicit funds from northern philanthropists for educational endeavors. A number of schools were created in Nashville during the post-Civil War era. In 1864 the American Baptist Church founded Roger Williams College. Similar schools were created that dedicated themselves to the education of formerly enslaved blacks: Central Tennessee College (1866), Fisk University (1866), and Meharry Medical College (1876), the first medical school for blacks in the south. African Americans also made countless efforts to build and sustain their own institutions of learning. After slavery, for instance, blacks started schools in vacant buildings and homes while literate blacks served as teachers. When a student completed a course, they moved up in ranks and instructed other pupils, just as Murray would do. Yet, these educational gains were gradual.[30]

* * *

Coming of age in Mississippi formed an important context for Murray's future philosophies on racial uplift. She soon experienced how her mother's early insistence on education opened doors that illiteracy had closed. In like manner, her move to Nashville, Tennessee at the age of fourteen aided in her initial transition from a youth to a blossoming educator. According to Murray, she excelled in her studies and left a positive impression on adults with whom she interacted at school. Within a few months of her arrival in Nashville they asked her to teach. Dressed in her finest attire, Maggie more than likely took her teacher's exam at the newly built, red-brick Brown County Courthouse, which opened its doors in 1875 in the center of Nashville. She passed the exam and became a certified teacher. It is unclear where she taught during her early years in Nashville, although it is unlikely that she taught in the city's public school system, given that no black teachers were represented among its seventy teachers in 1875. It is probable, however, that after passing her exam she joined other blacks in temporary school buildings and taught basic lessons in reading and writing.[31]

Now a Quaker in beliefs, Murray benefitted from the resources of that society. She also benefitted from the institutions in the black community, including Fisk University. A great deal of the credit for creating the institution is attributed to three northern teachers who moved south to educate African Americans: John Ogden, Edward P. Smith, and Erastus M. Cravath. John Ogden served as a lieutenant in the Second Wisconsin Calvary during the Civil War. Largely due to his experiences as the Principal of Minnesota State Normal School, he was appointed Superintendent of Education for the Freedmen's Bureau in

Tennessee, headquartered in Nashville.[32] Erastus M. Cravath served as a Chaplain in the 101st Regiment of Ohio Volunteers, and later accepted a position in the American Missionary Association (AMA).[33] Edward P. Smith was the final member of this trio. In 1863, Smith assumed the job of District Secretary of the Middle West Department of the AMA in Cincinnati. Smith and Cravath were directed by the association to establish a school for newly freed blacks. After an evaluation of the city, they concluded that Nashville would be the logical place for a school that extended beyond primary education. Nearly twenty years later their partnership influenced the life and trajectory of Maggie Murray.[34]

Owing to its sizable population, Nashville had the potential to service both the Border States and the deep South. John Ogden, the Bureau Superintendent at the time, agreed to financially support the new school that would become Fisk. With the added assistance of General Clinton B. Fisk, Assistant Commissioner for the Freedmen's Bureau of Tennessee, they secured abandoned hospital buildings for the school. At the start of the spring semester on January 9, 1866, the Fisk Free Colored School (now Fisk University) opened its doors as a designated high school. Maggie was just five years old.[35]

White backlash against black progress abounded supreme. Even though Tennessee was the only state in the South prior to the Civil War that did not legally prohibit reading and writing among enslaved blacks, whites in the state were not strong proponents of black education following emancipation. The new institution's founders were careful to avoid antagonizing locals with black education. Few whites supported black schools. They refused to rent or sell land to blacks for such purposes or provide housing for teachers of such institutions.[36]

As an educator, Maggie saw firsthand the resentment from whites at all levels of black advancement. White locals constantly threatened black establishments in Tennessee. For example, in 1866 Memphis experienced a race riot where forty-six blacks were killed. Ninety-one black homes, twelve black schools, and four black churches were subsequently burned to the ground. Furthermore, at least five black women testified to being raped during the riot, after having their possessions taken. The events in Memphis did not occur in isolation. Blacks were victimized across the nation throughout the late nineteenth century. Despite the risk of bodily harm, hundreds of students enrolled at Fisk. Its mere presence symbolized the possibility of something different for the race. When the doors of Fisk opened in 1866, that also opened the realm of choice for blacks to decide the type of education they would receive. By the time of Margaret Murray's enrollment, Fisk offered traditional academic courses in liberal arts and industrial training alike. Historian Joe Richardson credits Fisk for being a strong proponent of industrial education. Fisk's early administration, however, believed that blacks should have access to all levels of education, including courses in elementary education, industrial training, professional advancement, classical arts, and other subjects. In an 1889 editorial, the editors of the *Fisk Herald* declared that Fisk: "Believes in industrial education, but chooses to leave that work to other institutions which have that as an end. It wishes such schools, Hampton, Tugaloo, and kindred institutions the highest success, but its end is always and persistently higher education."[37]

In most instances, blacks were only permitted to preach or teach, leaving little room for mechanical or classical advancement. However, Margaret Murray and others came to realize that industrial education gave way to mechanical advancement and liberal arts training led to classical education, thereby minimizing the gap created by limitations.[38]

Financial insecurities left many blacks in the trenches, regarding higher education, as Fisk and other institutions struggled to keep their doors open. By 1871 Fisk experienced financial hardship that could have possibly led to its demise. George L. White, a teacher of music at the school, and later the Treasurer, placed the choir—the Jubilee Singers—on display, to bring white financial support to the institution. This initiative went so well that he took the singers into other venues that drew international attention to the school.[39]

Margaret Murray observed the positive transformation of the institution. This influenced her decision in 1881, at the age of twenty, to enroll at Fisk University's preparatory school as a part-time student (or a half-rater, as it was also called). Erastus Cravath served as the president during her college years.[40] Prior to Murray's enrollment, in 1876 Fisk had no college graduates and only two the following year. Along with inadequate finances, this may have been the reason she waited six years to enroll in college. Nonetheless, the school saw gradual improvements as years passed. By 1883, two years after her enrollment, there were thirty-three regular college students, and forty-eight students enrolled in college preparatory classes. These numbers continued to increase following Margaret Murray's 1889 graduation.[41]

While a student at Fisk, she worked in the homes of faculty members and taught preparatory classes in Nashville during summer months, to help fund her education. She also conducted field work. In June of 1886 she wrote to the editors of the *Fisk Herald* concerning her tours of schools and churches throughout the south. She spent two weeks in Jackson, Tennessee, roughly 130 miles from Nashville. This visit proved to be one of many. According to Murray, "about three years ago I visited Jackson and I can say with honesty that during three years, there has been a decided improvement in school facilities for the colored people." To help garner support from sympathetic readers and philanthropist, she also documented the dire need for greater collaborations and financial support. "The present system was inaugurated about seven years ago, and Mr. A. R. Merry of the class of '79 was appointed principal . . . [However] as yet, there is no convenient building but it is hoped and expected that there would be one soon." The school in mention was the South Jackson School for Colored Students started by Fisk University graduate Austin Raymond Merry. The school later became Merry High School.[42]

Faculty members at Fisk, as with other newly-founded black institutions, were predominantly white. Murray developed lasting relationships with black and white educators throughout her entire life. These collaborations, in her mind, created greater opportunities for the race. While still a student, she spent at least one summer in Pontotoc, Mississippi, where on the "13th of June [she along with other teachers] opened [a] school with 21 pupils," according to an 1887 letter she wrote to the *Fisk Herald*. The teachers were both black and white educators. Some elite blacks felt that a racially mixed faculty board created a more nuanced learning experience. Murray believed that when more whites worked alongside blacks as equals, the more difficult it would be for them to deny blacks their humanity and pursuit of first-class citizenship rights.[43]

Mary Church Terrell, a clubwoman from Memphis, Tennessee, echoed Margaret Murray's sentiments. In her autobiography, Terrell described the benefits of attending Oberlin high school and making friends with a white girl. She expressed the positive implications this relationship had on the race. According to Terrell, through an interracial learning environment, her white friend "would know that there are many such 'exceptions,' and she could never place such a low estimate upon the mental and moral qualities of the whole race as she would if she did not know from personal experience the desirable qualities of head and heart which at least one representative of the race possessed."[44]

* * *

Similar to her experience in Mississippi, Margaret Murray remained relatively poor and without many resources. Despite rampant poverty among southerners, Emmett Scott noted that those who did not have to work their way through school typically looked down on those who did. According to historian Joe Richardson, during winter months, some students were "forced to miss school because it was too cold to walk barefoot."[45] Murray's financial situation remained challenged throughout her college career. She also suffered from fragile health, stemming from her childhood. Margaret Murray was no anomaly, however, as many students suffered from poor health caused in part by overwork, poor food and substandard living conditions. In desperate situations some students subsisted on Nashville's soup-house which served cornbread and soup, as their only meal.[46]

Margaret Murray and other students endured undesirable conditions in their pursuit of a college degree. Despite these financial hardships, Fisk provided educational opportunities abroad which in turn impacted their teaching philosophies. Graduates of the University were sent to East Africa in 1883. The school maintained an interest in Africa and included African history and culture in its curriculum. Margaret Murray's presence at Fisk in the midst of this period of heightened concentration on Africa undoubtedly nurtured her later interests in African and African American history. This international focus also provided an important context to the possibilities that travel, both domestic and international, could provide for the complete development of the race. Of course, it would be many years before Murray's platform of travel abroad to help in the uplift of her black sisters would be fully realized.[47]

During her years at Fisk Margaret Murray developed lasting friendships. She worked closely with future race leader William Edward Burghardt Du Bois. Du Bois was born in 1868 in Great Barrington, Massachusetts. His mother worked as a maid and his father was a barber who left the struggling family when William was still very young. Great Barrington provided a unique setting for Du Bois. He grew up in a relatively tolerant community. After his mother died in 1884, the sixteen-year-old Du Bois was the first black to graduate from his high school. His move to Nashville proved to be a watershed moment in his life. In the south he experienced the brutal realities Jim Crow and racial discrimination had on the race. These lessons left a lasting imprint on his future politics of race and American slavery.[48]

Du Bois spent three years in the south before completing studies at Fisk University. Upon graduation he studied abroad in Berlin and afterward became the first black graduate to earn a Ph.D. from Harvard University. Du Bois went on to be a professor of history, sociology, and economics at Atlanta University, and one of the greatest sociologists of the twentieth century. In addition, after starting the Niagara Movement in 1905, he served as a founding member of the National Association for the Advancement of Colored People (NAACP) in 1909. Fisk classmates Du Bois and Margaret Murray would remain close friends until her death in 1925, despite the tumultuous relationship he would eventually have with her future husband.[49]

While a student at Fisk, Du Bois co-founded the school's newspaper, the *Fisk Herald*. Created and edited by students, the *Herald* suggested that the advancement of the race was the responsibility of the best of the race, which comprised around ten percent of black Americans. Du Bois asserted that the students at Fisk were all part of the Talented Tenth—a concept originating with Henry L. Morehouse, but for which Du Bois became a leading advocate. Margaret Murray joined the *Herald* staff after her fifth year at the University in 1886 and remained on the board until her graduation in 1889. Editorials were also written by non-students including future clubwoman Ida B. Wells. Throughout the paper, Murray and others documented the progress of the race. Although she appreciated collaborations by both races, she also highlighted that blacks were creating and maintaining schools of their own. In one issue she recalled visiting Jackson, Tennessee, about 130 miles west of Nashville. She most likely visited the Colored Methodist Episcopal High School, founded in 1882, which later became Lane College. Murray rejoiced in their progress as she wrote in the *Herald* that "the school [was] conducted entirely by the colored people," and their advancement "moved steadily on."[50]

The 1880s proved to be an important decade for black progress. As a journalist, and blossoming orator, Murray helped to document the advancement of the race and engaged in important dialogue about the future of black Americans. Discussions of the Great Race Problem saturated the minds of rising black intellectuals. Many were proponents of integration, some felt the race would only be able to grow and thrive in an all-black nurturing environment, then there were others who wanted the freedom to choose. Many whites, however, gravely contested the mixing of the race in all things public or private. Surely Murray, whose father was white, saw the contradiction in segregationist culture known as Jim Crow. Historian Neil McMillen referred to this as "Jim Crow's most vexatious problem": the absurdity that integration would instigate unprecedented race mixing. However contradictory, this ideology became typical of American whites.[51]

Margaret Murray and other associate editors of the *Fisk Herald* wrote of political and cultural developments, particularly in the South. In an 1889 article, the same year that Murray graduated, the editor of the *Herald* refuted the existence of a "New South," asserting that it still carried the same old prejudices and customs as the Old South. "A NEW SOUTH with old ideas, old customs, old prejudices and a desire for old conditions with respect to a certain class of its populace, is one of the inexplicable problems of the age," reported the editor. Within this article the column editors challenged prevailing notions that the South had abandoned its old plantation culture and gravitated more towards industrialized forms of production. The *Herald* editors wrote: "In our opinion there can be no New South without a complete reformation." These conversations were vital to the development of Margaret Murray as a social activist, journalist, orator, and educator.[52]

Like her experience in Macon, Mississippi, with the unrest caused by war displacement and uncertainty, the inner transformations taking place with Murray at Fisk University gave voice to inequalities and hardships she saw as normal occurrences among blacks. Still, the line between idealism and practice can sometimes be blurred. The extent to which a college or a college newspaper influences a person cannot be easily measured, but Margaret Murray, who would become one of the leading advocates of industrial and experimental education, clearly absorbed the elitist atmosphere that the *Herald* promoted. Although Fisk University students endorsed Morehouse's idea of the Talented Tenth throughout the newspaper, they assumed that people understood the information in different ways. This became evident when graduates of Fisk went to work in liberal arts and industrial education settings alike.

Outside of the increasing popularity of industrial schools, job scarcity was an apparent concern for educated blacks, as it became more common for blacks with classical educations to seek jobs at industrial institutions. In later years, Du Bois sought employment at Tuskegee Institute, asserting that he could bring to the industrial school his education from Fisk and Harvard, and his expertise in German, philosophy, natural science, and history. In like manner, Margaret Murray took courses in Latin, Greek, philosophy, science and literature, specializing in Shakespeare and Hawthorne. In many ways, race men and women brought a sense of prestige and caliber to industrial settings. It is also important to mention that the realm of opportunity for black intellectuals was extremely limited. Many blacks were forced to accept jobs and positions after graduation for which they were over-qualified, due to white supremacy and employment restrictions. The racism behind these measures was apparent. Thus, HBCUs and black communities proved crucial not only for the intellectual spaces they provided for students, but also for professional development of HBCU faculty, and safety afforded to blacks within a community. Such experiences were important for black leaders. The HBCU culture remained deeply ingrained in Margaret Murray as she transitioned through various phases of her life.[53]

Booker T. Washington, founding Principal of Tuskegee Normal and Industrial Institute since 1881, and Margaret Murray's future husband, visited Fisk during her 1889 graduation. The commencement program lasted for seven days, from June 6–12. During the second day of programming Murray was prominently featured, as she served as the president of the Young Ladies Lyceum, founded in 1882. The lyceum programming occurred on the evening of Thursday, June 7, 1889, and included topics on domesticity, fashion, and the penal system. According to scholar Paula J. Giddings "the 1880s saw the growth of black lyceums and literary societies across the country . . . [it] typically provided a forum for debates, readings, musical selections, and recitations in which instructors and other members of the community attended."[54]

It is unclear if Booker T. Washington participated in this event, however, he did take part in the graduating exercises of the college department on June 12th. He was seated at Murray's table. That day, Margaret James Murray, at the age of twenty-eight, along with one other female student, Emma Jane Terry, graduated from Fisk University with honors. Booker was not the keynote speaker for her commencement, though he did give a "happy after dinner speech," as the *Herald* declared. Murray, who described by others as attractive and bright, approached Washington and inquired about an English instructor position at Tuskegee Institute. News had circulated on campus that Booker Washington had designs to recruit some of the Fisk graduates for work at the Normal School in Tuskegee. While many classmates knew that Murray had already accepted a teaching position at Prairie View Normal and Industrial College in Texas, they did not know she had an earnest desire to join the staff at Tuskegee Institute.[55]

As early as March of 1889, nearly three months before her commencement, William Jenkins of Nashville wrote to Booker on Margaret's behalf, suggesting "I think you would do well to have her [Murray] among your corps of teachers next winter." Washington had received the letter and requested Murray secure a recommendation from Fisk's First Lady and Principal. It took two months for Margaret Murray to respond. In her reply which was still a month before her graduation, she declared, "I heard of Mrs. Washington's illness and so have retained the recommendation until now . . . I shall be very glad if you can give me work." Perhaps Murray did not want to disturb Washington with matters of employment in light of his second wife's fading health. However, the seating arrangements at her commencement provided her a perfect opportunity to boldly approach him and explain why she had delayed her initial response.[56]

Tuskegee Normal and Industrial Institute had gained high regard by the time of Margaret Murray's graduation in 1889. From its humble beginnings in 1881, it had grown into a leading institute for teacher and industrial training. Booker Washington was known to hire graduates of his alma mater, Hampton Institute. Because the success of the Tuskegee school depended a great deal on his faculty, he was very calculated in his attempts to hire teachers who held ideals similar to his about morality and racial uplift. One of his most important early hires and co-founders of Tuskegee Institute was his second wife, Hampton-trained Olivia America Davidson Washington, whose philanthropic connections were vital to the school's early survival.

Olivia Davidson and Booker Washington married in 1886; however, she died only a month prior to Fisk's 1889 commencement ceremony. Her death left Washington with two young boys, one of whom was barely three months old, and Portia, his daughter by his first wife Fannie Smith Washington, to rear. Margaret Murray may have read about Olivia D. Washington's death in the local newspapers. Although it was his first time actually meeting Murray, Washington had heard of her academic standing from William Jenkins months before her graduation.

It is also highly probable that with the recent death of his second wife, and the near-closing of the school, he had a heightened need for qualified assistance at the Institute. Olivia Davidson Washington's role at Tuskegee had been essential to the structure of the school. Her death left him with the burden of soliciting support for Tuskegee, and in need of a female instructor. Despite the circumstances that may have delayed their communications, upon this initial meeting Booker offered Margaret a position at Tuskegee as an English instructor.

Consequently, Margaret James Murray joined the staff at Tuskegee, shook off the visible layers of poverty, and walked into her destiny as the leading woman of Tuskegee's black elite. Although her childhood was filled with death, poverty and fragile health, Murray used the teachings of her mother and her experiences at Fisk to form her voice, and assist her transition into higher education, administration, and leadership. Most important, during the next phase of her life Murray developed the foundations of a strong, healthy, and safe home life.[57]

Chapter Two

A Family That Prays Together Stays Together

> There are a great many important subjects to which I might call your attention, but the time is too short, and I am going straight to the question, which, above all others, appeals to me—'The Negro Home,' the Negro home life.
>
> —Margaret Murray Washington
> (*The Negro Home*, 1920)[1]

On July 29, 1895, Boston clubwoman Josephine St. Pierre Ruffin called the first-ever national conference of black women to order. Forty-two African American women's clubs from fourteen states convened at the brick Berkeley Hall in Boston, Massachusetts. Margaret Washington's convention speech would be the capstone of a three-year-long series of events that had propelled her into the national spotlight. Her club work and marriage to race leader Booker T. Washington placed her amidst a class of elites that prior years in slavery and poverty had denied her. Newfound privilege allowed her to nurture her own aristocratic identity in ways that the broader black society could not. Through her own family, Margaret Washington reinforced the values of respectability such as thrift, hard work, self-respect, and religious convictions. The black home became the center of her outreach and helped to elevate the image of black Americans and alleviate allegations of black women's immorality. She challenged African American women to build their own communities, stock their own libraries, and educate themselves in all matters of black life, starting with the home. Washington understood the impact that seemingly inconsequential family accomplishments had on society's acceptance of African Americans as elites, leaders, and deserving recipients of full-citizenship rights.[2]

The city of Tuskegee was founded in the early 1830s, and by the time of Margaret Murray's birth in 1861, it had become a thriving market town for its white residents. Yet, remnants of the Civil War left Tuskegee a shell of its former self, leaving ample room for expansion and improvements. By 1881 the city had about twenty-five hundred inhabitants, several schools for white youth, and the recently established Mount Zion school for black students of all ages.[3]

Despite its display of black progress, Tuskegee was not immune to the backlash and resentment of local whites, especial in regard to education. By 1880 Alabama's legislature authorized the creation of a Normal School for blacks, which they initially intended to be run by a white principal. The mere presence of an all-black school with an all-black staff generated distress among Tuskegee's white residents. Many felt that education encouraged black crime, reduced agricultural labor, and fostered the illusion of equality. Most southerners were unprepared to accept black education, particularly when a vast majority of whites remained illiterate.[4]

Undaunted by this backlash, African Americans held firm to the belief that access to an education signified both the spatial and figurative freedom that emancipation promised. Due to their limited access to public education, especially in the Black Belt, it became imperative for blacks to create institutions that catered to their unique educational needs, in the belly of white resistance. A number of black institutions sprang up in the aftermath of Reconstruction. Historically Black Colleges and Universities (HBCUs), were a unique brand of schooling specifically created to train men and women with the skillsets needed to advance the race.[5]

In 1881 former slave owner George Washington Campbell and formerly enslaved Lewis Adams founded a school for the traing of black teachers in Tuskegee, Alabama. After soliciting the help of General Samuel Chapman Armstrong of Hampton Institute, they appointed Booker Taliaferro Washington the founding principal. He arrived at Tuskegee Normal in June of 1881. The school officially opened its doors on July 4th. Nearly ten days after opening, Washington assessed: "I find Tuskegee a beautiful little town, with high and healthy location. It is a town such as one rarely sees in the South. Its quiet shady streets and tasteful, rich dwellings remind one of a New England village."[6] Amid these clams of natural beauty, Tuskegee flourished as an incubator of black racial uplift and a model of progress that would be adopted across the nation and abroad.

Born into slavery on a tobacco plantation on April 5, 1856, Booker Washington seemed an unlikely candidate to lead the school and garner a national following that would change the nation. After emancipation, Booker and his family moved to West Virginia to be with Washington Ferguson, his mother's husband and father of his younger sister Amanda. Shortly after their move, Booker worked in the dreadful dungeons of West Virginia's coal mines. "I do not believe that one ever experiences anywhere else such darkness as he does in a coal mine," he later wrote. This darkness would heighten his hunger and drive for mental stimulation.[7]

Washington eventually enrolled at Hampton Normal and Industrial Institute in Virginia and graduated with honors in 1875. Four years later he entered Wayland Seminary in Washington, D.C., and upon graduation joined the staff at Hampton Institute. While at Hampton, Armstrong asked him to head a school in Tuskegee. Booker Washington accepted the offer and became the founding principal of Tuskegee Normal School for Colored Teachers.[8]

Ambitious in his endeavors, Booker Washington used the Hampton model of industrial training to advance the meaning and popularity of elitism, and the possibilities of black economic success. During the first seven years of the Institute, he supported the ideals he learned at Hampton, which provided blacks with lessons in industrial skills, mathematics, the English language, history, and biology. There cannot be equality, Booker Washington declared, "until there is industrial independence." The focus on industrial education as a path to racial uplift became an important vehicle for new black elite leaders, as it provided a tangible escape from white resistance and refocused on black progress. Margaret Murray completed her education from Fisk at the height of these new and invigorating ideals on black progress.[9]

Following her graduation, in the summer of 1889, Margaret Murray made the nearly-300-mile journey from Nashville, Tennessee to Tuskegee, Alabama. Her move marked an extension of her professional career, her passage into marriage and motherhood, and her transition from part-time student and teacher to full-time administrator and community leader in Tuskegee, Alabama.

By 1890 Tuskegee Institute became synonymous with industrial education. As a new faculty member, Margaret remained objective about the evolving educational platform associated with black progress. While adopting many elite pedagogical techniques, she continuously sought to expand its realms of inclusion. She frequently experimented with new approaches to education that improved the lives of her students, farmers and domestic laborers. Despite the overwhelming fascination middle-class blacks associated with a liberal arts education, during her initial years at Tuskegee she espoused the belief that "scientific cooking, dressmaking, and agriculture are subjects that should be in all of our schools" and taught to all girls, giving them a greater appreciation for their domestic responsibilities.[10]

As a Fisk graduate, however, Margaret Murray engaged with faculty who strongly supported the notion that industrial education was not sufficient to liberate blacks. While it was understood that not all blacks would be teachers, lawyers, and doctors, the contrary views elite-thinking blacks held to industrial training within the black community signified barriers that they had created as a means to separate themselves from the masses. Despite the growing unwillingness to choose industrial training over liberal arts, students at Fisk were fully aware of their commitment to the larger community. They were also cognizant that their intellectual pursuits did not always represent that of the broader black community. These challenges followed Margaret Murray to Alabama. By the age of twenty-eight, she began to use her position at Tuskegee to expand the realms of industry to include an appreciation for the arts and domesticity. Her timing proved impeccable and fit within the larger community's discussions of black life and social equality. As a relatively young, attractive and educated woman, she used her poise and intimate understanding of challenges that plagued the community to propel her leadership.[11]

Margaret Murray's mixed parentage may have influenced her reception amongst blacks, just as her southern background helped her to connect with residents in the Black Belt. Education, sex, and race were not only intertwined, but as the analytical framework espoused by Kimberlé Crenshaw suggests, the intersectionality of race, gender, and class are important factors in better understanding challenges black women faced in their racial uplift philosophies. This perspective also sheds light on the internal struggles race women endured. In many regards, black female leaders had limited realms in which to exert their spheres of influence. The new elite provided an important platform for Margaret Murray, and her skin color, whether she admitted it or not, impacted this ideological transformation.[12]

Scholars have recently compared the new black elites of the late nineteenth century to old black elites of the antebellum period. Following emancipation, the old guards, as the old black elites were called, placed very little emphasis on wealth. Although many of them were wealthy overall, ancestry and family lineage took precedence, which helped safeguard their ranks as formerly enslaved blacks began to obtain wealth through various business ventures. After Reconstruction, however, many believed that these identifiable characteristics were not enough to distinguish elites from the masses because of the inaccessible occupational pool, and limitations placed on education. In many instances, adopting the behavior of respectability politics, coupled with positive attitudes towards the system of capitalism, were used as determinant class identifiers.[13]

It is unclear at what point Margaret Murray fully realized the interconnectedness of race and class. While new elites placed less emphasis on skin color, this did not exempt them from the pitfalls of color bias.[14] Florence Ledyard Cross Kitchelt, a white graduate of Wells College and head social worker at the Little Italy House in Brooklyn, gave a description of Washington. In her 1901 journal, she declared that "Mrs. Washington is lighter than he [Booker T. Washington] and has beautiful features, arched brows, blue eyes, a Grecian nose, and a poise of the head like a Gibson girl. Her hands are white as mine and beautifully shaped."[15] The description of her skin color in comparison to her husband, who was also of mixed parentage, illustrates the variations in skin color that existed even within mulatto circles. Whether these perceptions led to better treatment is difficult to measure.[16]

After joining the staff as an English instructor, Margaret Murray soon realized that her talents and years of teaching could be better utilized at the Institute.[17] The Lady Principal at Fisk University, Miss Ballantine, noted Margaret's exceptional progress. In a reference letter to Booker, Ballantine added that Margaret was of sound mind and conscientious religious convictions and had the ability to capture the minds of her peers and those younger than herself, while also directing them. Other faculty members at Fisk considered Margaret a great scholar who possessed the attributes of a remarkable leader. Margaret Murray's work in the classroom resembled other black teachers at Tuskegee, who valued the importance of character building and racial uplift. The high praise she received from other leaders and administrators signified the influence Margaret Murray had as a young, effective leader and educator.[18]

On April 7, 1890, the trustees of Tuskegee Institute appointed

Margaret Murray to Lady Principal (later known as Dean of Women) of Tuskegee Institute, to start the following term beginning September 1, 1890. On that same day in April, Booker T. Washington accepted the resignation of Rosa Mason, who had held the position since the death of Olivia Davidson, while also commending her on an outstanding job. In the capacity of Lady Principal, Margaret Murray enhanced the professionalization of domestic work and stressed the importance of the home.[19]

At this stage in her blossoming career, Margaret was a young, attractive and unmarried woman. She came of age during a period that welcomed ideas of passionate love and frequently read romantic novels which expressed the pleasure and enjoyment associated with courtship and marriage. Yet, prior to her move to Tuskegee, very little is known about her romantic interests. Speculation did arise about a suitor who attended Fisk and presumably would accompany her to Prairie View Normal and Industrial College in Texas, where she had been expected to teach upon graduation. However, due to external pressures placed on black women and notions of sexuality during this period, it is probable that facts about this suitor were not disclosed. A respectable black woman during this era kept her romantic interest private, unless she was willing to endure public scrutiny and degradation to her character.[20]

By 1889 Booker had been widowed twice. Fannie Norton Smith Washington, his first wife, was from his hometown of Malden, West Virginia. She went to Hampton Institute and the two married in 1882, a year following his move to Tuskegee. Fannie worked on the faculty at Tuskegee while also maintaining the school's buildings. She was twenty-six years old when she fell terribly ill and died on May 4, 1884, leaving behind their infant daughter Portia Marshall. Washington's second wife, Olivia America Davidson Washington, was the co-founder of Tuskegee. The two married in 1885, nearly a year after Fannie's death. Born in Virginia but reared in Ohio, Olivia introduced Booker to a number of prominent northern philanthropists. During their marriage the couple gave birth to two sons, Booker Taliaferro Washington Jr., who went by Baker and Ernest Davidson, who went by Davidson or Dave. Following the birth of their second son, however, through extensive travel, teaching, and administrative responsibilities, along with a history of chronic respiratory ailment, which may have been triggered by a recent fire to the Washington's home, Olivia's health worsened. "In 1889 she died, after four years of happy married life and eight years of hard and happy work for the school" Booker later wrote. Olivia passed away in the Massachusetts General Hospital of consumption, the 19th century name for tuberculosis. Olivia Davidson left behind two young sons, one of whom was barely three months old. By the time Margaret arrived in Tuskegee, Booker found himself a two-time widower with the added burden of rearing three small children. His leadership position and conservative politics demanded that he follow the strict code of respectability and remarry a third time.[21]

After the death of Olivia Washington, rumors circulated that Booker had at least two possible love interests. One was Hallie Tanner Dillon, newly hired at Tuskegee and the first black female physician in Alabama. There appeared to be an initial jealousy in regard to Margaret and Hallie. Three months prior to her marriage to Booker, Margaret wrote to her fiancé, "Dr. Dillon will soon be here, sometime next week . . . I do not dislike her but I do not care to be at all intimate with her, and to avoid her I will go a mile." Margaret went on to write, "I never think of her without remembering that the bitterest words you have ever spoken to me were on her account, at least, they were the result of a conversation concerning her." Despite their uncomfortable beginnings, however, Margaret and Hallie would eventually mend their relationship and partner on numerous club initiatives. The other rumored love interest was Mary Moore, who the campus playfully teased Margaret about. Mary was also a good friend of Olivia Washington. As Lady Principal, Margaret had worked closely with both women, though this did not prevent her from accepting Booker's advances. In a small city like Tuskegee, it would have been difficult to keep their courtship private and navigate between their private and public spheres unnoticed.

This also may have created a competitive spirit between the women. Not immune to feelings of jealousy, Margaret expressed moments of insecurity about Booker's relationships with other women. "Her letters are more like love letters than are mine? You would laugh if I were to tell you that I am jealous of her," wrote Margaret, to Booker about Mary Moore. It is difficult to ascertain if Booker ever responded to Margaret's insecurities. Despite any initial uncertainty, however, the couple moved forward with their courtship.[22]

Margaret and Booker were officially engaged by 1891. After losing two wives it is possible that Booker remained closed to romantic notions of love. Minor glimpses of his affection can be found in the way he finished his letters to Margaret, always calling her Maggie. Margaret, on the other hand, appeared to share a romantic love for Booker, who was outwardly focused on his commitment to the race and his three children. Booker also traveled extensively, sometimes leaving the Institute for months at a time. Margaret eventually adjusted to the demands of a high-profile union.

To be effective as the wife of a race leader she had to be equally focused on uplift. A successful 19th century wife embodied identifiable concepts of respectability. Margaret's background made her an ideal candidate. Her respectability was inspired by her associations to Quakers since the age of seven, which mirrored Booker's own upbringing, her teaching experience since the age of fourteen, and her education at Fisk University. It is also not surprising that in an 1890 article titled "Training Our Girls for the Responsibility of Life" Margaret detailed the role of women to their homes and community. She would go on to assert their responsibility to their husbands. "Wom[e]n w[ere] created to be man's helpmate, helpmate in the sense that she is to be his teacher, his counselor, and his guide, not in one thing alone, but in all things. Her relation to man is such that neither one can get on without the other. They are supports to each other."[23]

Helpmate came to describe the couple. Margaret took great care planning their wedding ceremony. "If you do not object" wrote Margaret "we will marry here at Martha's," (Margaret's sister) adding that "[Martha] is very anxious to have us do so and it is most convenient for us both."[24] Most of her wedding plans were conveyed through letters, and despite the separation, Margaret moved forward with wedding arrangements. In a small ceremony on October 12, 1892 Margaret James Murray and Booker Taliaferro Washington exchanged wedding vows. Thus, Margaret immediately became the mother of three young children—Portia, Booker T. Washington Jr., and Ernest Davidson—and the third Mrs. Booker T. Washington.[25]

The relationship between Booker and Margaret was both political and public. Navigating the Jim Crow South, tackling administrative issues at Tuskegee and raising their three children were the strong ties that united the couple. However, they spent very little intimate time together. They would occasionally visit Massachusetts and New York for fundraising during their summer months together, but it was more common for Booker to travel alone. He typically spent up to six months away from the Institute and Margaret each year. In letters to Booker during his numerous absences, Margaret often complained about the infrequency of his correspondence and length of his trips. It became crucially apparent that Margaret Washington needed to devote more of her time to the community and her home, lest loneliness were to drive her insane.

Motherhood came with its own unique challenges. Margaret often vented to Booker about her lack of experience with kids. Until this point, she had lived thirty-one years of her life without children of her own. She often lamented that she knew very little about motherhood and needed him to instruct her on better ways to improve her approach. Through letters, Booker seemed to have little patience for her apparent failures. "You do not have much sympathy with me because I feel as I do in regard to little folk," Margaret confessed. She often felt emotionally detached from the children and annoyed with herself, expressing that "the feelings [were] there just the same." Though Margaret Washington did have younger siblings, she only spent a brief period in her home of origin before moving to Nashville while still a child herself. The role of motherhood proved to be more difficult than she had anticipated. However, she slowly adjusted. She sometimes sewed clothing for the children and took great care to ensure that their nannies were competent. This adjustment may have influenced her keen attention to black mothers and their home life.[26]

As mentioned earlier, Margaret Washington bore no children of her own. No references suggest that she was unable to physically have children, although her poor health may have been a determining factor. In an 1898 speech in Charleston, South Carolina, Margaret Washington spoke briefly about her views on childbirth, motherhood, and class. "Our educated women will not or do not become mothers and our less intelligent mothers let their little ones die," she stated. Considering her position on the matter, it is highly probable that she could not have children of her own, whether a decision of intellect or a consideration of health. Her siblings had similar fates. "My mother had ten [children], most of whom have lived long enough, but they have no children . . . In the whole ten of us, all grown, there are only two children, and they are the children of the youngest girl, who is now twenty-seven years of age, and there has never been more than these, and what is worse, there never will be." Margaret and Booker would eventually adopt her niece Laura and nephew Thomas Murray, following the death of her youngest sister, six years after this speech in 1904. Thomas was a teenager at the time of the informal adoption, but

Laura, who was much younger, would come to recognize Margaret as her mother. She even changed her name to Laura Murray Washington before attending Spelman Seminary (later Spelman College) in Atlanta, Georgia.[27]

Margaret Washington understood the symbolic importance of the black home in the Jim Crow South, despite struggling with the challenges of motherhood. Her relationship with her eight-year-old stepdaughter Portia began with visible tensions. Margaret frequently confessed to Booker that she did not have feelings for Portia, as she felt a mother should. She expressed embarrassment about her lack of feelings but had no way to control them. Portia, on the other hand, had experienced the loss of two mothers within a five-year span and was forced to welcome a third. Margaret Washington may have felt as Mississippi clubwoman Ida B. Wells-Barnett described: "if the mother does not have the training and control of her child's early and most plastic years, she will never gain that control." Under these circumstances it is understandable that Portia grew closer to her father, the only adult who had consistently been in her life since birth. Booker Washington's two younger boys were a different story, for Margaret Washington entered their lives at very early ages. The boys had been in the care of Tuskegee's nurses and in New England following the death of their mother. Margaret provided a more settled family structure, during their most impressionable years.[28]

By 1895 Margaret Washington had better adjusted to her role as mother and wife. Her initial challenges seemed to intensify her commitment to improving the community and presenting a positive image of the black home. In the mind of many middle-class blacks who subscribed to the politics of respectability, white America would grant blacks full-citizenship rights if they proved they could conduct themselves responsibly, as free citizens. For Margaret Washington, the quality of a home provided identifiable portraits about black America's ability to care for their children and community. Respectability also created very visible examples of self-governance and racial up-lift. "Where the homes of colored people are comfortable and clean," Margaret stated, "there is less disease, less sickness, less death, and less danger to others." The home, and its cleanliness, became the focus of many of her outreach initiatives. In many ways, the home was seen as the true black domain of influence. Booker's second wife, Olivia Washington also spoke of the home, stating, "what the families are, the race will be."[29]

Although these ideas became prevalent among race women during the Jim Crow era, what Margaret Washington and her husband created at home helped to solidify their position among other black elites. It also helped to counter notions that "black marriages [were] devoid of fidelity." Respectability politics shaped the way Margaret Washington viewed the role of blacks in their own demise. During the Progressive Era, marriage was not only a status symbol, it also provided black women with male protection, community respect, and symbolic gestures of freedom. While speaking to middle class women in Charlotte, North Carolina, she urged them to take note of the numbers of unwed blacks in various southern locales: "twelve hundred colored men and women, for whom there is no excuse, living immoral lives, handing down to their offspring disease and crime, and only three living in such a way as to advance the race. No spectacle can be more appalling." Although Margaret often included statistics throughout her writings that were exaggerated, her message and intent were delivered with an intended impact. It is clear that Washington was a woman of her time. An unwed woman could not help to rebuild the foundation of a community that had been shattered by the immoral system of slavery. In order for a black woman to be seen as a respectable woman during the Jim Crow era, she had to abide by very strict codes and could not be seen as promiscuous. These respectability codes in many ways, helped to justify the mistreatment of the race and the complete subjugation of its women. Uplift rhetoric forced those who used it to eliminate external factors and freedom of choice, and the Jim Crow south didn't afford them the privilege of being individuals at the expense of the larger black community. For Margaret Washington, in order for the race to be uplifted, she had to improve the character of women's lives in the home.[30]

Washington's focus on the home gave her a solid platform to establish herself as a leading figure within this new class of blacks. Her background with the Quaker community also did much to assist in weaving the core foundation of hard work and moral purity into her notions of character building. These were characteristics closely identified with both old and new ideals of elitism. Many black elites of this era, especially those classified as old guards, endorsed the teachings of Quakers. For example, clubwoman Josephine Bruce, exemplified these beliefs. Wife of Mississippi senator Blanche K. Bruce, Josephine was born in 1853 in Philadelphia, Pennsylvania to free parents. Her mother, Elizabeth Willson, was a singer and musician. Her father, Dr. Joseph

Willson, was a prominent dentist. Josephine was the eldest of five siblings and spent most of her childhood in Cleveland, Ohio after her family moved. Her parent's free status helped to situate Bruce amongst aristocrats of color.

Bruce attended the Pennsylvania Abolition Society's exclusive Clarkson School, an elite school started by Quakers. In 1878, she married Blanche K. Bruce, and like others in their class, the two traveled abroad before settling in Washington, D.C. Josephine Bruce eventually became a charter member of the Colored Women's League of Washington, D.C., and temporarily worked as the Lady Principal at Tuskegee after the 1898 death of her husband, and the brief sabbatical by Margaret.

Clubwoman Mary Ann Shadd also had close ties with Quakers. A Canadian American activist, Shadd was born in Wilmington, Delaware in 1823. Eldest of thirteen children, she grew up in an abolitionist household. Her father worked for the abolitionist newspaper, the *Liberator*, which provided useful tools and aid for enslaved persons who escaped to freedom through the Underground Railroad. Following in her father's footsteps, Shadd attended the Quaker Price's Boarding School in Pennsylvania, and later became the first female African American newspaper editor in North America. Like Bruce and Shadd, a close connection to the Quaker community in memory, schooling and customs created very symbolic gestures of class and played an important role in Margaret Washington's own identity of racial uplift. She adopted many of the Quaker ideologies, practiced them at Tuskegee, and encouraged other African Americans to do the same. These philosophies were linked to ideas of respectability and proved to be a moral compass for Margaret Washington.[31]

Booker T. Washington had similar teachings during his early years. He worked in the house of Viola Ruffner, a New England white woman and wife to Lewis Ruffner, owner of a saltworks.[32] As Booker worked in the Ruffner's home, he learned lifelong lessons that eventually followed him to Hampton, and later to Tuskegee. His biographer Robert Norrell writes: "Ruffner instilled in Booker the essence of what the German sociologist Max Weber later called the Protestant ethic, which taught that the values of industry, sobriety, thrift, self-reliance, and piety, accounted for success in modern capitalist societies."[33]

The home life that Margaret and Booker cultivated had as much to do with their upbringing as did the discriminatory environment in which they toiled. The strenuous task of working and laboring in the South took its toll on Margaret Washington. In 1892, two months prior to her marriage to Booker, she temporarily resigned as Lady Principal, and Booker hired Hallie Quinn Brown. The daughter of former slaves, Brown was born on March 10, 1850 in Pittsburg, Pennsylvania and was forty-two years old when she accepted the one-year position as Tuskegee's Lady Principal. A fellow clubwoman and notable lecturer, Brown had earned a bachelor's degree from Wilberforce, an institution founded by the African Methodist Episcopal Church. She later received an honorary graduate degree and became a college professor, but her true passion was public speaking. In 1895 she addressed an audience at the Women's Christian Temperance Union Conference in London, and while serving as a representative for the United States she spoke before the International Congress of Women in London. Similar to Josephine Bruce, Brown helped to organize the Colored Women's League in Washington, D.C. Her connection to the club movement, publishing record, and educational background, made Brown a perfect fit for Tuskegee and Margaret Washington's vision of progressive black womanhood.[34]

* * *

Secure in her selection of Brown as an example of black respectability, Margaret Washington used this opportunity away from administrative duties to spend more time with her husband, whom she felt traveled too much. Margaret also confided in Booker about her insecurities in relation to race work. "I often shudder to note the change which has come over me since I have been engaged in this work and I try too, to influence myself differently." she wrote. The degree of personal and public stress that Margaret Washington endured may have been enormous. Nonetheless, between 1889 and 1895 she had accomplished great feats. She graduated from Fisk University, became an English teacher at Tuskegee, was appointed Lady Principal, married a race leader and principal, became the mother of three young children and extended her realms of influence to the community. She did all this in juxtaposition to a system of racial separation and gender inequality. In addition, like most race women of the Jim Crow era, Margaret Washington had very few routes of escape from the daily woes of racial uplift. Despite these demands she attempted to maintain an inner sense of identity, sanity, and social integrity. Margaret Washington quickly regrouped after her brief respite, as she resumed the duties of Lady Principal. She would soon learn, through near-exhaustion, to strike a workable balance between her home life and professional commitments.[35]

Margaret Washington evolved as a leader and educator through personal diligence. Booker Washington's increased recognition also expanded her power and respectability throughout Tuskegee, the South, the nation and the world. Margaret Washington's status elevated when, nearly three years following their marriage, Booker T. Washington was asked to speak at the Cotton States and International Exposition in Atlanta, Georgia. "After preparing my address" Booker recounted in *Up From Slavery*, "I went through it, as I usually do with all those utterances which I consider particularly important, with Mrs. Washington, and she approved what I intended to say." With great anxiety as to the outcome, On September 17, 1895, Margaret, Booker, and their three children took a train to Atlanta. The address came to be labelled by his critics as the Atlanta Compromise. Washington proposed a solution for the great Negro problem of the post-emancipation South. Despite his critics, after the speech, Booker T. Washington became the leader of blacks in America, with his economic, social and political agenda drawing audiences from around the world. According to Louis Harlan, "Washington offered to trade black acquiescence in disfranchisement and some measure of segregation, at least for the time being, in return for a white promise to allow blacks to share" in northern economic growth. At the time of the speech, Washington's predecessor, Frederick Douglass, had just died and Republican dominance in the South had recently ended.[36]

Booker T. Washington's speech also helped to cement his family's position in the black community. Their national celebrity increased again when in 1901 President Theodore Roosevelt invited Booker to dine at the White House with his wife Edith and daughter Alice. While individual black leaders like Douglass had visited with presidents, no other black family could lay claim to such a request during Jim Crow. This invitation did not evade criticism from black and white leaders. It became a national sensation. Roosevelt and his wife, as well as Booker and Margaret, received backlash. According to the *New York Times*: "Among public men there is manifest a distinct aversion to be quoted about the matter. But the general tone of conversation points to a pretty general disagreement with the President as to the propriety of the departure from a traditionary avoidance of just such events."[37]

Still, these affairs brought nationwide exposure to the small town of Tuskegee and the Institute. This national visibility also helped propel Margaret Washington and her agenda of educating black women to the foreground, as the President publicly declared how he "admired [Booker] for his character, his devotion to the cause, and for what he has accomplished." The heightened attention on Booker Washington meant an increased focus on his work and the work of Margaret Washington. Their position on industrial training as the most plausible curriculum for the masses of African Americans and the black home now attracted a national audience of both supporters and critics. It is important to note that black women's limited access to public venues required they use the approach of sharing the platform with their husbands. This granted married black women areas of influence unavailable to unwed women of color.[38]

Publicity from the White House dinner presented unique opportunities for Margaret Washington to capitalize on her performative efforts in Tuskegee. This visibility led to additional duties in the community and at the Institute. Like most race women, Margaret Washington did not have the luxury of choosing between uplift work and wage-earning work. She had to do both. Many black women held jobs outside their homes. However, work in academia was particularly desirable. As mentioned earlier, Josephine Bruce, clubwoman and widow of Blanche K. Bruce, also held the position of Lady Principal at Tuskegee. Unlike Hallie Quinn Brown, Bruce's family had been free blacks in the Northeast. Her privileged background had sheltered her from a great deal of southern bigotry, and her complexion won acceptance among white Republicans and socialites. These factors influenced Bruce's experience as a working woman and Lady Principal in Tuskegee.[39]

Margaret Washington's wage-earning work also created a unique brand of leadership during the Progressive Era. While she identified with an aristocratic lifestyle and espoused a conservative approach to character building, at this time in her life she was not particularly endowed with personal wealth in comparison to other black elites. Nonetheless, many of her cultural achievements placed her amid the new black elite. As Du Bois suggests in *The Philadelphia Negro*, income and other identifiable characteristics were not the main determinants of the new black elite due to restrictions placed on the systematic access to wealth. Still, Margaret Washington's social adaptation to elitist living standards and her husband's continued success amongst the black masses spoke to their elevated status. Their social platforms also brought wide access to the resources of prominent American philanthropists. In 1903 Andrew Carnegie donated $600,000 in U.S. Steel Bonds to Tuskegee Institute's Endowment fund, earmarking $150,000 of them to be used solely for the Washington family and Booker's tours. This donation, among many others, provided the Washingtons with a financial cushion that enabled them to advance their social agendas for Tuskegee and other industrial institutions. In addition, Margaret and Booker would use similar philanthropic donations to promote the creation of model black communities.[40]

In Tuskegee, the Washingtons constructed the community of Greenwood. It served as a model black community and promoted citizens who understood the value of the black home and home ownership. It also housed members of Tuskegee's faculty as well as other middle-class blacks from surrounding areas. Margaret advocated home ownership. In addition, she saw women's role as critical to this endeavor. In a 1904 article "The Gain in the Life of a Negro Woman," Margaret declared that women "have helped their husbands to purchase homes by their thrift and economy." She went on to assert, "they are well designed, painted cottages of six and eight rooms, with bath and hot and cold water contrivances, well ventilated, and constructed with an eye to sanitary arrangements . . . The Negro women are un-modern in that they assume a share in working to pay for homes for their families."[41]

Tuskegee tended to be one of the more rural communities in the late nineteenth-century South. Whites owned the farms that surrounded the small town. Blacks continued to work the land of white farmers, and a vast majority of them remained in the agricultural sector. The Greenwood community represented a neighborhood of southern blacks who had a different place in the South: a population section of blacks who could be the national model of black life and culture.[42]

The school purchased over 200 acres of land from white planters and sold it to blacks at discounted rates. According to Harlan, "to demonstrate that blacks could live in a clean, orderly, middle-class way, the Village Improvement Association governed and patrolled the town." Greenwood had paved streets, a city park, and night lights. By 1906, Greenwood totaled well over 2100 inhabitants and represented what blacks could do in the midst of the Jim Crow south. Greenwood typified more than a model community, it gave blacks and visiting whites an image of black progress. Margaret Washington's home life became as much about the public image as Greenwood. This could also be seen in the attention to detail the Washingtons gave to their own home, The Oaks. The image of black progress, Margaret Washington learned, would be an important tool to turn the tide of racial and political inequality.[43]

Margaret may have been born enslaved, but she lived out her adult life with an elevated sense of privilege and class. A part of creating a model community in the Black Belt, Margaret and Booker extended their realms of elitism with their access to travel, and they both traveled extensively. Scholar Joel Williamson notes that until the 1920s, mulattoes successfully led separate lives and deserve a separate history. While this may be plausible, Margaret Washington and many other blacks could not avoid the larger black community. For one, they understood they were not seen as separate by the dominant race. Despite parentage, the one-drop rule made them black. Whites in America did, however, go to extreme lengths to enforce its segregation from black America. This did not prevent black aristocrats from forming institutions of their own that paralleled white associations, such as Masonic and fraternal lodges like the Eastern Star. As Mary Church Terrell would recall when reflecting on an event in Washington, D.C., the colored attendees "observed the same standards of conduct and culture as do those in the best [white] social circles in the United States."[44]

Margaret Washington used her ability to travel to extend her margins of respectability. On rare occasions when the opportunity presented itself, she vacationed in Colorado, California and Mexico, without the obligations of work. Travel afforded race women an occasional chance to rest, but it also allowed them an opportunity to interact with other cultures, often helping to bring the platforms of self-help and community betterment to a wider audience. In 1899, during her second leave of absence as Lady Principal, Margaret and Booker received a rare invitation from Mrs. Francis Jackson Garrison and her husband, to tour and rest in Europe for three months. The Garrisons, along with Northern friends, had raised money to pay all expenses for the Washingtons tour and absence from the Institute. While Booker initially expressed anxiety and fear to leave Tuskegee and the school for such an extended period for leisure, Margaret eagerly welcomed the break. From early May to July of 1899 the Washingtons traveled to Europe and made stops in Holland, Belgium, Brussels, Paris, London and France While in Bristol, England the couple spoke at the Women's Liberal Club. Of her experience, Margaret stated: "we saw English life and to me it was most beautiful." She described trips to Paris and London where she visited with the "dear old Queen [Victoria] and had tea in her banqueting Hall" at Windsor Castle, along with the leading American advocate of women's suffrage, Susan B. Anthony. Anthony and other white clubwomen held the third International Congress of Women in London from June 26 thru July 7, 1899. Margaret prided herself on her capacity to name-drop. Francis Jackson Garrison, a relative of the abolitionist William Lloyd Garrison, made sure that the Washingtons' trip to Europe was as comfortable as possible by ensuring they were looked after by former abolitionists. The Washingtons traveled extensively in Europe and Margaret Washington declared in a letter to Frances that it "would tire you if I were to attempt to tell you all we did and saw & heard & felt." It was not uncommon for race leaders like Mary Church Terrell to reflect on their international travels and suggest that, "reams upon top of reams I might write if I tried to tell the innumerable acts of kindness shown . . . through whose countries I traveled." This dialogue was not uncommon among the rising elite. E. Franklin Frazier, a black sociologist, later wrote of "the so-called rich Negroes [who] indulge in lavish expenditures and create a world of fantasy to satisfy their longing for recognition." However, it must be noted that the Washingtons were leaders in disseminating propaganda. These trips locally and abroad were status markers within black America, but more importantly, they served as projections of black opportunities to the outside world. It is thus not surprising that after their trip to Europe, Booker purchased the family a summer home on Long Island, where the Washingtons' and their children spent time on the beach. Through their travels, Margaret Washington, and her husband, personified the endless possibilities that were available to blacks in America.[45]

There were many elements to the black home. Black-owned communities, social work, adhering to politics of respectability, travel and the rearing of children were all identifiable markers of black home life. Education remained a central component. While instruction started in the home, the type of education one received said as much about their home life as their occupation. Despite Margaret and Booker's advocacy of industrial training, they eventually sent their children away for schooling. Due in part to the tense relationship between Margaret and her stepdaughter, Portia spent a great deal of time away from her home, but not without bouts of loneliness. She eventually lived in

Framingham, Massachusetts for three years with a classmate of her first stepmother, Olivia Washington, while attending school.[46] Portia later returned and graduated from Tuskegee Institute before entering Wellesley College in the fall of 1901, as a special student, to further her music career. She also studied piano in Berlin, Germany under Professor Martin Krause.[47] The Washington boys, Baker and Davidson, like Portia, spent a great deal of their childhood at boarding schools before going off to colleges such as Fisk and Talladega, living at home only for short periods.

Margaret and Booker received criticism for sending their children away from home to liberal arts schools. The children experienced difficulties adjusting and either transferred to other schools or returned to attend Tuskegee before completing their degrees. Margaret and Booker also ensured that the children possessed some industrial awareness. In an interview with the *Boston Globe*, Portia validated her parents' decision to extend her education past the realms of industrial training:[48] "My father has been anxious for me to attend college. He believes in the college education of girls where it is possible for them to have it, and my mother, you know, is a graduate of Fisk University. But for most of the girls at Tuskegee father sees that the industrial education and that which emphasizes the household arts is most needed. None the less, he encourages further study whenever it is possible for the student to get it."[49]

The Washington children fit squarely within Margaret Washington's focus on the black home. Her personal life was undeniably public, yet the success of her children illustrated the greater success of the black community. While the concept of the black home embodied all elements of black life and respectability, it spoke specifically to cultural refinements that could be found within the physical black home. According to Margaret, "this training of young women should begin early, for it is the young girl who develops into a full-blown rose." Thus it became imperative for the Washingtons to create a model home of their own. Toward the end of the nineteenth century Margaret and Booker began building what Isabel Barrows called a "substantial abode."[50] Built by the students of Tuskegee, this two-and-a-half story, fourteen-room home became an iconic image of the Tuskegee community and was given the name The Oaks. The house was situated on the Old Montgomery Highway at the edge of the Tuskegee campus. Custom-built, it included a handcrafted stairwell clearly made to accommodate Margaret Washington's short stature. The home presented a unique reinforcement of culture.

The Washingtons dressed in formal attire every day for dinner and frequently entertained other elites as well as residents of the Tuskegee community. Eating at a table was a privilege not afforded to many blacks and a practice that Margaret took very seriously within her own home and on campus. Booker recalled in his autobiography, "I had not had the privilege of sitting down to a dining table until I was quite well grown." Margaret took special interest in formal dining and this public display of refinement. Educators such as Mary McLeod Bethune of Daytona Educational and Industrial Training School for Negro Girls in Florida, Mrs. George C. Hall of Chicago, and Miss Lucile U. Miller of St. Alban's Industrial School in Florida were all guests at one time or another at The Oaks. Margaret Washington usually served as the hostess to out of town guests, as her husband had an extremely taxing travel schedule.[51]

The Washingtons entertained guests, held plays, and hosted banquets and extravagant weddings, demonstrating to the community the exemplary behaviors and interactions of the best men and women of the race. Margaret also used the home to showcase her love for lyceum and literature. In 1900, they held a rendition of Shakespeare's immortal tragedy *Othello* in their home. Margaret's love of theater and literature found a stage in Tuskegee. She hosted plays on women in Russia, Germany, and annual Christmas productions that added to their philosophy of culture.[52] In 1907 they hosted an impressive and dignified wedding reception for their daughter Portia, who married Tuskegee graduate William Sidney Pittman. Some local observers considered the wedding "the chief social event of the year." As a wedding gift Margaret and Booker purchased Portia a piano for her new home in Washington, D.C. Through tangible events like these the Washingtons and other members of the black elite were paradigms of obtainable black life and the black home.[53]

The decor of the home also spoke to refinement. Booker Washington confessed that when he worked in the home of Mrs. Viola Knapp Ruffner, she taught him lessons that stuck with him throughout his adulthood. They guided him when building and maintaining his own home in the Tuskegee community. "Washington entered an upper-class white household whose mistress was the prototypical New England Yankee schoolmarm, devoted to the Puritan precepts of thrift, work, truth, and cleaning," asserted Robert Norrell.[54] Margaret Washington also contributed ideas on the interior design of the home. She typically asked Booker to leave her money to buy new furniture, always preferring oak.[55]

Building up her home in the most refined ways gave Margaret Washington great pride. Born into slavery and later adopted by whites, Margaret Washington longed for a sense of belonging. She understood the importance of a physical home. Like many displaced African Americans, she carried with her the emotional scars that overt poverty and racism, had made on her mental health. She also understood how the inability to foster a healthy home impacted the psyche of women in her life and the emotional intelligence of the race. Home also nurtured the family. It provided comforts that restored one's energy and sense of place. As a wife and mother, Margaret took great pride in the comforts of her home. In reflecting on his travel, Booker asserted "it is such a rest and relief to get away from crowds of people, and handshaking, and travelling, and get home, even if it be for but a brief while."[56]

Margaret Washington's administrative work also provided her a platform to educate and influence the trajectory of young women, both in the home and the community. She imparted lessons of good character and domestic responsibilities. In an 1890 article, Washington declared, "nothing which goes to make a complete and entire woman, should be neglected. The happiness of the young woman depends upon this completeness of character." While her administrative work allowed her to meet the needs of young women, her club work allowed her an opportunity to reach the older community, who were similar to her grandmother and mother, to fill a social and cultural void between the generations. Club work also became a platform to advance her philosophy of the black home and black cultural life.[57]

In 1893 Margaret Washington started a local chapter of Mothers' Meetings and by 1895 she created the Tuskegee Woman's Club (TWC). The TWC served as a direct response to efforts by educated southern black women to join forces, as northern black women had done, and create outlets through which they could mingle on personal, professional, and social levels. The TWC was Washington's first attempt to join like-minded women together to educate themselves on the state of southern black women and children. The organization also catered to the social needs of the community. The women hosted plays, dinners, and dances. Clubwoman Jessie Guzman remembered: "She [Washington] had founded the Tuskegee Woman's Club, and it was really the center, from the point of view of the community, the center of the life of Tuskegee women." What Washington did in Tuskegee propelled her to the top of the Black Women's Club Movement and the black elite.[58]

In that same year, Washington and a group of black women met in Boston and formed the National Federation of Afro-American Women's clubs (NFAAW). Boston was home to many of the nation's old and new black elites including Josephine St. Pierre Ruffin. Boston clubwomen were usually descendants of antebellum free blacks, and in many instances, formed highly exclusive clubs. Yet, due to the rebranding of elitism, the group chose Washington, a formerly enslaved, Southern born, self-made woman, to lead the club, just as she was leading the women in Tuskegee in all things domestic and social. Some women, like Ida B. Wells-Barnett, believed this appointment was due to Booker Washington's influence with the U.S. President and white businessmen. It was no secret, however, that Margaret and Booker were at pivotal points in their careers. Not only was Booker T. Washington considered the spokesperson for black America, but Margaret Washington's new club affiliations placed her at the forefront of upper-class black women. Her position in the South gave her an unquestionable advantage to access and remedy the condition that blacks currently held in American society. Through the cultivation of the home and racial uplift she sought to improve the race from within. As most blacks remained in the south after emancipation, her platform made her the most qualified race leader.[59]

By the time the NFAAW was formed, Washington's TWC had already become the first club for upper-class black women in Tuskegee. During this period, middle-class women throughout Alabama were meeting regularly and conversing on ideas for improving conditions for blacks. Towns with black schools and HBCUs were often key locations for social and civic clubs, due to the number of professionals and upper-class residents.[60]

Unlike other black elites who initially rejected working directly with the masses of blacks, Washington welcomed working within the black home and social centers. She labored to remind elite black women that they were, in part, a component of that same community. Her approach, in many regards, separated women of the new black elite from old elites, but it did not exempt them from viewing themselves as different. Uplifting the race was primarily seen as a mission of education.[61] Yet divisions of class and prestige existed within the new black elite. Washington realized that upper-class blacks were judged by the worst of their race, and rather than working separately, they would have to work together in order to actually overcome Jim Crow racism.[62]

Margaret Washington understood that in order to live in the South she had to manipulate segregation laws in the least threatening manner. Regardless of her power within the community, her voice was sometimes muted, yet she believed some white Americans were committed to fairness and racial harmony. "You know that we often feel that every white man and woman south of the Mason and Dixon line is a real devil," she proclaimed to a women's group at Old Bethel church. "It is pretty bad down here, I will admit, but there are many fine and noble Southern white people, women as well as men," she added. New and old elites used their connections with whites, usually philanthropists, to help advance the race as a whole. Statements about the virtue of good whites were necessary to secure the support of southern whites. This rhetoric also helped calm the fears of southern blacks who were living through one of the lowest points in American history. As a race woman, Margaret Washington understood that in order to be an agent of change, she needed to outthink her contemporaries as she empowered black women to take their homes and lives into their own hands.[63]

Margaret Washington transformed into a nineteenth century race woman, and as she promoted ideals on improving the black home, she attempted to embody her teachings while simultaneously improving her class and community. Washington went from the Negro home to the streets as she positioned herself to lead women, improve their moral character, and uplift through her social work. She initiated many of these things in the classroom and on the campus of Tuskegee Intitute.[64]

Chapter Three

Building an Empire through Home Economics

> I was born in the state of Mississippi, educated in the state of Tennessee, and am a citizen of the state of Alabama.
>
> —Margaret Murray Washington
> (*The Negro Home*, 1920)[1]

As a new southern aristocrat of color, Margaret Washington understood freedom to be a constant struggle. She remained deliberate in her constitutional duty to the South and incorporating formal and informal curriculums of domestic sciences and respectability politics. In her role as Lady Principal of Tuskegee Institute, Washington had an invested interest in educating women of the South. "I see no reason why she [the black woman] should not take her place as teacher, homemaker, and in industrial pursuits such as millinery and dressmaking, filling an important place in her community, especially the South," she noted. This focus on industrial education provided southern black women with the tools needed to improve their financial conditions and to combat the toxic system of Jim Crow, sexism, and racial discrimination.[2]

Margaret Washington's exposure to independent black schools predated her move to Tuskegee. As an associate editor of the *Fisk Herald*, she routinely reported on the progress that private black schools, churches, and other institutions of learning were making. Blacks were taking their education into their own hands. Subtle progress in terms of black education existed in Alabama before the establishment of Tuskegee Normal. In 1873, Alabama established the first state Normal and Industrial School for Negroes near Huntsville, later known as Alabama Agricultural and Mechanical College. In 1877 the state legislature provided for a state system of public education with a state superintendent.

By 1880 the blueprint for Tuskegee Normal and Industrial Institute was underway.[3] "On November 16, 1880 . . . Representative Brooks introduced a bill appropriating the sum of $2,000 to pay the salaries of teachers at a normal school to be located at Tuskegee . . . it was signed February 10, [1881] by the President of the Senate and approved February 12, Abraham Lincoln's birthday, by Governor Rufus W. Cobb. In 1881 history converged on what was to become Tuskegee Institute."[4]

As previously mentioned, Booker T. Washington came to Tuskegee Normal School for Colored Teachers in 1881. With no physical buildings or staff, Washington took charge of the public school for colored children on Mt. Zion, forming the first cohort of Tuskegee students. Classes were held in Butler Chapel A.M.E. Zion Church. The structure was small, approximately 40 x14 feet, divided into two rooms. William Gregory, a student at Tuskegee, described the first few days as they took a series of examinations. According to Gregory, the first classes were comprised of young and very old students who were also teachers in the community. Booker T. Washington taught and instructed them for a week or so until he received assistance.[5]

During the initial years of the Institute, Booker struggled to secure funding and teachers, and to establish an Industrial and liberal arts institution like that of Hampton Institute. According to Albert Scipio, "no provision was made, however, for land, building, or equipment—these were to be provided by persons who benefited from the school; in other words, the black people." By August of 1881, Hampton graduate Olivia America Davidson joined the school as an Assistant Principal and co-founder. Washington and Davidson provided instruction until other teachers were hired. When Margaret Washington arrived in 1889, there were over fifteen faculty members at the Institute. With the help of General James Fowle Baldwin Marshall of Hampton Institute, Booker Washington secured the abandoned 100-acre plantation known as the Bowen Estate. In addition to constructing the school, raising funds, and employing staff, Tuskegee had the added pressure of producing qualified graduates. The demand for career-ready graduates, directly connected to teachers who displayed high moral character and a command of their discipline, was at an all-time high for conservative normal schools.[6]

At the time of Margaret Washington's 1890 appointment as Lady Principal, she was deeply invested in the advancement of the South. She labored under the guise that personal development went hand-and-hand with full-citizenship rights. However, she understood students were forced to learn these principles in the midst of violence. As she instructed students on the effects of having good character and home economics, on their advancement, she also warned them of the prevalent dangers that existed outside the Institute's walls.

Margaret Washington witnessed firsthand the discrimination towards blacks in Alabama, Mississippi, and Tennessee, where the Klansmen of Reconstruction wreaked havoc. Furthermore, she believed that "industrial education provided blacks with an economic niche in the country that would not threaten or antagonize white southerners,"[7] as stated by David H. Jackson Jr. This was not an accommodationist view, as many critics of her husband asserted, but rather a survivalist strategy. Calling it accommodationist placed it into a narrow box that shortchanged the metalanguage of race, where race over-determined other categories including sex, gender, and class. It also does not accurately assess the ability of blacks to disguise outreach as nonthreatening. As blacks fought against the Jim Crow laws of segregation, they also used that forced separation to build their own institutions. In the midst of this progress, domestic terrorism intensified. In fact, in the 1890s Alabama led the country in the highest number of lynchings per year. In the wake of this violence, black educational spaces became that much more imperative.[8]

Most southern whites were opposed to any efforts made to improve conditions for blacks. Moreover, whites found it difficult to see themselves as equal to individuals they once regarded as property. Margaret Washington believed that in order to gain the freedoms promised with emancipation, southern blacks needed to conceal their educational agendas. Although Tuskegee started as a Normal school to train black teachers, by 1891 it had added industrial training to its mission. A small number of southern whites who saw industrial training as a plausible substitute to classical or higher education, according to Joe Richardson, "grasped eagerly at industrial education as a method of satisfying blacks' desire for learning while at the same time keeping them in their 'place,' or so they believed."[9]

On the other side of white resistance, some supporters of liberal arts education considered Tuskegee Institute's approach lacking in intellectual and philosophical training; they saw it as inferior and unnecessarily narrow. In reflecting on her thoughts about vocational training versus liberal arts, leading clubwoman Mary Church Terrell asserted: "I appreciated Dr. Washington's effort to train the masses to earn a living . . . I felt that he emphasized industrial training to the exclusion of everything else."[10]

Nonetheless, black advocates of vocational training believed that learning a trade would gain black people more respect amongst whites and give them skills the South needed. It could also become an avenue to racial uplift and independence. The Washingtons program of race progress did not assert, as implied by Du Bois, that "the South [was] justified in its present attitude towards the Negro." Nor did they feel that industrial training should be the only form of education. Their own children attended liberal arts and industrial schools alike. They did, however, present industrial training as a viable alternative to no education at all. And to a class of blacks only one or two generations removed from slavery, this form of education provided the most practical route to economic independence.[11]

Whites remained on the defense. Though a liberal arts education was once seen as elitist, soon whites began to recognize the value of industrial training and forced blacks out of certain trades through various licensing practices. Margaret Washington, like her husband, realized its importance and continued to emphasize industrial training as an instructor of the female students at Tuskegee Institute. Domesticity, though once seen as an occupation under servitude, now carried with it the possibility of economic freedom, even as they better understood the chemistry in the foods they cooked. Margaret Washington promoted skills that many considered innate to women, such as Home Economics.[12]

Black industrial educators struggled to change the perception of black women's need for an education. Margaret Washington sought to prove that educating women benefited the race, and she made sure their curriculum in the domestic sciences reflected this belief. "When the same advantages [that] are given [to] boys in intellectual training are given to the young women . . . [she] will be equally fitted for the responsibility which is sure to come to her." Washington also believed that every aspect of life could be improved. "There are new ways and interesting ones even in sweeping a floor," she jokingly noted, while addressing a group of young teachers. The work being done at Tuskegee was not conducted in a vacuum and was highly publicized. It also gained the attention of race women.[13]

The number of black female educators who helped spread the gospel of domesticity in the classroom and throughout the community grew significantly at the turn of the century. Lugenia Burns Hope, wife of John Hope, and Lady Principal at Atlanta Baptist College (now Morehouse College) advanced studies in the domestic sciences and soon established the Neighborhood Union, an organization that helped to lay much of the grassroots efforts of the civil rights movement in Atlanta. Jennie Moton, like Hope and Washington, also worked within the walls of higher education. The wife of Robert Moton, successor at the Institute to Booker T. Washington, Jennie Moton taught classes and worked with the Tuskegee Woman's Club, helping to elevate the status of black women. This focus on home economics was also evident among other southern black female leaders in the early twentieth century. Trenna Banks, wife of Booker T. Washington's chief lieutenant, Charles Banks of Mound Bayou, Mississippi, and Josephine Bruce of Mississippi, worked in their respective communities and instructed women in various forms of domesticity.[14]

Educating women at the Institute took on various forms. Aside from directly teaching women the practical art and application of domesticity and imparting lessons on respectability, non-scholastic issues concerning students and teachers were brought to Margaret Washington, as Lady Principal. She handled matters that involved student salaries, laundry, and the hiring and firing of female faculty and student workers. She also helped to employ many of her graduates. In one instance, Margaret Washington received a request from Temple, Texas, "for someone who can teach broom and mattress making." Women with industrial training who worked under Washington were actively recruited for positions in domestic fields and in administrative posts a like. Tuskegee's reputation for well-trained female students resulted in alumnae obtaining good teaching positions throughout the nation. This brought recognition for the school, but it also helped to improve the financial trajectory of black families.[15]

Students like Julia Cunningham and others routinely turned to Washington for letters of recommendation. Washington also received numerous descriptive job postings, like an intelligent girl who can file papers. In one instance, however, Emmett Scott needed a new office assistant because he believed that "the little girl we have is willing and earnest, but simply does not know what I am talking about half the time."[16] Margaret Washington informed Scott, "I am going to do my very best in the next day or two to select you a good office girl," but with hesitation she added, "I would put Louise back there but I feel that I would just be putting the girl in the way of temptation because the girls are so unprotected in that office."[17] This was a rather strange comment for Margaret Washington to make, given that if she did not place Louise there, she would employ another female student. This may speak to the youth of Louise, or the ideas of respectability and separation of the sexes, rather than foul play on the behalf of the male faculty in this particular office. However, Tuskegee was not immune to toxic masculinity and unacceptable public behavior.

Prior to the 1972 Title IX of the Education Amendments Act, which prohibits discrimination on the basis of sex in education programs and activities, Washington was known throughout campus for her effective tactics in dealing with students and faculty members. She had a zero-tolerance policy. Female students in the presence of males, without proper supervision, were reported and closely monitored. Male faculty members who lingered around female work areas were quickly relieved of duty. Margaret Washington solicited the support of her husband in an incident in Alabama Hall, when male teachers, according to students and female faculty members, were standing in the halls and talking to the girls. One teacher, a Mr. Green, went so far as to ask for the company of one of the girls. Margaret Washington considered this behavior foolish and refused to tolerate it; Mr. Green's conduct was unacceptable, and breached notions of trust between female students and faculty. There were also incidents of male teachers smoking in public. While Margaret herself "enjoyed the odor of a good cigar" she strongly warned against its implied public messaging. In a letter to Dr. Moton, Margaret Washington wrote, "I just cannot bring myself to vote for a warning against boys who smoke as long as our men smoke so thoughtlessly, and carelessly anywhere the boys may see them . . . and therefore may be tempted to do likewise." Margaret Washington went on to assert, "I do not want to be considered as not wanting to see the teachers have a good time nor to in any way curtail their freedom, but freedom in my mind does not mean license." In her estimation, teachers were required to make sacrifices when it came to their public performance. Respectability was the conservative law and many things they were accustomed to doing should be "left undone."[18]

The heightened visibility of Tuskegee increased the emphasis for qualified teachers. Black educators as a whole were committed to improving the quality of instruction given to black youth. Ida B. Wells-Barnett, a fellow clubwoman and anti-lynching activist from Holly Springs, Mississippi, held strong views about black educators. Wells-Barnett attended Shaw University (later Rust College), located in Holly

Springs, before tragic family affairs forced her to leave at sixteen. After convincing an administrator that she was eighteen, she started teaching and became the primary caretaker of her siblings and eventually started her career in journalism. In 1895 Ida married attorney Ferdinand Barnett. They had four children together. As a wife and mother, Wells-Barnett did not retire from wage-earning work. She became an investigative journalist and her research brought attention to topics impacting the race, including the role of black teachers. Wells-Barnett openly criticized the hiring of black female teachers who had little to no mental and moral character. Teachers had a great responsibility to the race. Just as Wells-Barnett, Washington strongly believed that teaching was one of the few occupations that a respectable woman could occupy without compromising her social status. Education Administration provided Margaret Washington with the necessary influence to ensure students mastered a skillset, but equally important, that they received instruction on how to properly conduct themselves in public. This also directly impacted her hiring and firing practices in regard to instructors.[19]

Upon receiving a request for the recommendation of a Mrs. Kenniebrew, Margaret Washington declared, "I know Mrs. Kenniebrew very well, [however] I do not think that we should consider her at all for the work . . . Mrs. Kenniebrew is a woman of very strong mind, but I consider her unfit in a way for work here."[20] Washington considered herself curator of Tuskegee's public image. She strongly disapproved of the way that Kenniebrew performed respectability, as she and her husband had not lived together for some time. This became sufficient evidence to deny Kenniebrew an appointment at Tuskegee Institute, as broken marriages challenged ideas of respectability and raised doubts about character. It also went against Washington's emphasis on the importance of the black family and the mental and physical health of the black community. In nineteenth century racial uplift doctrines, the private and public were one and the same. African American leaders operated within very strict moral codes of conduct. Black women were no exception. The responsibility of racial uplift controlled most private sectors of an individual's life.

There was also the added pressure of teacher qualifications, especially in the field of domestic sciences. Margaret Washington understood liberal arts training to be equally as important as industrial training but knew they required different skills. She herself had a liberal arts background. According to Booker T. Washington's biographer Louis

Harlan, "most of the teachers in the academic department were college graduates, who felt a sense of superiority to the typical industrial or agricultural teachers, self-taught or half-taught men and women whose particular skills had earned them faculty status." Aware of these tensions, Margaret Washington learned to emphasize the importance of both industrial and liberal arts training at the institute. She ensured that night school teachers, full time instructors, and Normal school students were properly trained in their fields of study and curricular. She asserted, "these two things should be put on a par because no longer should these teachers feel that they must go out and have students doing such phases of work," in which they are not particularly qualified. Her keen desire to have the most competent faculty members train Tuskegee students in their respective fields was evident. With the constant attention placed on the school and its graduates, according to Margaret Washington, faculty members needed to be proficient in "mathematics and science that go along with these trades and certainly they should all have English," along with a grasp of black history—all fields of study taught during her years at Fisk University.[21]

Most instructors at the Institute took pride in merging the curriculums of history, domestic sciences, and liberal arts. Seasoned faculty like George Washington Carver, nationally-known inventor and artist, and activist Bess Bolden Walcott, curator of the George Washington Carver collection and the rural circulating library, took great pride in their race and academics. In fact, Walcot taught American Literature and founded the *Tuskegee Messenger*. In addition, in 1918 Walcott chartered the first black chapter of the Red Cross, in Tuskegee. Yet, there were some instructors who failed to see the connection between industrial training and black history. In reflecting on a story she heard a white woman share, Washington was shocked to learn that "a colored woman asked why it was necessary to study Negro history when the white woman had suggested it." This comment provoked her to declare, "Nothing will give these teachers whom we are training a more forward look than to get some sort of race pride" which could only come from race knowledge. Washington considered the appreciation of black history as a prerequisite to race pride, and sought the premier scholar in African American history, Carter Godwin Woodson, to teach a course at Tuskegee.[22]

Woodson was born in 1875 in New Canton, Virginia, and educated at Berea College, the University of Chicago, and Harvard. With a doctorate in history, he devoted his life to historical research and the dissemination of black culture and life. Woodson co-founded the Association for the Study of Negro Life and History (later named the Association for the Study of African American Life and History) in 1915, published countless works on black history, and in 1926, a year after the death of Margaret Washington, he established the celebration of Negro History Week. The week was recognized on the second week of February, to coincide with the birthdays of Abraham Lincoln and Fredrick Douglass. Woodson's efforts eventually led scholars of Black History to push for the entire month of February in 1970.[23]

Although Woodson never taught courses at Tuskegee, in 1915 shortly after establishing the association, he spoke to faculty and students at the Institute on the importance of black history, at the request of Booker T. Washington. Margaret Washington also used his pamphlets in her classes. She felt that the students "had gone too long without some well-defined systematic course with reference to the Negro." This keen desire to educate students in black history was personal to Margaret Washington; she embedded history into her educational pedagogy and club work. She believed that race pride placed confidence and esteem into a group of Americans who failed to understand their influence and impact on American history, largely due to the lack of positive black images offered to them. Promoting positive black excellence remained at the core of her outreach and racial uplift, especially in her role as second-in-command to Booker T. Washington.[24]

With all of the advancements being made at the Institute, Margaret Washington still took two sabbaticals during her tenure. In reflecting on the arduous task of tending to the race and personal matters simultaneously, clubwoman Terrell proclaimed: "it is possible for a woman to succeed . . . if she has nothing to do but look after her children and her home. But when exacting public work is added to her other cares, it is very difficult." When Washington stepped away from her position as Lady Principal in 1899 for the second time, a number of factors were at play. For one, she had a history of fragile health. The daily strain of race work forced her to be selective with her responsibilities. She also desired to be the president of the National Association of Colored Women, an organization formed in 1896 after the merger of the Colored Women's League and the National Federation of Afro American Women. There were also the added stresses of being in the shadow of her husband and her desire to travel more with him. Her loneliness, triggered by Booker T.

Washington's frequent absences, caused her great anguish. She sometimes also felt torn between her role as daughter and wife. In a letter to her husband, she confessed, "our mother [Lucy Murray] is rather old and not a strong woman and I do not think that I want to go there next summer for I am going with you." Margaret Washington wished to accompany her husband on a once in a lifetime trip to Europe where the quinquennial meeting of the International Congress of Women would be held in London in 1899. Though she did not win presidency of the National organization that year, she did travel to Europe. During the trip, she took her mind away from the day-to-day matters of the race and school, and for one of the first times in her life, took extended leisure. Booker T. Washington, as he had done in the past, accepted her sabbatical and sought the assistance of Josephine Bruce.[25]

Bruce temporarily replaced Margaret Washington as Lady Principal. Considering her friendship with Margaret and the prestige her appointment would bring to the school, Booker took full advantage of securing her for the position. Without any other notice of the hire, only a month before her appointment, he informed Bruce that "I have just sent you a telegram saying that we expect you next week," which left Bruce very little time to prepare for the transition. And although she asked for $90 a month plus room and board, and all other expenses, Booker Washington, who was noted for his low salaries, suggested that she receive "$80 per month and board, board to include all expenses except traveling." This was rather lucrative considering that upon initially accepting the position, clubwoman Hallie Quinn Brown, Margaret Washington's previous replacement, received a salary of $60 per month and board. Margaret Washington, however, earned $500 plus room and board per semester, which was roughly $100 per month. Booker T. Washington informed Bruce he would consider increasing her salary "if later on I can see my way clear to make it a larger figure."[26]

For the next two years Josephine Bruce helped to keep afloat many of the liberal and cultural aspects of the curriculum. According to biographer Lawrence Otis Graham, "she revised the curriculum and made sure that the young women were being offered a wide range of courses that supported Washington's industrial trade-skilled approach." Equally important to Tuskegee and Margaret Washington, Bruce provided the students with an example of northern high-class respectability. She also extended Tuskegee's agenda to the North, where she had many friends and philanthropic connections.

Living in Tuskegee after the 1898 death of her husband, proved challenging. In addition, Bruce realized that education in the South differed greatly from the comforts she received in the North, particularly at Howard University. Born into a free aristocratic family in 1853, Josephine Bruce knew a life of relative leisure. Her parents had respectable jobs and her husband, before his death, served as a senator.[27]

While Margaret Washington worked her way into aristocracy, Bruce inherited it. Notions of elitism ran through her blood. Bruce also had grown accustomed to teaching second and third generation college students who attended the best schools money could buy in Washington, D.C. At Tuskegee, however, she was charged with helping to educate, refine, and stimulate students who were ambitious, but whose first exposure to an education occurred when they entered the Institute. Bruce commented that the students at Tuskegee were "not well-poised or intellectually curious" as the more elite students she knew in Washington, D.C. According to her biographer, "these students [at Tuskegee] were largely from poor, uneducated families that lived in what many called the 'black belt.'" This unfamiliar terrain made Bruce feel isolated at Tuskegee. The lack of opportunities for social and cultural activities for a widow increased her desolation. The transition proved more than she could bear. Bruce remained at Tuskegee for two years but disliked the position and the elaborate schedule associated with it.[28]

Josephine Bruce's time at the Institute relieved Margaret Washington of her administrative responsibilities for two years. Her presence also gave Booker T. Washington a useful connection in Boston, through Bruce's son Roscoe Bruce, who proved to be a powerful lieutenant while a student at Harvard. Josephine Bruce continued to aid the Institute even after her term ended. In 1901 Margaret Washington resumed her responsibilities as Lady Principal and remained in the capacity until her death in 1925. She approached the position with more vigor and conviction than ever before. She also used her post at Tuskegee to cultivate her initiatives in the larger community, as Tuskegee's students kept her informed about the daily problems affecting blacks.[29]

Upon her return to campus, Margaret Washington refocused her attention to moral training. She instructed women on leadership practices and the importance of marriage and motherhood. In an 1898 speech, she declared, "today all who are willing to study facts with reference to our growth and strength in this country declare also that the most serious drawback to the race is its lack of careful, moral and healthy motherhood." Washington believed that true motherhood coupled with good character were key ingredients needed to uplift the race in the midst of white opposition. As she later recalled, lessons at the school included every aspect of home life including the maintenance of the garden, proper ways to store food, efficient methods of childbearing, the preparation of food, sewing, cleaning and even home décor.[30]

The number of female students grew rapidly at the turn of the century. The Girls Industry soon needed larger accommodations. In 1901 Tuskegee students constructed Dorothy Hall, the new girls industrial building. Numerous efforts were made towards the professionalization and modernization of education. The scientific method was applied to many fields of study. However, introducing these new skills to black women sparked debates, finding critics even among Tuskegee's administration. Some doubted the validity and usefulness of female Domestic Sciences. After the death of Booker T. Washington, Margaret Washington responded to the patronizing views of his successor, Robert Moton. In 1921 she wrote to President Moton, "I am also sending you some examination questions for all of those trades here so you will get an idea that we [women] do not just use our hands down here, but we also use our minds." Margaret Washington rarely held her tongue in defense of female education. Not even for the Institute's president. This indignation also speaks volumes to the atmosphere Washington must have confronted after her husband's death, struggling to keep the industrial fire burning in a society that looked very different than the one she first encountered in 1889.[31]

Washington maintained that Tuskegee women were more proficient in the art of domesticity than anything else. Not only did the lessons and curriculum prepare them to be effective mothers, in many ways it gave them the instruction needed to lead and teach proper nutrition, health and food preparation, to other women. On one particular examination, female students were asked: to "give the chemical action of yeast in bread . . . Just how does baking powder make mixtures light . . . what are the essential points in canning?" In regard to the nature of diet and health, the examiner asked: "How many calories of heat will be given off if you spend one-hour walking, 1 hour sitting, 2 hours in light exercise," then asked "has the proper amount been supplied through diet?" This exam, among others, demonstrated the complexity of the curriculum and courses given under Margaret Washington's directive. The exam also suggests that although women were seen as natural mothers and caregivers, the curriculum trained them to become more proficient in the art of home economics and to better comprehend the science behind things they were already doing—an important step to uplifting the race. Washington rarely kept silent in order to allow men to undermine the work being done by women in the field of domesticity and character building. Such private acts would have had grave implications on the race as a whole.[32]

Respectability Politics called for its followers to engage in a public performance of culture, and racial uplift embodied respectability. Washington's administrative role, in juxtaposition to the Jim Crow South, required that she produce female students who were well-trained in their discipline, and well-groomed in their culture and communication skills. "If a person reads well, writes well and spells well, he makes a good impression and very often is able to secure work where otherwise he wouldn't," Margaret declared.[33] A Tuskegee graduate who later became a principal herself wrote Washington thanking her for all of her advice and guidance, crediting Washington for her stern tactics which ultimately prepared the student for a career in administration. The former student closed the letter by urging Washington to continue to show girls the right way and assured her that in return they would enter the world more prepared and equipped for success. This letter reveals the positive impact Washington made on women as wage earners in highly desirable fields. Tuskegee Institute stood as the modern incubator of black propaganda. Of letters that made their way to the Tuskegee archives, few were from disgruntled or unsatisfied students.[34]

Washington filed countless letters from former students who either became teachers or administrators. These individuals spread the Tuskegee gospel across the nation. Margaret Washington succeeded in promoting industrial trades as granting access to economic freedom, while also encouraging a moral lifestyle. In October of 1907, former student Charles P. Adams found himself in Grambling, Louisiana, attempting to rebuild at a school that lacked the foundation of Tuskegee Institute. He wrote: "Seeing that it is a lack of industrial and moral training . . . that is causing so much crime, vice, poverty and immortality among our young people, we are determined . . . to build an institution as will supply the deficiency."[35]

As a consequence of Booker T. Washington's frequent absences, he established an Executive Council. The Council, made up of fifteen to twenty officers and department heads, assisted with many of the minor decision-making aspects of the Institute. Members of the community regularly sought Margaret Washington's advice on behalf of their children. She routinely sent the parents to the Council, who attempted to handle the disputes. She did not, however, always side with the parents. In one situation, the concerned mother of Devotion Greene wrote to Margaret Washington. According to Washington, Mrs. Greene asked, "if there was any possible way of getting Devotion back in school to finish her course. She said she was going to bring it up [to the] Council and asked me if I would vote for it." Margaret Washington, who believed that moral character and respectability were of the utmost importance, responded, stating that: "I told her distinctively that I would vote against it." Mrs. Greene responded with disapproval. Although Margaret Washington was the Lady Principal and second-in-command to Booker T. Washington, Mrs. Greene intended to take the matter to the Council. This did little to shift Washington from her original position. She informed the Council that "the girl who was playing cards and drinking liquor at Mr. Spalding's house was a woman downtown instead of a student," and should not be readmitted into Tuskegee. Consequently, Devotion Greene never earned a degree from the Institute.[36]

Respectability was a crucial issue among middle-class women and men. Anything contradictory to dominant middle-class values stood to jeopardize the advancement of the race and their progress towards uplift. Margaret Washington frowned upon public smoking and games, excessive dancing, and gambling. She believed she was training the best and the brightest and thus responsible for their success. Booker Washington's reputation, as well as her own, required her to take this position, given that graduates represented the accomplishments of Tuskegee. Furthermore, these women were expected to become race women. For this reason, Margaret Washington remained stern when it came to the complete education of women, particularly when it came to their moral character.

Blacks required an education to lead productive lives. "I believe that you expect our children to be decent citizens. This they cannot be if there is no improvement made in the amount of character and education now given them," Margaret Washington noted. Character building was the signature social reform of nineteenth century black elites. Within that concept, respectability reigned supreme. Significant changes occurred in the mid-nineteenth century. Reformers created separate spheres of respectability for white men and women—which came to be known as the "cult of true womanhood." Men were designated as natural leaders, while women were subjugated to their domestic responsibilities. Closer attention was therefore placed on the moral character of women and children. Certainly these myriad efforts towards raising the standards of the poor did not suddenly appear in the aftermath of slavery; however, race women adopted such principles as piety, purity, and domesticity, to refute white stereotypes about the inherent promiscuity and immorality of black women.[37]

Washington also concerned herself with the girls' appearance and attire, since these elements were assumed to be outward signs of respectability. She routinely expressed doubts concerning the appearance of the post-graduate girls. They were not required to wear uniforms but were expected to dress in modest clothing. Because they were older than the traditional student body, she naturally held them to higher standards. In an apparently frustrated state, she rebuffed their conduct, remarking that "they come in just as they feel like it. At one time these girls came to their meals as they should and there is no reason why they should not do so now." She went on to declare that "Dress has a great deal to do with the impression which a woman makes." In addition, the women were routinely not eating at the tables. Although a simple defiance, this practice of refinement spoke to the race as a whole. As mothers in training, learning to sit at a table during meals, in Margaret's eyes, better prepared these women for the responsibility of freedom. Washington's credibility among clubwomen would also be questioned if the women being trained at Tuskegee did not publicly perform to standards of respectability. Going far beyond education, or a skillset, black women fought against ruthless claims of sexual immorality and low moral conduct.[38]

Margaret Washington protected the image of black girls and the school, routinely reprimanding students and faculty. This authoritative posture made her appear unapproachable. In fact, in response to Margaret Washington's demeanor, faculty member Elizabeth Benson suggested "to look at her, a little high school kid would probably be afraid. But when you talked with her or when you heard her talk, you found that she was a very warm and concerned person for her students." She was also a stickler of punctuality and procedures. According to a former student, one afternoon when Washington called the horse barn for her horse (whose name was Dan) and buggy, they did not have a boy to send. She then requested the help of a female student to bring her horse and buggy to Dorothy Hall. As compensation, Washington offered to take the young student with her downtown. However, as was the custom, female students were not allowed off campus past 4:00pm without prior written approval. According to the student, Mrs. Washington looked at her watch and said, "No, it's too late. I can't take you because it will be after 4:00 before I get back . . . I don't have time to go back and call Mrs. Landers." This incident left the student perplexed. "I couldn't understand why . . . [with] all of her status . . . she had to ask . . . but I understood it years later. It was procedure." Just as Margaret enforced proper protocol on the instructors, she practiced them herself. However, she also expressed frustration to rules without compromise. As was the case when she requested two-dozen eggs from the commissary for visitors on campus. Mr. Attwell, who was in charge of the commissary, "refused to give me the eggs, saying that I would have to wait until the Business committee met today at two o'clock which would be all too late to be used when I wish to use them," Margaret wrote to Mr. Logan. She went on to conclude, "as far as I am concerned—a thing like this does two things; it makes you lose interest in trying to do a thing of this kind and tempts one to break the school's rules." Though she understood why the rules were in place, exceptions existed in most all situations.[39]

Margaret Washington sometimes deviated in standard punishments on campus. In a letter addressed to the Executive Council at Tuskegee, Washington brought mention of a prospective student, Irene Burroughs, who taught before attending Tuskegee, and had stood accused of "permitting her cousin to use her Teacher's License." The case reached law officials who, along with the assistance of Irene's parents, were able to resolve the dispute without any penalty to Irene.[40]

When Irene applied for admission into Tuskegee, the Executive Council sought the recommendation of Margaret Washington. "There is no doubt in my mind that Irene did let her cousin use her Teacher's License," Washington conferred. Despite Irene's guilt, however, she was admitted to the Institute. "I consider the act like that of a child who knows it is not right to take its mother's sugar and does not understand all the wrong of such an act. I think the humiliation of the whole thing has been quite punishment enough," concluded Washington.[41] There are few documented situations where Washington admitted to the misstep of a student, without reprimand. She made it a practice to be fair with the girls as far as such a thing is possible.[42] Yet, rules and guidelines were not etched in stone and many times she used her own discretion to determine the severity of an infraction. Unlike Irene Burroughs, who falsified documents to obtain employment for her cousin, Devotion Greene violated customs of female respectability and highly respected notions of womanhood, which was inexcusable. Greene's willingness to hang around men went against the era's fundaments of respectability and also reinforced negative stereotypes about black women's character and their alleged promiscuity. Washington built her career attempting to refute and rectify these claims, as she, like most middle-class women of her era, believed that the best of the race was judged by the worst of them.[43]

The responsibilities of racial uplift required a full-time commitment. Administration proved to be a 24-hour occupation and female pay continuously made headlines. Tuskegee provided waged jobs for as many students as possible. Along with the task of managing a marginally funded budget, on many occasions Washington became a mediator for the female students who performed all of the laundry duties for the entire Institute, with deficient equipment and meager pay. Female students received ninety cents for thirteen days of laundry work. She complained to the male staff that the female students were working in the laundry without the means and appropriate equipment to properly and effectively complete the task of laundry in a timely manner. "We are behind with the laundry work this week" and "we are still without irons except a little over one a piece which means that every few minutes eighty-six girls have to stop and wait for irons to get hot," Washington lamented in an official letter to Scott.[44] She contacted Scott to resolve the issue. "I hardly know what to suggest but it seems to me that something must be done," she asserted. The issue was temporarily resolved, and students were eventually better compensated. However, Washington continuously rallied against the glaring inequalities shown to female students' education and labor.[45]

She used her resources to solicit outside funds for the Girls Department, particularly for the purchase of efficient equipment, supplies, and additional buildings. The Girls Department budget required constant attention. "I am doing my best to cut down expenses," wrote Margaret. However, she usually found her resources void of finances. The constant scavenger hunt for equipment and funds was not unique to Tuskegee. Many black schools during this time had to contend with skeletal budgets. Her alma mater Fisk regularly experienced financial hardships in its beginning years, with poor salaries often in arrears.[46]

Administrators at HBCUs understood the key position their institutions held in the community. In many instances, they lobbied on behalf of one another. Despite the monetary problems Tuskegee Institute encountered, and amidst their aging equipment, it was a relatively well-funded black institution. Margaret Washington even solicited donations from white philanthropists. At the beginning of the twentieth century she was successful in helping Fisk secure a needed Carnegie Library grant. Fisk officials had unsuccessfully approached Andrew Carnegie on numerous occasions throughout the years. However, Carnegie "finally in 1908 gave the school $20,000, in part as a favor to Margaret Washington, whom he admired," writes Richardson.[47]

Margaret Washington also received aid and financial assistance from black businesswomen, most notably Madam C. J. Walker. Born Sarah Breedlove Walker in Louisiana in 1867, Walker grew up very poor and worked as a washerwoman and cook. She married at age fourteen and was a widow by nineteen. After struggling to "tame" her hair, Walker created a cosmetic business. She eventually amassed a fortune, making her one of the first black millionaires in the nation. Walker was also very generous with her funds and in support of the industrial model and philosophy of "pulling yourself up by your bootstraps." Walker gave generously to Tuskegee and the Girls Industry, in particular. By 1915 she had established a scholarship fund in her name for women at Tuskegee to complete their studies. She also wrote to Margaret after Booker's death asserting, that he was "the greatest man America ever knew." A year after his passing in 1916, Walker visited Margaret on the campus of Tuskegee, along with students who were recipients of her scholarship. When Walker died in 1919 she left money to both Tuskegee Institute and the National Association for the Advancement of Colored People.[48]

Maintaining an industrial institute in the south produced a number of moving parts. Students were typically first-generation students who lacked the financial resources to pay for their schooling; many worked on campus for low wages to cover tuition and living expenses. Most of the faculty did not fare much better, and pay remained a contested budget issue. In one situation the threat of losing a valuable faculty member, because of the Institution's inability to provide pay raises, drove Margaret Washington to formally request that Booker T. Washington reconsider the issue of increasing teacher salaries.[49]

He generally offered his faculty lower wages than were seen at other HBCUs. Booker Washington expected his staff to be so dedicated to the cause of racial uplift that they willingly accepted a significantly lower salary. But Executive Council members at Tuskegee received the best salaries of all. For example, in 1903 Council members earned over $1000 a year plus board, compared to junior faculty who made under $300 a year with board. Margaret Washington believed that if the teachers were not making enough money to take care of basic necessities, then achieving goals of lifting others to a higher purpose would be impossible to attain.[50]

Many faculty members eventually left the Institute. Roscoe Conkling Bruce, a Harvard graduate and son of former Senator Blanche K. and Josephine Bruce, was an open proponent of industrial education. He served as supervisor to Tuskegee Institute's Academic Department from 1903 to 1906. Bruce documented that the frequent departure of faculty members from Tuskegee coincided with low salaries more comparable to those of elementary school teachers, than college level faculty. In a rare turn of events, on July 3, 1915, the Cleveland *Gazette* reported that on his 25th wedding anniversary, Julius Rosenwald "distributed $5,000 among the teachers of the Tuskegee Normal and Industrial Institute, Alabama, on the basis of faithfulness" and length of service. Faculty members who had served fifteen-plus years received the monetary award.[51]

Amidst the challenges of pay, students continued to graduate from the Institute, remaining highly marketable and well prepared for the responsibilities that came with education. "I shall never forget 'the Tuskegee Spirit'" declared a graduate, expressing an enduring sentiment among students. These letters were also published for mass consumption, citing comments such as: "I am always pleased to hear the progress of my dear alma mater."[52]

Frequent positive articles like those in the Cleveland *Gazette* praised the work being carried out at Tuskegee: "It is more than a crystallization of a masterful idea—it is a GENERATOR from which a mighty current of industrialism is flowing through the southland and gradually bending its course in other directions." There were also critics of the Institute. For example, William Monroe Trotter's Boston *Guardian*, and white southern papers were on the leading edge. Due primarily to negative press, which Booker T. Washington typically silenced, Margaret Washington advised faculty members to document and spread the positive news of their departments. In addition, Tuskegee was the cradle of the Washington's greatest influence. Emmett Scott ensured that the news and business of the institute were meticulously kept and that the

Washingtons' stayed abreast to any negative press or threats to the Institute. During Booker Washington's frequent absences, Scott provided detailed updates on the daily operation of the school, and any external threats to the institution or its mission, or threats to the leader himself. It was only natural that Scott and Margaret Washington would work closely in matters concerning the maintenance of the school, positive propaganda, and the hiring and firing of personnel and students alike. On one occasion in particular, Emmett Scott informed Margaret Washington that he saw and heard of many interesting things that were going on "in the Domestic Science Division, including the way the girls are working this year in cooking, [and] serving at the teacher's dining hall."[53] Scott went on to suggest that these things along with others should be included in the student paper. This practice of spreading positive propaganda was not new to Tuskegee. Booker Washington regularly curtailed the dissemination of negative information about Tuskegee and himself. According to historian August Meier, "the most sensational charge leveled at Booker Washington during his score of years as a leader of national importance was that he subsidized newspapers and magazines in order to silence criticism." Booker Washington went so far as to purchase stock in the black press to better control what was written about him and the Tuskegee Machine.[54]

Publicity along with respectability served as important components of racial uplift, culture, and the field of Home Economics. Margaret Washington prioritized these values into the daily lives of students, ensuring a holistic learning experience for graduates. In her administrative role, she handled the day-to-day concerns that impacted the Institute, including recommendations, issues of pay, hiring and firing, and the dissemination of positive propaganda. She remained stern, but fair in her capacity. Washington also fought for gender equality, while simultaneously adhering to concepts of nineteenth century respectability. Her position at Tuskegee, although taxing, positioned her for greater social reforms. The Tuskegee platform also launched her into a work that extended beyond the duties of the classroom and administration. Her desire to help improve black life propelled her into the Tuskegee community and expanded her racial reform into club work. African American women's clubs, according to Ida B. Wells-Barnett, were "the new power, the new molder of public sentiments, to accomplish the reforms that the pulpit and the law have failed to do."[55]

Fannie N. Smith, Booker T. Washington's first wife. The two married in 1882 and moved together to Tuskegee, Alabama, where Washington had taken a position as principal of the African American school. Smith died suddenly and of unknown causes in 1884.

Olivia America Davidson, Booker T. Washington's second wife. The two married in 1886. Davidson served as the cofounding principal and the first Lady Principal until her untimely death in 1889.

Margaret Murray Washington, pictured in middle, with friends in Jackson, Mississippi, circa 1906.

The Booker T. Washington Monument, also known as "Lifting the Veil of Ignorance" was sculpted by New York artist Charles Keck and dedicated to Tuskegee Institute in 1922. Casted in bronze and mounted on a marble base, it is inscribed with multiple texts, including speeches from Booker T. Washington.

Margaret Murray Washington's workstation with images of her homelife and the American flag.

Dorothy Hall. Originally built in 1901. Remodeled several times and is currently part of the Kellogg Hotel and Conference Center.

A younger Margaret Murray draped in an embroidered dress.

Girls Industrial Building. Dorothy Hall. Originally built in 1901. Remodeled several times and is currently part of the Kellogg Hotel & Conference Center.

The young Washington family, circa 1899. From left, Earnest, Baker, Margaret, Booker, and Portia.

From left, rear: Earnest, Baker. From left, seated: Margaret, Booker, and Portia Washington.

Booker, Margaret, Portia, Earnest, Baker, and Laura Murray (Margaret's niece and the Washington's adopted daughter).

The executive council of Tuskegee Institute, circa 1906, which includes Margaret Murray Washington.

An older, more experienced Margaret Murray Washington.

An aged portrait of Margaret Murray Washington
that clearly reveals the physical impact of race work.

Chapter Four

Tuskegee Women Unite

> There is no question which affects any part of the South in which I am not interested and for which I am not willing to give both time and strength.
>
> —Margaret Murray Washington
> (*The Negro Home*, 1920)[1]

On March 2, 1895, nearly a dozen educators packed into the small room of Dorothy Hall, located on the campus of Tuskegee Institute. Under the direction of Margaret Washington, the women created the Tuskegee Woman's Club (TWC). The organization facilitated their political, social and intellectual advancement. For years race leaders, black women in particular, lacked the social, political and economic means to change the dominant ideologies of white America. However, the end of the nineteenth century saw a shift in black female activism. Black middle-class women used their limited resources to uplift their communities from within. They went into the prison complex system, built schools on former plantations, and created platforms for the liberation of the entire race. Club work allowed Margaret Washington to assert her political autonomy as she created alternative platforms to combat vicious attacks against the race and its womanhood.

The commitment of local autonomy attracted Washington to club work. As she began to identify as an aristocrat, new standards of elitism offered her a respectable course to advance the community. After four years at the Institute and a year of marriage, in 1893 she made her first public attempt to organize women through the creation of a local chapter of Mothers' Meetings. This network of working and middle-class black women helped to improve standards of living among women and children in the Black Belt. Washington's creation of Mothers' Meetings paralleled the initiatives made in the North by white women like Jane Addams and Ellen Gates Starr, who co-founded Chicago's Hull House in 1889. Their social reform efforts effectively assimilated newly-arrived European immigrants, with a primary concern for women and children. Still, closer to home, as her husband desperately gave farmers new ideas, new hopes, and new aspirations, the revelation came to Margaret Washington that the community of Tuskegee could serve as a focal point to "correct certain evils among women and girls and to bring about needed reforms."[2]

The triumph of Jim Crow in the 1890s and early twentieth century coincided with the rise of the Black Women's Club Movement and efforts to improve conditions of blacks in America. However, Jim Crow did not merely separate the races, it legally reduced blacks to second-class citizenship in public and private life. Race leaders were tasked with the daunting responsibility of "lifting as they climbed" through the trenches of racialized violence, bigotry, inequality, sexism, white supremacy and a legal system that sought to strip them of their very humanity. According to scholar and theologian Howard Thurman in his 1965 book, *The Luminous Darkness*, Jim Crow gave "rise to an immoral exercise of power of the strong over the weak, that is to say, advantage over disadvantage. The restrictions affecting the disadvantaged, the Negroes, are mandatory, while there is a voluntary element in the way the same restrictions affect white persons." In order for white supremacy to succeed, blacks had to accept racist rhetoric about their inability to thrive separate from the watchful gaze of inequality, and black immobility. Margaret Washington and other black women used this forced separation as a tool to uplift the race from within. Economic independence of a people less than three decades removed from servitude remained an important tool in the larger movement of black freedom, and women continued to play a central role.[3]

Mothers' Meetings were inspired by the first Tuskegee Negro Conference held in February 1892. Booker T. Washington invited farmers and their families from rural areas to discuss their unique place within the southern economy. Washington challenged the prevailing perceptions associated with black farmers, self-governance, and their economic stability. Through the troupe of respectability he stressed the importance of dressing well, understanding best practices, political consciousness, and community leadership. To race men and women, these strict codes of conduct disproved black farmers' inferiority and inability to govern themselves without white supervision. In addition, they proved blacks were fit for full-citizenship rights. The politics of respectability, according to Booker Washington, gave farmers a greater respect for their labor which in time would shift the dominant narrative surrounding their black bodies. White supremacy, however, proved reactionary as it continuously remodeled itself to fit the challenges of black progress.[4]

Twenty-eight years removed from slavery, black families continued to mend their broken ties and to find their place in the American South. A great majority of families remained in agriculture and women were actively seeking ways to better influence their home, economically and domestically. Black women attended the first Tuskegee Negro Conference. However, they were not represented on the program. Nineteenth century gender politics required that black women create separate spaces within the race to address concerns of sex, domesticity and labor outside of the household. Margaret Washington's Mothers' Meetings served as a political and social outlet. Through efforts of the local chapter, racial uplift in Tuskegee extended its realms of protection to women and children.[5]

The Mothers' Meetings represented an honest attempt to organize women in the community and to empower them through collaborations and the dissemination of best practices. The Mothers' Meetings headquarters were established on the top floor of an old store located on the main street of Tuskegee. The first meetings resembled town hall assemblies. Local working women discussed southern violence, childcare, and black life in general. According to Margaret Washington: "That first meeting I can never forget. The women came, and each one, as she entered, looked at me and seemed to say, 'Where is it?' We talked it all over, the needs of our women of the country, the best way of helping each other, and there and then began the first Mothers' Meeting, which now [1920] has in its membership two hundred and twenty-nine women."[6] After the first few years the meetings were held in a large hall on the main street of Tuskegee in property owned by a local black merchant and graduate of the Institute.[7]

Mothers' Meetings soon caught the attention of black women across the state. Many traveled great distances with their small children to attend the sessions. More than fifty youth under the age of twelve attended regular meetings. "What should be done with the children?" women asked. Washington eventually created a small library for them. Instruction consisted of the three R's—race, respectability, and reading. More often than not, black children had limited learning experience in childhood. Blacks witnessed first-hand the inequalities associated with blackness which greatly impacted their psyche. Many toiled in the field at young ages and had few outlets to cultivate their imagination. The small libraries did more than provide the youth with necessary reading materials. They served as a refuge from discrimination and as a safe harbor for the development of black childhood.[8]

Female students at Tuskegee promoted the work of Mothers' Meetings. The Institute's newspaper, *The Tuskegee Student*, devoted a vast majority of its attention to the student body and graduates of Tuskegee. It also gave attention to the way Mothers' Meetings had beautified the city, and how the children were behaving better than in previous years. The paper credited the improvements to the leadership of Margaret Washington. Sewing circles were organized for the young girls and reading groups for young and older males. The women established a day and evening school for parents in a local cabin. These initiatives promoted community pride and support of Tuskegee Institute. It also led to the recruitment of future students and created a healthy association to education and physical labor. Without fail, however, these sacrifices of leadership weighed heavily on race leaders.[9]

Washington's close friend Cornelia Bowen also took lessons from the creation of her Mothers' Meeting initiative. Just a few miles away in Mt. Meigs, Alabama, Bowen chartered a local chapter of Mothers' Meetings. By 1900, local papers reported that Mothers' Meetings in Mt. Meigs had influenced the lives of over two-thousand people. Residents received weekly lessons from the women on childcare, race consciousness, and job opportunities. What Washington created in Tuskegee began to spread to communities throughout the south and nation.[10]

During the formative years of her social work, Washington engaged the campus and the community. Racial uplift often carried an unavoidable strain. The myth of the superwoman caused many race women to work to the point of exhaustion, sometimes creating resentment among blacks. Washington expressed occasional discontent with expected duties to her race. Other clubwomen like Janie Porter Barrett, the daughter of a domestic laborer and the president of the Virginia State Federation of Colored Women's Clubs, verbalized the stress associated with uplifting the race. While still a student at Hampton Normal and Agricultural Institute (now Hampton University) in Virginia, she lamented on the strain race work caused, confessing "I did not love my race." While speaking with Florence Lattimore, "a smile play[ed] about her lips"[11] as Barrett said 'I didn't want the responsibility of it. I wanted pretty things. At the institute, we were always hearing about our duty to our race, and I got so tired of that! Why, on Sundays I used to wake up and say to myself, 'To-day I don't have to do a single thing for my race!'"[12]

Washington came to understand the lifelong responsibility of race work. "I often shudder to note the change which has come over me since I have been engaged in this work and I try too, to influence myself differently," she wrote to her husband. She often expressed self-doubt and fatigue. She took brief sabbaticals from administration, however, her private life was inextricably intertwined with her social work. She was married to a race man and to racial uplift. For many race women, in order to live a life of usefulness, they sacrificed their personal interest and took very little time for themselves. The success of the movement also required race women to train the next generation in the doctrine of racial uplift.[13]

Jim Crow laws demanded that a collective body of individuals rally in defense of the race. While Mothers' Meetings were well received and emulated in other cities, the women needed a stronger organizational network. Margaret Washington knew she would soon be forced to expand her realm of influence. In 1895, two years after the first Mothers' Meeting, she formed an alliance of women to share in the responsibility of community building. A few months before Booker T. Washington gave his famous speech at the Cotton States Exposition, in Atlanta, Georgia, Margaret Washington drafted the blueprint for the formation of the Tuskegee Woman's Club, the first-ever black women's club in Tuskegee, Alabama. The local chapter of Mothers' Meetings came under the umbrella of the new organization and helped to enhance Margaret Washington's influence among race leaders across the nation.

On March 2, 1895, at the age of thirty-four, Washington's leadership culminated, as she connected a network of middle-class women with interests similar to her own. Four of the initial twelve founding mothers were: Mrs. James B. Washington, a teacher at Tuskegee and wife of Booker's adopted brother; Miss Susan Helen Porter, a principal for Tuskegee's Training School; Mrs. Adella Hunt Logan, activist and wife of Tuskegee's Treasurer Warren Logan; and Miss Elizabeth E. Lane, an academic teacher. The remaining eight women were also wives of prominent men of the Institute and throughout the community. The TWC began as a private organization. In fact, during its early years, members could only join through the recommendation of Margaret Washington and other founding members, thus ensuring an exclusive membership.[14]

By 1905 the TWC had a total of ten departments, ranging from spiritual teachings, self-improvement and education, to assistance for the elderly. Each division had a chairwoman whose responsibility it was to educate themselves in their respective areas. As they formulated best practices to improve the conditions of the race, they went into the community and engaged in an experimental form of uplift, providing local residents with proper tools to effectively ameliorate their mental and physical conditions. Departments of the TWC included: The Jail division, Thompson's Quarters, Temperance division, Vesta Club, Margaret Murray Washington group, Humane Society, Suffrage division, Ednah Cheney Circle, Mothers' Meetings, and the Elizabeth Russell Plantation.

As president, Washington espoused the doctrines of uplift leadership, and its codes often straddled the proverbial fence of elitism. TWC members created a network where middle-class values and social expectations were cultivated. In their minds, however, they were raising the moral standards of black southerners. This they did while often simultaneously adopting many of the attitudes of whites towards separatism—a practice not uncommon in Jim Crow America. The TWC's early constitution instructed working-class women on the importance of adhering to codes of respectability, and the interconnectedness of moral character with first-class citizenship rights. Club members also treated the organization as a forum for their intellectual, educational, and spiritual growth, but they were unavoidably bound to guiding the race.[15]

Clubwomen were tasked with leading the race while also remaining linked to the community. Scholar Willard B. Gatewood writes: "Aristocrats of color readily joined other blacks in pursuit of economic and political objectives, but distance and exclusiveness marked their social relationship with those below them on the social scale. The aristocracy, in fact, embraced a version of Booker T. Washington's famous hand-and-fingers analogy: in all things purely social the aristocrats tended to be as separate from other blacks as the fingers, yet one as the hand in all things for 'progress of the race.'"[16]

Margaret Washington claimed to reject class separation. In an 1898 address at Old Bethel Church in South Carolina, as she gazed down at the women, she stated that "we cannot separate ourselves from our people no matter how much we try; for one I have no desire to do so." She frequently expressed the importance of blacks from all societal and political classes working together. These sentiments appeared more idealistic, as the exclusive nature of the TWC suggests that in practice, certain levels of class differences were inevitable. Furthermore, Margaret Washington's entrance into the upper-class further illustrates inherent distinctions from the masses of blacks. Nonetheless, she promoted race solidarity as she sent the clubwomen out into communities. Because black middle-class men and women were closer to the masses than were their white middle-class counterparts, they could make greater strides in progress within the larger black community. And while some race leaders benefitted from the self-imposed class distinction that uplift promoted, other elite blacks took on the responsibility of transforming the race from within.[17]

According to clubwoman Mary Church Terrell: "Colored women of education and culture know that they cannot escape altogether the consequences of the acts of their most depraved sisters. They see that even if they were wicked enough to turn a deaf ear to the call of duty, both policy and self-preservation demand that they go down among the lowly, the illiterate and even the vicious, to whom they are bound by the ties of race and sex, and put forth every possible effort to reclaim them."[18]

The TWC started their outreach in forgotten backwoods near the city. They first formed the Elizabeth Russell Plantation as a major reclamation project. Because public health and other government agencies typically ignored blacks, especially those in the South, reforms on the plantation were imperative for the very survival of those working and living on the property. Black women across the nation were leading efforts for improving health, as healthcare initiatives were strategically placed within the woman's sphere. Clubwomen saw healthcare as another voluntary social-work extension of their professional endeavors. It is not surprising that Washington placed such great emphasis on wellness programs, given that she herself suffered from a history of poor health. In the aftermath of slavery, many blacks lived through undocumented and persistent bouts of illnesses. Conscious efforts toward improvements made to black mental and physical health became an integral step in the philosophy of uplift.[19] By 1916 the TWC worked in a number of healthcare campaigns including Baby Week and other joint efforts with the Health League of Alabama. Through such initiatives, the perpetuation of high ideals of education, cleanliness, and improved community life were enhanced.[20]

Club work allowed black women a mutual space to serve in their communities outside of the home. Southern women in other cities used the TWC as a blueprint to extend their middle-class values onto the masses. For example, Lugenia Burns Hope created the Atlanta Neighborhood Union. Hope, a St. Louis, Missouri native, organized middle-class women in 1908 after the death of her neighbor. In Burns's imagination, a lack of community collectiveness ultimately aided in the neighbor's death. This, amongst other grievances, served as a catalyst for the establishment of the Union. Women, especially black women in the South, had a social and moral responsibility towards improving the health consciousness of blacks. That they were compelled to perform these roles while upholding concepts of femininity afforded club women access into traditionally male spaces. These affiliations expanded their realm of influence as their community activism extended beyond conventional female spheres to spaces that men and women shared: political organizations, mutual aid societies, universal organizations and schools.[21]

The TWC's Elizabeth Russell Plantation was located approximately eight miles outside of Tuskegee. Heavily populated with former convicts and those completing prison sentences, the clubwomen assumed the responsibility of a halfway house. Many were released from jails in Macon County to serve out their remaining time in agricultural labor. The convict lease system, common in the South, exploited the labor of blacks. In Alabama alone, according to historian David Oshinsky, "convict leasing generated about 6% of the state's revenue . . . giving Alabama the most profitable prison system in the country." Many of the residents lived in small dilapidated cabins that had survived the period of slavery. Leaking roofs and dirt floors elevated the transfer of disease and bacteria while simultaneously clouding the windows of possibilities. Washington described the former inmates as being thrown together without a sense of community. She went on to assert "they had little or no idea of the proper ways in which to bring up their children." Dwellings were very run-down, children were unwashed and undisciplined, homes were typically unkempt, while notions of legal marriage eluded them. For nearly twelve years members of the TWC worked to transform the settlement into a thriving community.[22]

Amidst uplift, Washington believed that stable Christian homes produced wholesome, well-balanced, and race-conscious children. She even required Tuskegee students to attend chapel services every Sunday and nightly chapel exercises, although they were "strictly undenominational." With the black home serving as the incubator of race progress, a religious framework for respectability and order remained imperative. Washington insisted that no job outranked that of motherhood, and she provided the women of the neighborhood with tools on becoming better mothers. This belief may be the reason she informally adopted her niece Laura and nephew Thomas. Homes became centers that produced the next generation of young men and women who would carry on the traditions and values necessary for continued racial improvement and uplift. And though Washington espoused these views within the club, she too battled with the difficult task of working in the community while also caring for her new family. The performance of respectability required that she not only embrace these views, but that she abide by them, in part to prove that black women were Christians, responsible mothers and deserving of protection under the law.[23]

Black women's alleged immorality was used to justify the inhuman treatment of the race. But, just as Tuskegee's Chaplain Reverend Whittaker preached, 'women [are] looked upon as inferior to her brother, man," which he concluded was a mistake. As an administrator and clubwoman, Washington sought to refute many of these exaggerated falsehoods through a strategic network of like-minded women. She asked Tuskegee teachers to assist her with the community residents. In the beginning years of the TWC, women went to the Russell Plantation only on Sundays. On that first Sunday Washington selected the most promising cabin and asked the resident if she could come back the following Sunday to hold a meeting. The woman agreed, and the clubwomen along with women from the neighborhood, went there early the next Sunday morning with cleaning utensils. This random cabin served as the prototype for other residents in the community. Through the simple task of cleaning, the clubwomen attempted to instill pride of self and home in the residents. These efforts were also meant to help repair untreated emotional bruises left in the wake of Reconstruction; bruises that many blacks learned to suffer through, despite visible signs of pain.[24]

Washington recommended that everyone take part in cleaning the house before all of the residents arrived. One of the neighborhood women took a broom and "half-heartedly" swept part of the room. Washington volunteered to finish the job. She had not gone far with her half before the same woman said: "Oh, Mis' Washington, lemme take de broom an' do mah half ovah." Long after the moment had passed, Washington confessed, "I have always thought that one unconscious lesson in thoroughness was the foundation of our work on that plantation." She was correct. The women of the community looked up to Washington and assumed the lessons being taught would eventually help to improve their morale and quality of life. This is not to say there were no objections from any residents about the invasive manner in which their homes, dress and health were inspected, but most welcomed the assistance.[25]

Eventually people came out to the meetings in large numbers. After a few Sundays, residents accepted the offer to have a day-school opened. The owner of the Elizabeth Russell Plantation donated the use of an old cabin, to house an instructor and classrooms. The teacher was a Tuskegee Institute graduate, Anne Davis. With a few simple household belongings Davis moved into the schoolhouse, and began daily lessons for the children at the plantation.[26]

The Elizabeth Russell Plantation, as a component of the TWC, served as a blueprint for black women's prison reform work. Less than thirty miles from the Institute in Mt. Meigs, Alabama, Booker Washington solicited the assistance of another Tuskegee graduate, Cornelia Bowen (also known as Nellie), to head a similar school. Bowen was born enslaved in 1858 on what became Tuskegee Institute.[27] By 1885 the twenty-six-year-old, tall, mixed-race and slender student, earned a first-grade diploma, in a class of ten, of the first graduates of Tuskegee Institute. Upon graduation, she became the principal of the local training school, the "Children's House," in Tuskegee. After serving in this capacity for many years, Bowen recalled, "feeling that I could be of more service to my people, and could better teach in the outside world the principals for which Tuskegee stands, I resigned my work at Tuskegee . . . for a broader field of usefulness."[28] Bowen returned to the South in 1888 at the request of Booker Washington to head the Mt. Meigs Colored Industrial Institute and later Reformatory in Mt. Meigs, Alabama.[29]

Similar to Margaret Washington's work with the women of Tuskegee, Bowen helped to turn Mt. Meigs into a thriving town of informed and educated citizens. A testament to her impact could be seen in their new motto "buy land," a stark departure from the oversaturation of tenant farming that populated the town upon her arrival. As she built the school, Bowen became increasingly interested in extending its influence into the greater community. Prior to her arrival to Mt. Meigs, there were no local farmers' conferences, Mothers' Meetings, town and gown collaborations, Improvement Societies, or Women's Clubs. By 1900, however, Bowen, Margaret, and other clubwomen had successfully formed local and state clubs. "Women's organizations, like all others, [did] not spring up like mushrooms, but [were] called into existence by necessity to establish or meet some great truths." These organizations focused on the special needs of blacks. Black women's clubs, in particular, were completely governed and operated by women of color, placing at the forefront, the special needs of black youth. Many of these women, however, subscribed to notions of respectability politics which focused heavily on adopting a moral public life and the constant policing of black bodies.[30]

Throughout the years, the Elizabeth Russell day-school in Tuskegee continued to grow. After a stay of three years in the old cabin, the school required larger accommodations. TWC members soon purchased ten acres of land that adjoined the plantation, and became acreage owned by black women. The grounds included a wood-frame house with three rooms. One room served as the schoolroom, another as the teacher's quarters, and the third room was designed for the study of home economics. Without the assistance of governmental aid, the residents of the community were encouraged to be self-sufficient, which reduced the amount of exploitation they received from whites' overpriced groceries. The community raised crops and cattle. 'From farm to plate' became their motto. The food grown on the plantation also fed the day-school students. This renewed pride in the land helped many black children see the personal benefits of working with their hands. For too long American slavery produced feelings of shame and a mental detachment from manual labor. Generations of blacks toiled the soil where their malnourished children died, that their loved ones were sold to preserve, and where streams of their blood flowed after failed attempts at freedom. For many blacks the soil was inextricably linked to attempts to destroy their very humanity. But through TWC efforts, black men, women and children were given a new lease on life from a regenerated sense of pride and social consciousness, toward a land fully connected to their freedom.[31]

These endeavors made by the clubwomen to provide necessary resources to the community became increasingly essential after the Supreme Court's ruling in the *Plessy v. Ferguson* case of 1896, which affirmed the concept of separate-but-equal as a legal practice. The ruling further separated blacks and whites, driving blacks, like Washington, to be more inclusive in their outreach. Black public facilities such as libraries and healthcare institutions were inferior to those of whites, if they even existed. Black schools that received used and outdated texts from white schools were fortunate to have any books at all. In many ways, the 1896 decision heightened the need for social organizations that placed the health, education, and stability of blacks foremost.[32]

Measurements of the Russell Plantation's success were ascertained in monitoring how rapidly the working-class residents conformed to respectability, and abandoned customs deemed racially stereotypical, such as women wrapping their hair with a cloth, a practice closely identified with slavery. While women gave up wrapping, they reverted to the wearing of black veils. This type of progress was not welcomed by everyone. To the dismay of many clubwomen, young white women in the community were offended and felt black women were taking their uplift too far. This tension highlighted the precarious position of many race women. On one hand, they sought to pass ideals of respectability onto the masses of blacks as a means to showcase their refined culture. On the other, middle-class women, especially new aristocrats, went to great measures to display their class as a distinct elite group within themselves. In instances where Victorian ideals were infused with African traditions, many of the clubwomen became embarrassed and displeased.[33]

Respectability required a public performance. In many ways, it demanded the skillful balancing act of a double consciousness, a term coined by Du Bois that called for the wearing of two masks. One mask displayed in public affairs, while the other showed in the privacy of their homes. Those who adhered to its doctrines used the public sphere as a stage to showcase improvements made by the race. Through efforts of the TWC, working-class women took notice of their public dress and ensured their hair remained neatly kept. Fewer women went barefoot, and even less socialized on the street with men. The community begin to display public attributes deemed appropriate of American citizens. The clubwomen took their outreach further through the acknowledgment of birthday celebrations. Due to the disproportionate lack of access to birth certificates for formerly enslaved blacks, the celebration of birthdays grew increasingly vital to claims of freedom. As many older residents did not know their exact birth year, Washington usually had them recall some incident in their lives as near as possible to the time they were born, in order to approximate their ages. These practices helped to garner a sense of citizenship among the local residents.[34]

Despite overwhelming restrictions created by the implementation of Jim Crow laws, TWC members recognized that massive improvements had been made in the daily affairs of the residents. By 1925, when reflecting upon the Elizabeth Russell Plantation, Washington noted that they were "a pride to themselves and a pride to those of us who have given our time." The house-to-house activities of the TWC did not go unrecognized by others. In 1911 Dr. John A. Kenney, medical director of the Tuskegee Hospital, gave praise to the efforts and keen attention to detail displayed among the clubwomen:[35] "The smallest details are looked after, as how to prepare and serve their food, how and when to bathe, how to ventilate their houses, how to care for their hair, the washing of their clothing, cleaning of their teeth, sleeping between sheets, and all such subjects as tend to improve their home conditions. The special subjects of tuberculosis and typhoid fever have been discussed before the people in the most elementary manner possible."[36]

Ten years after the formation of the TWC, Washington and the women of Alabama were continuing to do impressive things in the name of social reform. The ladies of the club contributed liberally toward several barrels of food, which they distributed to the community. In March of 1905 when the club undertook the responsibility of finding the means to provide a suitable home for an orphaned boy without proper supervision, the men of the community, although not members of the TWC, compassionately contributed twenty-five dollars and sixty-five cents toward the expenses of placing this young boy in a nourishing home and giving him a healthy start in life.[37]

As a direct outgrowth of their efforts on the Russell Plantation, Tuskegee clubwomen also provided outreach to prisoners. The state of Alabama provided inadequate resources for black inmates. In addition, Jim Crow laws made legal the disproportionate incarceration of black bodies. Many boys and men were arrested and jailed for minor offenses such as vagrancy or breaking curfew restrictions. The number of black males wrongly jailed and convicted by the court of white opinion was staggering. These statistics prompted clubwomen to intervene through the creation of their Jail division. Functioning as an outreach and support component, TWC members conducted at least thirty visits to the prison per year. In many ways, they confronted the very laws that branded the men as criminals and sought to further reduce them to new forms of slavery.[38]

Clubwomen saw to it that those incarcerated knew they were loved. Religious services were held at each visit. The prisoners were given fruit and clean clothing, and in return expressed their gratitude. They also made strong efforts to present a tidy appearance during the visits. However, all inmates were housed in the same facility and treated as hardened criminals, regardless of their age or crime. One incident in particular appalled Washington and TWC members. They discovered that four small boys, who were imprisoned for robbery, were placed in the same cell as four adult men. The women pleaded with the city to discontinue the practice. In the interim they saw to it that the prisoners in Macon County, regardless of their ages, were given basic lessons including hygiene and behavior modification. They made it a priority to invest time in their well-being, personal development, and in the condition of their souls. At Christmas, the TWC occasionally brought small gifts to each prisoner. The women also made extravagant dinners for the Christmas season. Magazines with pictures were left behind for their entertainment and Bible students volunteered their time to help inmates with scripture.[39]

Sunday School, as a tool, promoted Christian culture in accordance with the divine commands of both the old and new testaments in the daily life of its followers. The Thompson's Quarters department proved an important addition to the TWC and provided weekly Bible lessons to the community. The women who worked within the Thompson's Quarters did not confine themselves to Bible teaching alone. They extended a hand wherever needed, visiting the sick and adding somewhat to the comfort of the afflicted. For instance, in a very deprived home of eight children, one child became very sick and died. The family had no means to give him a proper burial. Through the kindness of teachers and the Bible students, the TWC raised money to help with his funeral expenses. This lifted a financial burden from the parents who had only recently moved to the Tuskegee area.[40]

Attendance to Bible studies, however, was relatively low. The usual attendance ranged from five adults to roughly thirty or so children. In the winter of 1905, however, the Thompson's Quarters saw a greater increase than at any other time in its ten-year history, the overall number of adults and children nearly doubling in number.[41] This may be in part to Margaret Washington's initiative to extend the Bible sessions to the community. Thompson's Quarters occasionally had small parties with very light refreshments including candy, cake and iced lemonade, to attract families. On warm days, they found that the parties not only brought the community together, but people were less inclined to brawl. Much of the stress that local residents faced during their day-to-day lives was forgotten, if only for a moment. Through the parties, the public use of alcohol also came into focus. Some residents sought the comforts of spirits, where the laws had failed them. Others used alcohol to fill the void they had been subjected to, that second-class citizenship had created.[42]

Throughout the years, Margaret Washington enthusiastically sought to keep the work of the Temperance Division of the TWC relevant in the minds of local Tuskegee residents and students. In the 1870s white women started the Women's Christian Temperance Union (WCTU). This organization, formed in Chicago by Annie Wittenmyer, first attempted to shut down saloons with a rather Christian approach. In the years that followed and with the term of its second president Francis Willard, in 1879 the movement became more militant, and classified as the temperance movement. Black women were included in the WCTU's membership, such as Frances Harper, but their involvement was usually splintered and oftentimes limited by white women. As with the Atlanta Progressives, who pushed prohibition so that liquor would not be available as a means of buying votes in wet areas, the TWC also strove to inform the community and students about the importance of prohibition work being done throughout the country by prominent citizens and organizations. This became useful in helping to suppress the use of alcohol and its associated evils.[43]

Mrs. J. H. Palmer taught at the Institute on the importance of temperance. In reflecting on lessons given to the men and women of Tuskegee:

> (1) All of the young men of the school were addressed, the subject having been considered from a social, economic and hygienic, as well as moral standpoint. (2) The entire company of young women of the school was given a thorough review of the work of the Women's Christian

> Temperance Union and also a full report or statement of the life and work of Frances E. Willard. (3) On "Temperance Sunday" a talk was made before the Young People's Society of Christian Endeavor and an earnest plea being made for each one who listened to the talk there, and Christians everywhere, to use their influence always in favor of the suppression of the liquor traffic. (4) A talk was made on the subject "Temperance and its effects" to a rural school, composed of seventy-five or more children who repeated the pledge against the use of alcohol as a beverage, the use of tobacco and profanity. (5) Many private talks to individuals and special classes were given annually.[44]

Alcohol in fact contributed greatly to the destruction of black families. Drunken husbands routinely spent what little money they made on alcoholic beverages. To make matters worse, abuse against black women rose when alcohol was part of the equation, making it a central concern for the Tuskegee Woman's Club.

Margaret Washington also constantly encouraged men and women enrolled in Tuskegee's night school to help in promoting a health-conscious community. In 1901 several students took a pledge not to drink, lie, gamble, or steal. The clubwomen believed that the efforts to create a sentiment against the destructive use of alcohol would prove effective. A large number of young people participated in this work, endeavoring to establish habits of purity, temperance, and total abstinence. These efforts by the TWC were similar to broader temperance efforts such as those made by Harper of the WCTU.[45]

There existed as well, a great interest in the suffrage movement during the years of the Progressive Era. Black women understood the importance of the ballot. They believed it meant the social equality of the sexes. The ballot would place the needs of blacks on a national agenda and change the role of women in society. "Women must become familiar with social and economic conditions; she must be a working force in the larger influences that affect her trade as home-keeper," stated Mrs. Nellie F. Francis of St. Paul Minnesota, in *The Women's Journal*, the official organ of female suffragists, whose national headquarters were in Warren, Ohio. She also sent helpful and encouraging information to aid the TWC suffrage department.

Margaret Washington advocated for women's suffrage and ensured its inclusion in the TWC and her other club initiatives. Adella Hunt Logan, an original member of the TWC and wife of Tuskegee's treasurer, Warren Logan, led the suffrage department until her emotional breakdown and death in 1915. Her efforts were considered sincere and enthusiastic, amid overwhelming disapproval of black suffrage. Although an important component to full-citizenship rights, Logan and Washington understood that voting alone would not solve the issues between the races. It was but one means to combat the system of Jim Crow and second-class citizenship. Many platforms were needed. Logan also did not envision black women gaining the right to vote in the near future. Nonetheless, she appreciated the importance of clubwomen remaining in the struggle and staying abreast on political issues. Their knowledge and public positions ensured the needs of black women were brought closer to the fore of national concerns. These efforts proved taxing, but necessary.[46] The TWC engaged in work that many of the founding mothers would not live to actually witness. They also made sure to provide spaces for young and old women of the community as a means to keep them stimulated as the struggle for first-class citizenship waged on.[47]

The Ednah Cheney Club mirrored other TWC concerns, in its importance to Tuskegee's elderly community. The club was founded in honor of the noble Mrs. Cheney, who died at her home in Jamaica Plain, Massachusetts, on November 18, 1904.[48] Aside from being a notable author, lecturer, and reformer, she also co-founded the New England Women's Club, where she devoted her life to advocacy for women's rights and human rights. Mrs. Cheney worked diligently with the Tuskegee Woman's Club, and Margaret Washington sought her advice on numerous occasions. Mrs. Cheney proved to be a friend of the weak and a champion of women's causes. Out of respect for the dedication Cheney exemplified, this department insisted that its highest aim would be that of service.[49]

Tuskegee's Vesta club consisted of women in the Institute's senior classes. By 1905 it had a membership of over twenty-five women. They expressed their desire to be of service to the poor and unfortunate people in the vicinity of the school. Just as the Cheney Club provided an outlet for elderly women, the Vesta club consisted of young women who were students at the Institute and residents in the community. This division provided a space for young adults to cultivate their intellectual curiosity through reading circles used for intellectual discourse.[50]

At this juncture in her life, Margaret Washington's greatest work was the TWC. As the club expanded, the women added divisions of interest. Washington continued throughout her tenure at the Institute to guide and instruct women of the South on the concept of self-help, self-sufficiency, and social reform. She did all of this in a time and era that remained hostile toward blacks, or to the idea of uplifting the race. While she imposed many standards of the societal majority onto Tuskegee's local residents, she believed that through respectability the race would rise. In the midst of working with various clubs and school initiatives, Margaret Washington was also diligently building her status as one of the leading figures of the black elite, spreading the Tuskegee gospel throughout Tuskegee, Alabama, and the South. Washington's success with the TWC proved equally effectual for the school. She soon used the success at Tuskegee to better position herself for joining forces with women of the North, and to head the National Federation of Afro-American Women's Clubs and the National Association of Colored Women.[51]

Chapter Five

The National Shall Rise

My women were left to drift and to pick up their ideals
and ideas too, by chance.

—Margaret Murray Washington
(*The Negro Home*, 1920)[1]

The poem below, quoted by Margaret Washington in a speech to clubwomen, gives a detailed yet brief account of the responsibilities that black clubwomen faced after Reconstruction and throughout the Progressive Era.

> What is a Woman's Club . . .
>
> A meeting ground for those of purpose
> great and broad and strong,
> whose aim is toward the stars;
> whoever longs to make the patient,
> listening world resound with sweeter music,
> purer, nobler tones, a place where kindly,
> helpful words are said and kindlier deeds are done;
> where hearts are [fed]; where wealth of brain
> for poverty stones,
> and hand grasps hand and soul finds touch with soul.
> This is a woman's club,
> a haven fair where toilers drop and lose
> their load of care.[2]

Although secondary literature has included information about the activities of black women's clubs, particularly the National Association of Colored Women (NACW), few have placed Margaret Washington's work with the NACW at the center of their research. Washington, like other clubwomen, had the daunting task of creating sustainable institutions in the midst of hostility and rejection, from both blacks and whites. However, she was unafraid to take leadership positions in various organizations. She was instrumental in creating the Tuskegee Woman's Club and served as chairwoman, vice-president, and president of the NACW. Under the NACWs umbrella, Washington founded the Alabama Federation of Colored Women's Clubs in 1898 and the Southern Federation of Colored Women's Clubs a year later in 1899. Her efforts with the NACW solidified her position as a national leader of clubwomen.

For generations clubs served as meeting grounds for men who shared the same interests and goals. However, the period just before and after the American Civil War marked a substantial increase in women's clubs and associations. It was also within this period that saloons became a symbol of disgust throughout black and white communities alike. Alcohol was considered by reformers to be the leading cause of domestic abuse of women and children.[3]

Through the Women's Christian Temperance Union (WCTU) and its leaders, the movement did more than attempt to control saloons, it brought together white middle-class women who shared similar concerns and interests. Along with social outreach agendas, the women also used the organization to pursue cultural activities. This public display of women who were socially active outside the home was a new and fairly unheard-of phenomenon. Whereas many of the earlier women's clubs and associations were primarily anti-slavery societies, the clubs and associations that were formed in the late nineteenth century took a more secular approach.[4]

The temperance movement opened doors for women in the public arena and became a blueprint for future clubs. The organizations brought together communities of women with a common interest. They initially fulfilled cultural aspirations, but quickly shifted to civic reforms. The organizational structure was similar to white men's associations, but the women's club agendas focused on community issues. Members were generally educated and involved in public affairs.[5]

Unlike the temperance movement, which had a specific agenda, the initial goals of these women's clubs tended to be very broad. According to Nancy Woloch, those who participated in women's clubs believed they served as "an order which shall render the female sex helpful to each other and actively benevolent in the world." Club work ultimately tended to be equally vague and stressed the need to collectively organize women into a unified way of thinking and acting.[6]

In 1892 several women's associations affiliated to form the General Federation of Women's Clubs (GFWC). Although the need to associate remained one of the key tools in bringing women together, it was after the women's clubs consolidated on a national level that their missions expanded. Where critics of the temperance movement portrayed women as manly and aggressive. the GFWC women maintained their images as Victorian ladies. The clubs of the GFWC, unlike the temperance movement, were comprised mainly of white middle-class women. A very small number of black women were admitted.[7]

Black women's clubs, like Margaret Washington's TWC, were not allowed into the Federation. Fannie Barrier Williams, whose husband Samuel L. Williams worked as a prominent lawyer in Chicago, was the first and only black member of the Chicago Women's Club in 1884. In 1893, while addressing a group of white women, Williams stressed the needs of black women. We want, she asserted, "liberty to be all that we can be, without artificial hindrances . . . a thing no less precious to us than to women generally." Josephine St. Pierre Ruffin was also a member of a white women's club. Her husband George L. Ruffin, a Harvard-educated attorney, was a Boston legislator and prominent city judge. Ruffin joined the New England Women's Club in the 1890s.[8]

At the turn of the century, Jim Crow laws forced blacks to create separate, racially segregated organizations and institutions of self-help. Moreover, by the late 1890s charities that were run by whites were often unwilling to work with impoverished blacks. Scientific racists claimed that black people were mentally deficient and unable to compete with whites on any level, and that any effort to improve their condition would be futile. Armed with this information, "many white charity workers, who had never really embraced working with poor blacks, welcomed the excuse to concentrate on poor whites instead."[9]

Black women like Washington were in a constant struggle. At times, rejection of women in the public sphere came from men within their own race. Toxic masculinity, white supremacy, and debilitating circumstances for black Americans became central reasons black women began forming black women's clubs.[10]

In the eyes of some black men, these public and social spheres of black womanhood made African American women too vocal and thus too manly. In a 1908 article published in *Colored American Magazine*, titled "How to Keep Women at Home," an anonymous black male writer expressed his discontent with women who felt that their influence was better served outside the household. He urged men to hold a convention in order to discuss this unfortunate situation in the black community. "Women are getting very bold, and instead of using the freedom that civilized men are allowing them, for adding to the comforts of man, they are abusing them," he wrote.[11]

African American men struggled desperately to find their place in post-Reconstruction American society. The *Colored American Magazine* article suggested that black men adopt middle-class white values after emancipation. The author went on to declare that the home "is her [the black woman's] place, her center of influence, her throne, where virtue and love sit enshrined."[12] While women like Washington did not completely reject the author's argument, they understood that clubs could be vehicles for personal improvements as well as the betterment of their homes and communities. Of course, the opinions of the magazine article's writer were not held by all black men.

According to Tuskegee Institute's Chaplain, Reverend Whittaker, "man holds his superior position wholly in consequence of his greater physical strength." Yet, he adds, "the same brute force, which made her a salable commodity in the early history of the world, makes her the plaything and football of men today." He concluded that "before we can have better women, we must have better men." Margaret Washington shared Whittaker's sentiments. In an 1890 article she rebuffed the idea that the proper place and rights of women were different than that of men. She asserted "those who try to prove that the rights of wom[e]n, and her work in life are separate from the rights and the mission of man are yet far from defining these satisfactorily to women." Through the clubs, these middle and upper-class women created social outlets, courses on leadership, and facilities for children that supported their place alongside men outside of the household. It was the belief of many clubwomen that through the efforts of the clubs, households, and civic initiatives, the race would elevate to a position that warranted recognition from whites and black men.[13]

Another catalyst for the establishment of a secular black women's club was an effort to counter notions that black women were barbaric, sexual, and mannish in nature. On March 6, 1895, four days after Washington created the TWC, John W. Jacks, President of the Missouri Press Association, sent a response letter to radical suffragette Florence Belgarnie, secretary of the British Anti-Lynching Committee. Belgarnie sent an international letter to American journalists to help battle the horrors of lynching. In an attempt to derail the anti-lynching efforts of Ida B. Wells-Barnett, Jacks responded and asserted "the Negroes of this country are wholly devoid of morality [and that] the women are prostitutes and are naturally thieves and liars." An outraged Belgarnie sent the letter to Josephine St. Pierre Ruffin, editor of *The Woman's Era* magazine, the organ of the New Era Club in Boston, in hopes of creating a stir among black clubwomen.[14]

While these myths and stereotypes were already being spread in America, Jacks' letter carried the ruthless allegations abroad. Washington and other leading females rejected these slurs. They used women's clubs to train and educate the masses of African Americans. Although separation from the lower class of blacks was a mainstay within some black middle-class circles, Washington knew that she and others were judged by the same assumptions. She also believed that despite racism and the history of enslavement, whites expected blacks to prove that they were fit for citizenship. Following the letter by Jacks, secular black women's clubs formed throughout the country in increasing numbers and strength.[15]

Because black women were generally not allowed entry into white women's clubs, black women instituted programs that nourished their particular interests and concerns, just as white women's clubs had done. Fannie Barrier Williams, clubwoman and journalist, stated: "it is possible for us to work out, define, and pursue a kind of club work that will be original." She concluded that black women sought to "distinguish our work essentially from white women's clubs." They did so by improvement of the race, through working with families in an effort to redefine black women's roles in society, along with their image.[16]

Washington's Tuskegee Woman's Club (TWC) was an excellent example for numerous clubs and in most cases it served as a prototype for organizing. With a membership of 35 to 100 women, the TWC offered women social, political and literary outlets. The clubwomen also educated themselves on ways to improve the health and welfare of their families and communities. Ultimately, black women answered the call to redefine the black woman's image.[17]

The national Colored Women's League Club (CWLC) pre-dated

the TWC. It was organized in June of 1892 in Washington, D.C., and incorporated on January 11, 1894. According to Terrell, Chairwoman of the Educational Committee, "a goodly number of these women decided to band together to raise the standard of their group." The CWLC sought "industrial and educational purposes, and educational and improvement of Colored women and the promotion of their interest."[18] Helen A. Cook was elected president and among the signees were Josephine Bruce and Mary Church Terrell. As early as 1800, however, black women had organized in New York, Boston, Chicago and D.C. The CWLC's mission was the education and improvement of black women. While the CWLC invited other club women to be a part of their association, their efforts to unite black women on a national level failed. In 1895, Josephine St. Pierre Ruffin, the president and founder of the New Era Club in Boston, became so outraged by Jacks' slander of black women that she put out a circular and on the editorial page of the *Women's Era* magazine, printed the call to action which was titled, "Let Us Confer Together." The "First National Conference of Colored Women," to defend black womanhood, took place in July 1895. However, initiatives for a mass meeting were underway months prior to Jacks' attempt to undermine Ida B. Wells-Barnett's anti-lynching campaign and black women's character. Black club women were already diligently planning to create a national organization. Prior to the June 1895 call to gather printed in the *Woman's Era*, Josephine Silone Yates of Missouri wrote in 1894 "by all means let us have a congress of colored women at some time in the near future to give solidity, unity of purpose, national character, and other requisites of success necessary to a movement so broad and far reaching as a race organization should be." The stimulus for women to join forces on a national level had been laid. Black women were collectively propelled into action.[19]

On July 29, 1895, over 104 delegates representing fifty-four clubs convened in Boston to develop plans for a national organization. It was no surprise to many that the call to unite black women came from Boston. Due to the area's sizable black population, Boston housed many of the nation's black elite and a militant black press. Elite blacks in Boston, as in Washington, D.C., usually came from multiple generations of free blacks, and in many instances, they formed local clubs among themselves that were highly exclusive. The opening day's speakers included Ruffin, Helen Cook, and Anna J. Cooper. Margaret Washington spoke on day two, along with Victoria Earle Matthews, journalist and founder of the 1897 White Rose Mission, a social center for black migrants of New York. Three men attended the meeting and they included William Lloyd Garrison, abolitionists and journalist, T. Thomas Fortune, American journalist, and Henry Brown Blackwell, co-founder of the American Women's Suffrage Association and reformer. The men took part in a session on "Political Equality." Washington's speech, "Individual Work for Moral Elevation," challenged women and men to be leaders in their communities. By the end of the conference, the National Federation of Afro-American Women (NFAAW) was formed, for the "purpose of establishing needed reforms, and the practical encouragement of all efforts being put forth by the various agencies, religious, educational, ethical and otherwise, for the up-building, ennobling and advancement of the race." Ruffin later stated that the work of the NFAAW was not to isolate black women from the men of the race, but to implement a movement that would be led by women. "We are not alienating or withdrawing, we are only going to the front," she declared.[20]

At the Boston conference, Ruffin also had this in mind when she said that the movement was not only "created for the sake of fine, cultured women" but also for: "the thousands of self-sacrificing young women teaching and preaching in lonely southern backwoods, for the noble army of mothers who have given birth to these girls, mothers whose intelligence is only limited at their opportunity to get at books."[21] Margaret Washington was elected president, mainly because of her exceptional work with the TWC. This election also positioned her as a national leader of African American women.

Although the Colored Women's League members were present at the Boston meeting, they did not officially join with the NFAAW. They were distraught over the fact that Ruffin, who called for the meeting, was not elected the first president. Although Ruffin was offered the position of treasurer, she "positively" declined. Once organized, the NFAAW united over thirty-six black women's clubs in more than twelve states throughout the United States. To be sure, in 1895 Margaret Washington became the very first president of a national organization formed by African American women, before Booker T. Washington became the leader of black Americans. Victoria Earle Matthew was elected chairman of the executive committee.[22]

Soon after the NFAAW was organized, they were invited to participate in a number of community functions, the first being the 1895

Cotton States and International Exposition in Atlanta, Georgia. Booker T. Washington gave a keynote address which called for racial unification and self–help from many of the clubwomen who attended. He was also a clear advocate of initiatives made by women's clubs. While at the exposition, the NFAAW helped to demonstrate the culture, skills, and various talents that existed amongst black women. They did so in the same way that Booker T. Washington promoted black manhood through his National Negro Business League, which he established in 1900. Booker Washington did not have a direct hand in the NFAAW affairs, but his presence and philosophy were extended through efforts made by his wife, Margaret Washington.[23]

In 1895, under Margaret Washington's leadership, members of the NFAAW attended the Republican National Convention in Detroit, Michigan. Richard T. Greener, head of the Colored Bureau of the National Republican Party, the first black graduate of Harvard and a former professor of law at the University of South Carolina, understood the significance and impact that a national body of African American women could have on his election, despite their continued struggle at suffrage. For the first time, he succeeded in obtaining representation of black women at the political meeting. Greener also noted the influence that a national African American women's club could have on the progress of the race and the betterment of its women and children.[24]

The NFAAW, under Washington's direction, made a positive and strong impression throughout the country. Washington made earnest efforts to get the organization's agenda into the public mainstream: "We have formed chapters, or branches, in Charleston S.C., Memphis, Tenn., Philadelphia, Penn., and Brooklyn, N.Y. Since our organization, we have called public meetings to our churches to discuss topics affecting the interests of the race in the Southland and in our own section, with beneficial results."[25] However, despite the progress of the NFAAW, the CWLC continued to call itself national and had a platform that resembled that of the NFAAW. Margaret Washington, along with other members, declared that the two clubs could not thrive as separate entities. According to Terrell, "the Federation of Afro-American Women, whose president is Mrs. Booker T. Washington, declared that even if the League were the first to suggest that there should be a national organization, the federation was the first actually to *become national* in scope." This created some obvious "bitterness of feelings" among the two groups and its officers. Margaret Washington was adamant about "breaking the chains" of the CWLC. However, her first attempt to merge the CWLC with the NFAAW failed because, according to Washington, the CWLC would not give a definite layout of the scope of their club and were even less forthcoming about its membership.²⁶

The existence of two separate groups that seemingly promoted similar objectives proved unproductive for them both. The CWLC held their first convention in Washington, D.C. from July 14–16, 1896 at the Fifteenth Street Presbyterian Church. Days later, the NFAAW held their second convention in Washington, D.C. from July 18–20 at the Nineteenth Street Baptist Church. With the club women all in the nation's capital a "remarkable" event occurred. Washington's NFAAW merged with the CWLC. Following the merger, a committee, including seven women from each former organization, was created. The joint committee, or committee of seven, was tasked with selecting an official name and officers. After much debate over the use of "Colored" or "Afro-American" the committee decided upon the name, the National Association of Colored Women (NACW). Fredrick Douglass's only daughter, Rosetta Douglass, spoke at the meeting: "While the white race have [sic] chronicled deeds of heroism and acts of mercy of the women of pioneer and other days, so we are pleased to note in the personality of such women as Phyllis Wheatley, Margaret Garner, Sojourner Truth, and our venerable friend, Harriet Tubman, sterling qualities of head, heart and hand, who hold no insignificant place in the annals of heroic womanhood."²⁷ Of the many women who Douglass honored, the legendary Harriett Tubman also attended this historic meeting. Tubman, an abolitionist and conductor in the Underground Railroad, represented a new era for black women in club work. To be sure, at this 1896 meeting clubwomen had successfully created a unified national organization of political and socially savvy women who would "Lift as They Climbed" to transform the nation in unimaginable ways.²⁸

The more difficult question of the committee of seven became who would serve as the organization's first president. Because tensions were high and personalities were wide ranging, the voting process took hours. The committee convened in the parlor of the Nineteenth Street Baptist Church on July 19 as the convention carried on in the main chapel. The women prayed for divine intervention as they placed the name of every female leader in the United States into the hat. Every organization member voted for their own members to lead the newly founded group. Washington's name was voted upon with a seven-to-seven tie vote from the committee. After many deliberations, and tie votes it seemed the women would never select a president. After countless hours of deliberation, it was almost six o'clock when Mary Church Terrell's name was entered a second time. A majority vote was finally secured. Terrell became the first president of the national organization. Terrell later commented: "The most difficult task of all confronted us! Who should be the first president of the new Association? It is safe to assert that while we were in the throes of electing the president, the name of no colored woman who had achieved success or prominence anywhere in the United States failed to be presented for consideration . . . This went on indefinitely, so that most of us had little hope that anybody either in the United States or out of it could ever be elected."[29] Terrell was confirmed president at the NACWs Nashville convention in 1897. There were seven vice presidents in all; representing the Northeast, Midwest and the South. Victoria Matthews was elected national organizer. Washington was elected chairwoman of the NACW's executive board. Members decided to meet biennially. During the initial years the officers included a first and second vice president of each region, recording and corresponding secretaries, a chairwoman of the executive committee, a national organizer, and a treasurer.[30]

Mary Eliza Church Terrell, the organization's new president, was born in 1863 in Memphis, Tennessee to formerly enslaved parents. Her mother Louisa Ayres Church was a maid in the Ayres household and opened a hair salon after emancipation. Her father, Robert Reed Church, was enslaved to a white riverboat captain Charles B. Church. Mary's parents divorced during her childhood, after which she and her brother lived in New York with her mother. During Reconstruction and the early years of the yellow fever epidemic in Memphis, her father survived gunshot wounds in an attempt to save his family and business. Robert Church still became a very successful businessman and probably the wealthiest black man in the South during those times. Her parents' business acuities were qualities that Terrell carried with her during her two-terms as president of the NACW. She attended Oberlin College where she majored in classics and earned her bachelor's degree in 1884, making her one of the first African American women to receive a college degree.[31]

Terrell also studied in Europe for two years, becoming fluent in French, German, and Italian. A high school teacher and principal, she was appointed to the District of Columbia's Board of Education, the first black woman in the United States to hold such a position. In 1901 she married fellow teacher Herberton Terrell and the two had one daughter and adopted another. Terrell later become nationally known both for her support of women's suffrage and her opposition to racial segregation. She also served in an influential role in the establishment of the National Association for the Advancement of Colored People in 1909.[32]

As NACW's chairwoman to the executive board, Washington played a vital role in laying the organization's foundation and policies during its formative years. However, the club's motto "Lifting as we Climb" did not spare this exclusive group of women from controversy. The NACW experienced a number of internal issues, including colorism, jealousy, pettiness, limited resources, and sometimes unsynchronized visions. Yet, Washington's impact remained consistent until the club moved forward in its missions of reform, childcare, and self-improvement.

As chairwoman, Washington gathered her cadre of women supporters. This group of friends and long-time supporters included the likes of Josephine Bruce, Mary McLeod Bethune, and women of Alabama like Adella Hunt Logan, Cornelia Bowen and later Jennie Moton, who consistently served as her eyes and ears during her years of influence.[33]

The NACW set out to make a difference in the black community through social reforms and ideas of uplift. The purpose of the club, as spelled out in its preamble, stated: "We the colored women of the United States of America, feeling the need of united and sympathetic effort, and hoping to furnish evidence of moral, mental and material progress made by our people, do hereby unite in a National Association."[34] The NACW endeavored to remove the veil that hundreds of years of slavery had created. It was also through the three C's of cooking, cleaning, and caring that cabinet members worked together to formulate key agendas aimed at reaching unschooled black women. NACW women worked together (despite their different approaches to the race problem) and attempted to spread a unified philosophy.[35]

There were obvious areas of disagreement between Terrell as president and Washington as chairwoman, especially considering Terrell's initial feelings about Washington's NFAAW and the limitations of Tuskegee Institute's industrial model. However, in an 1898 speech delivered before the thirteenth annual convention of the National American Women's Suffrage Association in Washington, D.C., Terrell promoted industrial and domestic training, stating: "object lessons are given in the best way to sweep, dust, cook, wash, and iron, together with other information concerning household affairs." Proving that Terrell was not completely opposed to industrial training or ideas of domesticity, which Washington endorsed. Terrell also came to understand that "no race [could] hope to stand on a firm financial basis without a well-trained laboring class."[36]

The philosophy of industrial training as promoted by the Tuskegee Machine also manifested itself in the early structure of the TWC. It can be assumed that Terrell and Washington did not agree on every matter, however, their ability to keep public controversy and turmoil within the group at a minimum allowed positive news to circulate about the race.[37]

During the early years of the NACW, the clubwomen established the first cohesive network of communication among American black women. These reform efforts emphasized the role of educated women in their drive for social stability. The NACW was a well-connected network that fostered leadership skills among women and sometimes men. They were not a feminist organization in the modern sense of the term, they were, however, advocates of inclusivity. The NACW did not seek to take away the domestic nature of the woman, instead they wanted to make them better mothers and wives. Fannie B. Williams stated, "In our day and in this country, a woman's sphere is just as large as she can make it."[38]

By 1897 Washington became the editor of the NACWs newly established news organ, *National Notes*. Prior to this publication the NACW used the periodical *The Woman's Era*, published by the New Era Club and edited by Josephine Ruffin, as its official publication. Members of the NACW used *National Notes* as one of their channels of communication. Washington started this process by gathering all the information from the meetings and later publishing the information at her own expense at Tuskegee. Once Washington began publication of the *National Notes*, she became the key distributor of its press.[39]

The *National Notes* identified Washington as an active participant in the circulation of black news within the association and it increased her visibility, philosophy and platform within club work. Her influence was so great that in 1904 she successfully rallied to move NACW's meeting center from the grounds of the St. Louis World's Fair because of their unequal hiring practices and discrimination against black patrons. However, her work with this and other endeavors were met with criticism. After newspapers reported Washington's confrontational stance, she relinquished any claims of participating in the protest. NACW members felt this radicalism undermined their cohesiveness and critics attributed this abdication to her husband's influence.

As previously mentioned, in 1900 Booker T. Washington established the National Negro Business League. The League brought together black businesswomen and men. Booker Washington wished to keep the black market informed and to circulate positive media to encourage high morale and energy in reference to black business, land ownership, and home ownership. It is thus less surprising that Margaret Washington would take such a strong stance in reference to the black dollar. Signature goals of the business league were to promote financial independence and to ultimately promote black business. Speaking to her commitment to the cause she become a life member of the business league in 1916.[40]

The incident at the 1904 World Fair would not be the last time that Jim Crow discrimination and violence angered Washington. She refused to bow to racial prejudice, and she understood the buying power of black America. In a 1919 letter to Tuskegee's president, Robert Moton, she asserted, ". . . there is so much restlessness everywhere, much fighting between the white and the black . . ." She then suggested a meeting with white merchants before threatening to prohibit black teachers and students from patronizing their shops. "This will put the town 'on its metal' and will make the merchants see to it that the colored people are respected. This town [of Tuskegee] depends largely upon us and what we want to do is to remind them of [it] every once in a while."[41]

Margaret also expressed much of this discontent with white Americas disregard to black life and business in the *National Notes*. Ida B. Wells-Barnett did not think too highly of Washington's work as editor of the paper or its content. Furthermore, the *National Notes* was both subsidized and printed at Tuskegee. In 1909, at the NACW meeting held in Louisville, Kentucky, Wells-Barnett stated that delegates had complained about "the irregularity of the *National Notes*, about its failure to publish matter sent, [and] about the dissatisfaction of subscribers who had never received the paper." Wells-Barnett requested a formal election to be held to elect "an editor who would be responsible to the body." Despite these concerns, Wells-Barnett, who had not attended a meeting in ten years, was dismissed by NACW members who felt her comments were meant to undermine Washington's position. Similar sentiments about Wells-Barnett's intentions circulated at the second election of Mary Church Terrell as president. Some members even felt that Wells-Barnett may have been acting selfishly and capriciously because of a vendetta against Booker T. Washington.[42]

NACW officers, nonetheless, understood the value of positive reinforcements within the black community. Washington and Terrell were two of the many leading African Americans who contributed to the journal, *Voice of the Negro*, co-edited by Jesse Max Barber and John Wesley Bowen. *Voice of the Negro* circulated monthly to thousands of readers and spoke out against racial injustice in the United States. It also called attention to discrimination among all non-Europeans around the world.[43]

In 1898, three years after the formation of the TWC, and two years after the formation of the NACW, Washington set initiatives in motion to expand the influence of black women in Alabama. Fully aware of the inequalities placed on blacks at the time, she knew that more had to be done to improve race situations in the South. This reform could not successfully be done in isolation. At the turn of the century, countless attempts were made by black elites to improve the conditions of the South. In the "Atlanta Compromise" address, Booker Washington pleaded for southern whites to "cast down your bucket where you are" among southern blacks, as he also encouraged blacks to improve their conditions in the South. "Cast it down in agriculture, mechanics, in commerce, in domestic service, and in the professions," Booker pleaded. In 1898 Margaret Washington drafted a blueprint for the Alabama Federation of Colored Women's Clubs(AFCWC), which served as an essential organization for the women of Alabama to convey their goals on a regional platform. Other women throughout the region began to organize. Clubs sprang up across the state of Alabama. The city of Mobile had at least four separate women's clubs ranging from religious education to reading circles. In Tuscaloosa women formed the Three Times Ten Club and in Montgomery clubwomen created the Sojourner Truth Club. The Women's Mission Congress was an incorporated body which also operated a hospital in Birmingham. Cornelia Bowen founded the Women's Club of Waugh. Bowen's club "was first called the Anti-Wrapping Club, [where] each member pledging herself to abandon the habit of wrapping her hair," until they broadened their scope.[44]

According to the Alabama Federation's 1907 resolution, the women made countless pledges, including an oath to black youth. "We pledge ourselves anew to the work of child-saving, realizing that in our young lies the hope of the race, and that when we save the boy or the girl of to-day, we save the man or the woman of to-morrow." The organization was initially led by Margaret Washington. Cornelia Bowen was elected president in 1904. Still, Washington's TWC remained the model club in Alabama and throughout the region. "Few clubs possess opportunities for higher literacy study superior to those of the Tuskegee Woman's Club, which, among its eighty-nine members, has fifty-two who are teachers in the Tuskegee Institute," asserted clubwoman Hunton.[45]

Being reared and educated in the South, Washington knew firsthand that "the country woman [was] sorely neglected, not only ours but the white country woman," as well. In a 1913 speech to clubwomen she declared of the southern women:[46] "Her home is of pictures and books; her churches and Sunday Schools are filled with ill-prepared men and women; her schools are poorly taught; she and her children are left alone in the majority of cases, to do both the work of the home and field, and thus to eke out a most desolate and miserable existence." These sentiments galvanized the momentum needed to join more women together under a regional platform.[47]

In 1899 after American troops returned from fighting in the Spanish American War, Washington organized the southern Federation of Colored Women's Clubs. She called a meeting of Southern women in Montgomery, Alabama. Addie W. Hunton commented on the event in a 1905 article in *The Voice of the Negro* titled "The Southern Federation of Colored Women. "Nearly six years ago there came together in the charming and historical old city of Montgomery, Alabama, a number of women representative, of the club spirit of several southern cities." She went on to credit "the efforts of Mrs. Booker T. Washington," who had organized and presided over the Alabama Federation of Colored Women's Clubs. The women "had been invited to Montgomery to discuss race conditions, especially those coming within the province of women to improve change."[48] As clubs rapidly appeared throughout the south, Washington wanted to ensure that the organizations had a clear and obtainable mission with annual agendas. She used her TWC as a prototype for the new regional federation, and for the formation of other local clubs throughout the south.[49]

Creating local and regional organizations offered the clubwomen clearer lines to address the unique problems of their states and cities in particular. As an educator in Alabama, Washington understood better the inequalities and possibilities for improvement across the state. As a daughter of slavery in Mississippi, she understood all too well the need for social improvements. Washington visited Mississippi, her native state, to join together its upper-class black women. By 1903 Mississippi had a series of black women's clubs and in 1913, a year after Washington was elected president of the NACW, Mississippi clubwomen joined the NACW. Washington could now institute meaningful change to a sector of black women and children in her home-state who had been largely forgotten.[50]

The Alabama Federation and the Mississippi clubs eventually came under the umbrella of the Southern Federation and the NACW. According to Washington, "The Southern Federation of two hundred and twenty-five clubs is devoted to work in the Southern States, but its clubs are affiliated with the National organization." The women were able to solicit support and assistance from state and federal institutions, white philanthropists, and most importantly under the initial presidency of Margaret Washington, they attracted a larger pool of African Americans for membership and community awareness then they had been able to do independently. Washington used her platform in Montgomery to reach a broader audience. As Addie Hunton noted: "by an intense and lofty purpose to make the colored woman her own emancipator from conditions and customs bequeathed her by a bitter past, and by a mighty desire to help in the warfare against vice and ignorance wherever it might abound, the women at Montgomery resolved themselves in the Southern Federation of Colored Women Clubs [SFCWC]."[51]

The SFCWC was able to branch out and make lasting contributions in Alabama and the Southern region as a whole. Hunton credited the women of Alabama for being: "Exceedingly wise in placing themselves under the leadership of Mrs. Booker T. Washington, for not only has she wider opportunity than other women to study the questions affecting our welfare, but she is a pioneer in club work among colored women and an untiring sympathetic and wise worker."[52] The Southern Federation implemented programs that served as examples for other regional clubs. They initiated and sponsored the state's first black history program, commemoration of the birthday of race leader Fredrick Douglass, and they helped to sponsor an essay contest which highlighted the achievements of various African Americans.

Shortly after the SFCWC's first convention, the NACW met in Buffalo, New York and elected its second president, Josephine Silone Yates, in 1901. Yates was born in 1859 to a prominent family in Mattituck, New York. She later organized the Kansas City Women's League in 1893. In 1901 Washington was elected first vice-president of the southern region of the NACW. She increased her visibility in the organization and continued to expand her realm of influence. The prison complex system remained a constant reformation project for the NACW and Washington in particular.[53]

The South was notorious for charging black youth with petty crimes. According to clubwomen, "by 1890, convict leasing in Alabama had become a huge operation, supplying bodies like the slave trade of the world. Black males, age twelve and older, went directly to the mines." On top of this injustice, they were sent to correctional institutions for adults because juvenile facilities for blacks did not exist. Homeless black youth were also sent to adult institutions when foster-care homes refused to extend assistance. There were a hundred and five reformatories in the nation, however, only seven were housed in the south, and the one in Alabama was all-white.[54]

These figures were staggering. However, in this laissez faire society of self-help, black women were on their own in matters of prison reform. Washington believed that children who committed crimes could be rehabilitated at a faster rate if there were institutions that nourished their needs and concerns. According to Washington, "ten or more years ago, one or two of us went to Birmingham to see an honorary judge, to ask for the small boys who came before the courts." To the surprise of Washington, "he kindly consented, provided we could show that we had a place to take these youngsters and a person to hold and to control them."[55]

At that time, the women of Alabama could provide neither. However, nearly one year after the meeting with the judge, the clubwomen had acquired twenty acres of land for five hundred dollars and a small house. From that acquisition, the Alabama Federation raised funds and awareness and helped to create the Mt. Meigs Reformatory for Juvenile Negro Law-Breakers. Washington credited the NACW as the direct stimulus for the reformatory. The masterminds behind the initiative were Josephine Washington of Montgomery, Cornelia Bowen of Mt. Meigs, Washington, and clubwomen across the state.[56] According to Josephine, the project was for "small boys and boys not quite so small, but all boys who linger still in the lap of childhood." Their collaboration ensured the success of the reformatory, and clubwomen soon purchased land, "a small house for twelve hundred, and a man for more or less," and built a five-room cottage in Mt. Meigs. The reformatory survived on small donations from clubwomen in the amount of $2,000 a year, a difficult sum to raise annually. By the second year of operation thirty-one boys lived at the center. For several years afterwards the number rarely dropped below fifty. The Mount, as it was called by the youth, provided the boys with kindergartens, playgrounds, trades, and reading courses. Lessons were given on proper ways to brush teeth and the necessity of baths. These routines were done in an effort to correct the injustices committed against black males and to see an end to the convict lease system, especially for black youth. Through the intuitive leadership of these clubwomen in the first five years of the reformatory, over 300 boys occupied the quarters, at one time or another.[57]

In 1911, with the hard work and dedication of the Alabama Federation, the Mt. Meigs Reformatory had become a state institution, by an act of the state legislature. Until that point "two thousand dollars in cash [was] spent each year to say nothing of food, clothing, [and] implements . . . by the Colored women of the state of Alabama."[58] At the Alabama Federation's fifteenth session in 1913, the organization's president Cornelia Bowen praised the women for "the work done for the Negro boys and the new work about to be launched by the federation for Negro girls." Washington was cognizant of the way black girls were neglected in the South and sought to expand reform efforts to include them, "wishing to give our attention to the girls of the state and feeling that the school for boys should be enlarged and cared for by the state" declared Washington. She added that "we have succeeded in getting the legislature to take over the property." The state provided over $8000 to improve the facility; in 1911 that money went a long way. Also included were additional funds for maintenance and expansion of the home. In December of 1911, Alabama Governor Emmett J. O'Neal appointed nine trustees, and the state assumed control of the reformatory.[59]

The Alabama Federation's influence had not been eliminated by the state's administration. The trustees of Mt. Meigs appointed an advisory board comprised of women who were members of the AFCWC, including Washington. In 1912 more than sixty-one boys were committed to the reformatory and by 1913 the number rose to nearly eighty-seven. In order to cover their cost-of-living fees, the boys picked cotton on neighboring farms. The clubwomen made sure the boys were not being exploited for cheap labor by the white landowners. Later that same year the federation petitioned the trustees to build an annex to be used as a trades skills learning center, and a water system which prevented the spread of typhoid fever. This initiative directly correlated to initiatives accomplished at the Tuskegee Institute and within the TWC. The expansion also guaranteed that the young men would receive a sufficient education and most importantly learn a trade so they could make an honest living once they were released.[60]

In 1918, future baseball legend Leroy "Satchel" Paige was sentenced to five years—or until his eighteenth birthday—to the Mount. Born in Mobile, Alabama in 1906, and raised by his single mother, the twelve-year-old Paige found himself at the mercy of the courts after a minor infraction of stealing a handful of snacks from a local store. In addition to the claims of theft, he was also involved in a rock throwing brawl with a group of white kids, just days prior to his arrest. Considering the racial climate of the day, his mother had few options in the wake of white retaliation. The Mount became his refuge.[61]

The educational experiences at the reformatory reached beyond practical lessons in the classroom and extended to community service and athleticism. Clubwomen soon realized the benefit of sports to reform. Paige and other boys enrolled in classes, joined the choir, and competed in outdoor sports. They learned race pride through hard-work and instruction. In addition, sports became a useful tool for practical lessons in accountability, teamwork, consistency, and brotherhood. This experimentation in sports reform proved to be beneficial to the boys and community at large. Sports activities, along with other extracurricular events, brought the city of Mt. Meigs and the educational facilities together, creating a synergy and an appreciation for black creative expressions. The success of the reformatory also spoke to the benefit of club work and social reform.[62]

Over the course of nearly twenty years, Margaret Washington positioned herself as an influential clubwoman and reformer. She demonstrated her ability to lead by successfully bringing women together to actively challenge the ills of society. Despite her administrative duties at Tuskegee Institute she worked tirelessly to aid in the betterment of southern youth. After years of progress, Washington was elected fifth president of the NACW in 1912 at the Hampton Biennial Convention in Virginia, where 10,908 members were reported. At the time of her election, the NACW had amassed property in the sum $113,832 and special attention was placed on children, lynching, and prison reform. In fact, at the 1912 meeting the clubwomen protested against the execution of a seventeen-year-old girl in Virgina.[63]

Booker T. Washington gave a brief speech prior to the closing of the convention. The exact content of the speech is unknown; however, it probably benefited Margaret Washington to have her husband there in support of her at the height of her involvement with the Black Women's Club Movement. Although Margaret Washington had a meaningful influence on the NACW's presidential administration before and after her tenure as the organization's chief executive, there was impressive progress made during her administration from 1912–1916. For example, by 1916 more than 300 new clubs had joined the NACW under Margaret Washington's reign.[64]

Her marriage to Booker T. Washington aided her success throughout her participation in women's clubs, and ultimately throughout her life. Marrying men of achievement undoubtedly positioned clubwomen to make influential changes in a male-dominated society. However, once women established their platforms they used their influence to make positive changes. Anna Julia Cooper, wife of a minister for two years before he passed away, asserted: "The question is not now with the woman 'How shall I so cramp, stunt, and simplify and nullify myself as to make me eligible to the honor of being swallowed up into some little man?'"[65] Instead the issue "rests with the man as to how he can so develop . . . to reach the ideal of a generation of women who demand the noblest, grandest and best achievements of which he is capable."[66]

Strong women profited from connections to strong and secure men. Booker T. Washington was more than willing to promote and advance the interests of his wife. He regularly supported her involvement with the TWC and the NACW, mentioning their achievements throughout Tuskegee and in his business endeavors. It is also important to mention that Margaret Washington's reform work fit directly in-line with the Tuskegee Machine. Despite his critics, Booker Washington was able to reach tremendous heights within the black community and encouraged Margaret Washington to do the same within her civil commitments.[67]

The NACW recorded many improvements made in the daily lives of the black race, but there were still barriers that were not yet broken. Blacks were the target of increased mob violence, specifically as it pertained to lynching. Margaret Washington spoke out against lynching, asserting, "there is a strong and growing feeling against this form of punishment for any cause whatscever."⁶⁸ This type of barbarity could not be tolerated in a civilized society. Margaret Washington probably became even more vocal in her protests against lynching after her husband was severely beaten and almost killed by Henry Ulrich, while in New York in 1911. Violence against black men was rationalized due to the alleged protection of white womanhood. It was not surprising that Ulrich engaged in vigilante justice after accusing Booker T. Washington of attempting to solicit the services of a white woman. After this incident, which hit home, Margaret Washington's public position against racial violence became more determined and authoritative.⁶⁹

In addition to the Ulrich incident, Monroe Nathan Work's investigative research deeply impacted Margaret Washington. Work joined the staff at Tuskegee in 1908 and created the Department of Records and Research where he collected and cataloged information on African Americans, creating the first Negro Yearbook. In 1912, Work also created the first Lynching report at Tuskegee. These biannual Lynching Reports influenced Margaret Washington and her awareness of the magnitude of mob violence across the nation.⁷⁰

The year 1912 was no exception to public brutality, and violence seemed to worsen in the years that followed. Margaret Washington continued to maintain that through self-improvement and community awareness blacks could eventually be liberated. It was easier for elite clubwomen to be optimistic about the possibilities for change during the Progressive Era. Although they experienced discrimination, their class allowed them a level of mobility that the masses of blacks did not possess. For most blacks, the era was plagued with disenfranchisement, increased lynchings, denial of civil rights, and an intensification of Jim Crow.⁷¹

In 1913, a year after her election as NACW president, Margaret Washington gave a speech to the NACW annual national convention. As she spoke to the group she reminded them that they were "the best women of the race" and credited the efforts of clubwomen for advances the community had made, both small and great. They were the first to initiate placing Bibles in public facilities like hotels. Washington recalled receiving a letter from a male prisoner who had been incarcerated for two years. In reflecting upon the usefulness of supplying the public with Bibles he concluded "the Bible you sent me has been my constant solace. I leave here next month and this book will go with me, and I know it will keep me from wrong-doing all of the days of my life."[72]

The clubwomen were also the first to call for the separation of black children from adults in prisons and their efforts led the courts to create a juvenile court system. Washington had felt that "the world at large realizes that the child must be saved in order to have the women and men needed for its development." The clubwomen placed special emphasis on the youth of the race, and many of their reforms were designed with young people in mind.[73]

In Margaret Washington's speech to the clubwomen she also addressed Jacks's letter that had degraded black women's character years earlier. Washington stated that in 1895 when the call was made to counter his attack, many were "eager to prove that with equal opportunities to make a living, equal chance for an education, we were not unlike other women of other races." She understood that black women, as with women of other races, were not where they could be, making it imperative for women to unite. This was a belief that Washington stood by and a theory she sought to prove throughout her entire adult life.[74] In an essay written for *Outlook Magazine* she declared: "Moreover, you can no more find the 'average' Negro woman than you can multiply eggs by treaties. Just as eggs are different from treaties, so good Negro women are different from bad Negro women, and no average can be struck. The best we can do is to estimate the size of the various groups of Negro women, but even this is not enough; the influence, efficiency, significance of one superior woman's life may be infinitely more than that of ten dull drudges. And so the statistical method could not do justice to this essentially human problem; statistics negate individuality."[75]

Washington concluded that the worth of different women (black or white) could be measured in various ways. She mentioned the absurdity of suggesting that "all black women" were the same, for each race had their share of good and bad women. Class rather than race, in her assessment, was the most identifiable difference within all races of women. Whether Washington truly believed this is unclear. However, it fit directly in line with a respectability politics and capitalist framework. If the clubwomen could get the masses of blacks to understand and appreciate the value of land ownership and wealth, then their black bodies could be saved from white discrimination and violence. This performance of respectability, Washington learned, would not be enough to save the race. However, it raised their active participation in improving their economic and social situations.

During Washington's tenure, the NACW, like the TWC, functioned through different departments. There were over twelve in total including departments on social living, Mothers' Meetings, rural conditions, education, temperance, health and hygiene, juvenile, music, suffrage, public prints and posters, a big sisters department, and a "railroad" conditions department. All of the departments saw progress under Washington's presidency.[76]

The railroad division in particular was a very important component, especially during the Jim Crow era when mass transit was restricted and dangerous for African Americans. Black women responded in different ways to this struggle, as had Ida B. Wells-Barnett in the 1880s. In 1884 Wells-Barnett paid for a first-class seat in the "Ladies Coach" of a train going from Woodstock, Tennessee to Memphis. A white conductor demanded that Wells-Barnett leave the first-class car and sit in the smoking car which had been set aside for blacks. Wells-Barnett refused and was subsequently thrown off the car, kicking and biting. In Memphis, she filed charges against the railroad company and won her suit in local courts. The *Memphis Daily Appeal*, first of many newspapers to write an article, ran the story Christmas Day 1884, with the headline: A DARKY DAMSEL OBTAINS A VERDICT FOR DAMAGES AGAINST THE CHESAPEAKE & OHIO RAILROAD. Unfortunately, the verdict in her favor was later overturned on appeal.[77]

Segregation laws in Alabama were not unlike laws across the American South. However, the legal and social policies of segregation were not official until after the Alabama Constitutional Convention of 1901. Through this legalized separation of the races, public spaces were either segregated or reserved for whites only. Washington was also no stranger to discrimination when it came to public transportation. In 1916 a newspaper published a story headlined "White Cab Driver Refuses Mrs. Washington." On August 4 while in Wilmington, Delaware, Washington and a group of black clubwomen on their way to Bethel African Methodist Episcopal Church, were refused a ride to the event. Black and white residents of Wilmington were outraged. A prominent white judge of the community stated, only "a fool driver could not distinguish between colored women of culture and refinement and common, worthless ones." This statement reflects again on Washington's earlier claim of class. The judge went on to state that Washington and her entourage had no recourse under the laws of Delaware unless they filed a civil action, but reports or newspapers do not suggest that Washington took any legal action against the taxi driver. However, she used this incident to illustrate the discrimination to which blacks were subjected due to race, and regardless of class, which countered her earlier statements.[78]

The Mothers' Meetings section of the NACW was also very dear to Washington. Through her initiatives this component of the NACW saw great improvements and advances. "All mothers, young and old, educated and uneducated, need to confer together, to study the best things in the rearing and caring for their children, to understand how to select and direct the reading, the music, the company of their boys and girls, to be able to steady the life of their older sons and daughters, and last but not least, to be a wife and a mother."[79] This department grew substantially during the years of 1912 and 1916. This may have been prompted by her own struggles in balancing public and domestic duties. She stressed the need for further improvements and growth in this capacity and remained vocal about the improvements it made on local women and children. The mothers' section of the TWC was also one of the catalysts that brought the NACW's increased publicity.[80]

The issue of suffrage greatly intensified during Washington's tenure as president. Contrary to beliefs some men held that women should not be involved in political affairs because it made them appear too manly, black and white women alike fought for the right to vote, albeit separately on most occasions. Washington had been involved with the Tuskegee community suffrage agenda as early as 1895. Adella Hunt Logan, wife of Tuskegee Institute's treasurer Warren Logan and also Margaret Washington's next door neighbor, presided over the TWC's suffrage department and worked closely with the NACW's department.[81]

In a 1912 speech published in *The Crisis* magazine, Logan defended the right of women to vote. She suggested that although in previous years women were obliged to say they would not get involved with politics, they soon realized that politics affected the way their communities and homes operated.[82] Margaret Washington constantly reminded clubwomen in speeches and articles that their approach to suffrage was conservative. More dangerous than no vote at all, proclaiming before a group of clubwomen that "we shall be ready to cast our votes intelligently and there shall not be the general accusation that our votes are for sale . . . all the way from a drink of liquor to two dollars." Washington contended that "our attitude toward the suffrage is of the conservative kind, we have not blown any houses with dynamite, nor have we been engaged in parading the streets in men's attire . . . but of one thing I am certain," declared Margaret Washington, "we are reading and studying the great question . . . and when the vote is given to women," we will be ready.[83]

Her stance was remarkably similar to that of her husband who, only a few years following emancipation, believed that political agitation was not the best answer for blacks whom he considered "ignorant and inexperienced" with politics. Margaret Washington supported universal suffrage; however, she preferred limiting it to educated blacks and whites. Some critics suggest that she opposed suffrage because she once stated: "The colored women of the country, thus far, have done little or nothing, however, for the suffrage movement. There have been and are still other questions of vital importance to us as a race of women and it is with these questions and problems that we have been engaged." In other instances, she admitted she never lost sleep over the issue of suffrage. Taken out of context, these words can be misconstrued and falsely interpreted as a denigration of women's suffrage. Washington's club affiliations and her support of suffrage education prove the contrary. She supported informed voters rather than those who were exploited due to their political ignorance. Furthermore, once the nineteenth amendment was actually ratified in 1920, Washington was one of the few southern women in Macon County, Alabama, who actually casted a vote.[84] According to Harriette Booth: "My mother died in [19]46 and she had been voting, I guess, 20 years before she died. But the average Negro did not realize the value of voting and didn't bother with it. But a few women got together, and they decided they were going to vote. Mrs. [B.T.] Washington got them together."[85]

Outside of the vote, Washington asserted that a positive identification with one's own race was very important. She also strongly believed that racial issues in the South had to be resolved by everyone who lived there. Believing that a small portion of white Americans were committed to fairness and racial harmony, she often encouraged southern blacks to trust them. "You know that we often feel that every white man and woman south of the Mason and Dixon line is a real devil," Washington proclaimed to a women's group at Old Bethel A.M.E. Church, in 1898. "It is pretty bad down here, I will admit, but there are many fine and noble Southern white people, women as well as men."[86] These beliefs could very well have stemmed from the fact that Margaret Washington's adolescent years were spent with a white Quaker family. She never spoke harshly of them and credited them for her early education. Uniting with other races was also a belief that her husband Booker T. Washington publicly subscribed to and one of the reasons he became so successful and influential throughout his life.[87] Tuskegee Institute's benefactors were white philanthropists who supported industrial education. Margaret Washington believed that civil injustices could be eradicated if they were brought to the "good" white folks by the "best" black men and women of the race.[88]

In 1913, Margaret Washington informed women of the NACW that the group would be joining the National Council of Women (NCW), a historically all-white organization which Washington considered the most progressive organization of white women. Washington felt that this alliance could bring many of NACW's initiatives to a broader audience. NACW would have one representative on NCW's executive council. While the NCW agreed to the merger, the cost of membership for the NACW into this organization was more than the $100 fee charged to white clubs. The higher fee caused a great uproar among NACW women who knew their membership would be limited to only one black woman and that person would only be allowed to attend executive sessions.[89]

The disgust that the NACW expressed as a whole reflected upon an incident that occurred years earlier in 1900 when Josephine Ruffin was sent by the New Era Club of Boston to the General Federation of Women's Clubs biennial national convention in Milwaukee. The GFWC informed her that she could not join the convention representing a black women's club. Ruffin later refused their offer to enter under a white women's club. NACW members were incensed by this affair which they called the "Ruffin Incident." However, Washington stood firm in her belief that this merger with the NCW would be a benefit rather than a hindrance to the NACW and maintained that through this type of racial cooperation black women would have another channel to voice their concerns and greater access to financial resources to execute their many initiatives.[90]

Washington selected Josephine Willson Bruce to represent the NACW at the National Council of Women. Wife of former United States Senator from Mississippi Blanche K. Bruce, and former Lady Principal of Tuskegee Institute, Josephine Willson Bruce was a well-rounded candidate. She held a prominent place among black women in Washington, D.C. and had promoted the welfare of African Americans in general. She was a strong advocate of industrial education and co-founder of several women's clubs including the Booklover's Club and the Colored Women's League. It is important to note that Bruce was so fair-skinned, if she desired she could pass as white.[91]

At the National Council of Women's convention in 1913, she addressed the issue of the unfair membership fee placed on the black organization. After she had spoken, the fee was lowered and revised in the NCW constitution to be the same as that paid by white organizations. Bruce was also able to present concerns of black women and the NACW to the group. As she addressed the all-white council of delegates and the audience, Bruce conveyed that, just like white women: "Colored women were responsive to the same ideals; that they [saw] the needs of humanity with the same eyes, and that they [were] giving their strength—physical, moral and spiritual—toward solving the same problems that occupy the minds of our sister women throughout the land; and though laboring under many difficulties, Colored women [were] fully abreast in the struggle to raise the level of life generally, and open up opportunities, of usefulness for our people."[92]

In Washington's mind, positive images of the black community also benefited both blacks and whites. She gave special attention to the prints and posters department of the NACW. When newspapers published advertising that grossly exaggerated the features of black men and women, Washington wrote the publishers and informed them of the harm these images caused. While some of her concerns were met with genuine remorse, she realized that many publishers cared little about the feelings of black readers and paid little to no attention to correcting this disparity. But this did not deter Washington who was determined to promote visually positive black images.[93]

Race vindication and its ability to shape the way blacks saw themselves rose in importance to the NACW. Margaret Washington worked diligently to incorporate positive black images everywhere possible. She firmly believed a person's self-image was directly related to the way they acted, ultimately determining whether or not they would take control of their future in a racially oppressed society. Washington relied on many of the works of Carter G. Woodson to assist her efforts of introducing a curriculum of African American history into black schools.[94]

Washington was reelected as president for a second term at the 1914 convention in Wilberforce, Ohio. During the convention the women endorsed women's suffrage, prohibition, and a national awareness for tuberculosis. They recorded reform work with children in urban slums while also expressing dissatisfaction with what they considered "extreme" fashion attire of girls. The clubwomen approved a literary award that encouraged the citizens to engage in higher realms of thought, similar to efforts being carried out with the National Urban League and the National Association for the Advancement of Colored People, founded in 1909.[95]

In October of 1915, during Margaret Washington's second term as president of the NACW, Carter G. Woodson and four others founded the Association for the Study of Negro Life and History. A year later Woodson launched the *Journal of Negro History*. Washington encouraged her fellow NACW members to support Woodson financially and to use his material in their communities and classes. Women from various clubs within the NACW conducted door-to-door campaigns in an effort to promote Woodson's black history materials. This initiative helped Woodson's "Negro History Week Movement," ultimately expanding awareness and appreciation of African American history.[96]

Under Washington's presidency, local clubs and federations developed and staffed libraries and reading rooms with materials on historic figures of the African and African American past. This representation increased societal awareness of black progress. It also served as cultural reinforcement for the community and clubwomen.[97]

Margaret Washington's humble beginnings showed her the value of race pride, economics, and maintaining good health. Her days at Fisk helped to lay a solid foundation towards her ideas about poverty. Though her health was often poor even before she moved to Tuskegee, this did not stop her from fulfilling the responsibilities of Lady Principal after her arrival. Her health challenges also did not reduce her extensive travel or her concepts of domestic feminism.[98]

By 1911 Booker T. Washington's health began to deteriorate. He received numerous warnings from doctors and friends to lighten his workload. George Foster Peabody, one of Washington's friends, advised him to: "Let up in your quite too strenuous life." Washington ignored these warnings for a while. For the majority of his adult life he had been so full of determination to make a change in black communities he could not enjoy leisure and derived his pleasure from succeeding at his work, in many ways becoming obsessed with it.[99]

Margaret Washington, despite her strenuous work schedule and her own delicate health, continuously urged her husband to take better care of his diet and overall wellbeing. Their 1899 trip to Europe had been the longest stint of time in their nearly twenty-three-year marriage that Margaret observed Booker on extended rest. Years later in 1913, Emmett Scott, Booker's personal secretary, coordinated annual fishing trips in the Gulf of Mexico for the race leader. Still, these small gestures did little to slow the frequent headaches, fatigue, weight loss, failing vision, and chronic high blood pressure. Washington had worked himself literally to death. On November 8, 1915, Booker T. Washington went to St. Luke's Hospital in New York where he was seen by specialists for a scheduled screening. Once in the hospital, on November 10, after an apparent nervous breakdown, Booker's health took a turn for the worse. With little hope for survival, he requested that his wife come immediately. Upon her arrival, Booker literally hung to Margaret as they returned by train to Tuskegee, Alabama on November 12. The Washingtons' arrived to The Oaks just before dawn on November 14. A few hours later, with Margaret and other family members by his side, Booker T. Washington died.

The nation mourned the passing of the "Wizard" of Tuskegee. After hearing the news, Charles Banks of Mound Bayou, Mississippi, immediately wired a message to Emmett Scott: "With the entire race I am bowed in mourning the loss of the greatest man the race has produced in any epoch. One of America's foremost citizens regardless of race." The death of her husband impacted the whole country, but Margaret Washington suffered the most. On November 17, 1915, thousands gathered at Tuskegee's Chapel to pay homage to the leader of black America, similar to how they had done two decades earlier with the passing of his predecessor, Fredrick Douglass.[100]

The years of his declining health could not prepare Margaret for the passing of her best friend, mentor, protector and life partner. Whatever thoughts consumed her mind at Washington's last breath, she knew that she had a great responsibility ahead of her, and because of this she gave herself very little time to grieve.[101]

Together the Washingtons worked for the liberty and dignity of black men and women in America and abroad. What they built at Tuskegee was incredible, given the harsh realities of the era. They worked for racial uplift so that black men and women in the United States and abroad would not be judged by the color of their skin, but as Martin Luther King would pronounce fifty-years later, "by the content of their character." After Booker Washington's death, Margaret Washington continued her work. She did not give up her position as president of the NACW or the TWC. Margaret also never remarried. She stood committed to the cause. In many documents, including census records, she simply wrote her name as Mrs. Booker T Washington. After all, she had another marriage to attend to—social reforms.[102]

It was the persistent will of Margaret Washington that carried her through her years as head of the NACW and made her strong influence linger well after her presidency. In 1920 the women held the NACW's twenty-fifth anniversary celebration at Tuskegee Institute. Perhaps it was a tribute specifically for Washington, the fifth president of the NACW. The presence of the club at Tuskegee for such a grand occasion signified the impact that Washington had on the group. Seven hundred women attended, representing over 100 black women's clubs. It is also interesting that although the NACW was incorporated in 1896, 1920 represented a combined celebration of Margaret's National Federation of Colored Women's Clubs which was formed in 1895, and absorbed into the NACW. Either way, the clubwomen paid homage to one of the mothers of the Black Women's Club Movement in their selection of venue.[103]

By the tender age of fifty-one and after nearly twenty-seven years of club work, Margaret Washington showed no visible signs of slowing down. As the NACW grew and additional departments were established, Washington would remain on the Executive Council of the group until her death in 1925. She continued to guide and instruct women at local, regional and national levels on concepts of self-help, self-sufficiency and social reform, ultimately carrying the Tuskegee model to the national stage. She was a builder, a founder, and a devoted humanitarian in every sense of the term. Washington became a visionary leader and advocate of women's rights, and her determination to change the situation of blacks soon reached international levels.

Chapter Six

Beyond City Limits

> A great many people complain that we are leaving the farms, we are leaving the country.
>
> —Margaret Murray Washington
> (*The Negro Home*, 1920)[1]

By the summer of 1916 Washington had served out her term as president of the NACW and President Woodrow Wilson had won his reelection—partly due to the popular campaign slogan "he kept us out of the war." Despite his attempt to remain neutral, by April of the following year Wilson petitioned Congress to declare war. Blacks were generally split on their support of World War I. Socialist organizer A. Philip Randolph attacked the war efforts as imperialist while Emmett Scott, Special Assistant to the Secretary of War and his supporters, believed that the war would help to confirm the black man as patriotic and manly.

Despite conflicting views on African American involvement in the war, black men who served in France were able to identify themselves with the African Diaspora. Their enlistment also challenged stereotypes of black male inferiority and citizenship rights. Nevertheless, while black men participated in war efforts, many of their civil and human rights were violated in the United States.[2] A newspaper clipping in 1918 asserted that Rafe Clemmings, a race man of Alabama, was given "a severe lashing by . . . twenty-five masked men," later identified as members of the Ku Klux Klan.[3] Another article asserted that "reports from Texas, Oklahoma, Louisiana, Tennessee, Mississippi, Alabama, South Carolina, Georgia and Florida indicate that the Klan is getting together in hundreds of communities."[4] Then, in Mobile, Alabama four black siblings accused of murder, two of whom were women, "were taken from the jail at Shubuta, Miss., tonight and lynched." Incidence of vigilante justice and terrorism against African Americans in the South rose during the First World War; however, violence was not solely a Southern or war-time phenomenon.⁵

By 1918 black American soldiers were returning home and many were disillusioned by the state of violence and discrimination that awaited them. "Military service had brought little of the honor and less of the glory that pro-war patriots had led them to expect." However, change was on the horizon: just as the Civil War had opened doors for enslaved blacks, WWI would ignite an international movement. Migration of blacks from the South to Northern and Western cities helped set the stage for the "New Negro,"—one who traveled to escape Jim Crow and was willing to fight for equality. Black philosopher Alain Locke is credited for the New Negro Movement. World War I also saw a rise in the number of black intellectuals and an increasing realization that change required constant and direct agitation.⁶

The "New Negro Woman" also rose during this period. Many black women served in war efforts; however, all women were excluded from military combat. Washington was fully aware of the changes taking place among enlisted soldiers. Black soldiers "have had to develop themselves physically, mentally, and morally; they have traveled and had contact with culture, and necessarily, they are going to be superior to our girls."⁷ She asserted that the "directing class of Negro women indicate[s] lines along which these new problems can be worked out," so that black women could be just as prepared as black men for the new era.⁸

Black soldiers from the United States were fighting alongside soldiers of African descent around the globe. This new pan-African brotherhood signified a revolutionary movement across time and space. Washington's nephew, Roscoe Conklin Simmons, a young orator from Mississippi, unofficially served as an advisor to president Warren G. Harding, Calvin Coolidge, and Herbert Hoover. During a speech in 1917 in Hampton Virginia, the charismatic thirty-six-year-old pierced into the audience as he attempted to dismantle an incensed crowd of African Americans. Simmons declared: "The American Negro knows but one government, speaks but one language, and claims but one flag." He went on to suggest, " . . . the Negro, with no voice in his government, has but one request . . . He ask for the guns of war." Many black males longed for an opportunity to join the war efforts, wear the soldier's uniform, and join in the international fight for black liberation. These sentiments helped to form deeper roots to the black freedom struggle, especially for the soldiers who served abroad.[9]

Following WWI some progress was made within this turning tide. Women secured their long-awaited right to vote with the 1920 ratification of the Nineteenth Amendment to the United States Constitution, the Harlem Renaissance brought national exposure to black poets, writers and culture, and Jamaican-born Marcus Garvey launched the largest social mass-movement of blacks in America, the Universal Negro Improvement Association (UNIA). However, many of the prewar hopes remained unrealized. The Ku Klux Klan resurfaced, and black Southerners and Northerners alike were subjected to increased forms of racial terrorism. The boll weevil destroyed cotton production and many southerners migrated North. These setbacks, and countless others caused clubwomen like Washington to look abroad for answers to problems confronting the race.[10]

Washington was confident that the black experience in America was similar to the experience of blacks across the globe. However, her club affiliations did not exclusively support international outreach. During the NACWs 1920 conference, held at Tuskegee, Alabama, the women continued earlier discussions on women in politics and the vote. Even more, during their 1922 conference in Richmond, clubwomen showed appreciation for West African Culture and spent considerable time on efforts being done through the Pan African Conference. However, their main focus remained domestic in nature. Rather than adding this to the mission of the NACW, in 1922 Margaret Washington stepped away from the club to form the first independent international organization of black women, the International Council of Women of the Darker Races of the World (ICWDR), in Richmond, Virginia. She became, in her own way, a Pan-Africanist.[11]

The term Pan-Africanism became popularized after 1900, though the idea had appeared prior to the American Revolution. According to Pan-Africanist scholar P. Olisanwuche Esedebe, Pan-Africanism, "represented a reaction against the oppression of blacks and the racial doctrines that marked the era of abolitionism. It also found expression in the independent church movement in the New World and Africa as well as in resistance to European colonial ambitions in Africa."[12]

Female involvement with Pan-Africanism emerged at the turn of the century. New conditions called for greater collaborations and strategic approaches to improve race relations across the globe. In 1905 when W. E. B. Du Bois and William Monroe Trotter formed the Niagara Movement, twenty-nine black men from various states met in Fort Erie, Ontario, Canada. The Niagara Movement's platform sought to obtain equality in education, housing and neighborhoods, suffrage, the military and economics. They believed in human brotherhood, the right to be men, and "that this class of American citizens should protest emphatically and continually against the curtailment of political rights."[13]

Although the movement was centered on men, at its second meeting in Harper's Ferry, West Virginia in 1906, clubwomen like Gertrude Wright Morgan held influential positions. In later years other women affiliated with the NACW such as Carrie Clifford, Addie W. Hunton, and Mary Church Terrell also collaborated with the Niagara Movement. It is not surprising that these women later joined with Washington to form the ICWDR. As early as 1904 Terrell had delivered a speech at the International Congress of Women conference in Berlin, Germany, on behalf of the NACW.[14] "I am the only woman speaking from this platform whose parents were actually held as chattels and who . . . would have been a slave herself . . . My happiness is two-fold, rejoicing as I do, not only in the emancipation of my race, but in the almost universal elevation of my sex,"[15] Terrell stated.

According to the *National Notes*, there were four clubwomen selected to be a part of this international auxiliary. The president of the NACW at that time, Josephine Silone Yates from Kansas City, Missouri, selected three women from the NACW including Margaret Murray Washington, Josephine Beall Bruce, Mary Church Terrell, and a woman who had no affiliations with the club, Coralie Franklin Cook. Although Washington was not selected to represent the club in Berlin, her 1899 tour of Europe and her connections with this committee suggest her early involvement in international initiatives. She collaborated with women within the NACW and those affiliated with white organizations such as the International Council of Women, formed by Susan B. Anthony and others. Washington's involvements with these initiatives were limited, thus fueling her greater ambition to create an independent organization.[16]

Although the Pan-African movement unified people of color on many fronts, there is still much debate surrounding its precise purpose. Some scholars refrain from using concrete definitions because the term has taken on various forms at different historical moments. Others suggest that Pan-Africanism united black people around the globe, serving to promote their interests. Hakim Adi and Marika Sherwood define Pan-Africanists as "women and men of African descent whose lives and work have been concerned, in some way, with the social and political emancipation of African peoples and those of the African diaspora." Scholar Tony Martin suggests that "Pan-Africanism became inevitable with the inception of the Trans-Atlantic slave trade."[17]

The ICWDR marked a defining point for African American women's international activism. The purpose of the council was to accumulate information on women of color outside as well as inside the United States. This information could be used for self-improvement of its members and also could be disseminated to the broader public "in order that there may be a larger appreciation of their history and accomplishments." Washington, along with other women, "declare[d] that the many handicaps, barriers and embarrassments from which the women of the dark races suffer because of color prejudice can and must be overcome by a powerful organization working intensively along definite lines."[18] The organization was Washington's creation and seemingly important to fellow clubwoman Mary Jackson McCrorey. In 1924 McCrorey drafted a proposal, describing the group's origins already underway prior to the 1915 death of Booker T. Washington. She first sent it to Margaret Washington for her approval:

> ... There lay in embryo in the heart and mind of Mrs. Booker T. Washington the plans for an organization having its chief objective some kind of definite cooperation among the women of all the darker races for the purpose of studying the condition under which each subgroup lived and progressed, of disseminating knowledge of their handicaps and of their achievements, and of simulating by closer fellowship and understanding to higher endeavor. From her we learn that she talked over with Dr. Washington. ... He heartily approved of her ideas. Then came suddenly the sorrow and heavier responsibility caused by his death. This delayed any onward action toward organization except as she discussed the idea with a few whose view on such a weighty undertaking she valued.[19]

Washington wanted her mission to include the study of black women's history throughout the world. ICWDR encouraged elementary and secondary schools as well as colleges to incorporate women of the

African Diaspora into their curriculums. They sought to achieve racial fairness through international activism by insisting on defining themselves in global contexts, seeking support from the international community, and publicly challenging white supremacy.

While some black men feared the public involvement of black women, during his life Booker T. Washington supported and encouraged his wife's activism. His endorsement of her international involvement was evident through a number of endeavors. His willingness to attend the 1899 international conference with Margaret during their trip to Europe. Also, his heightened interest in the Pan-African Congress of 1900, created "in view of circumstances and the wide-spread ignorance which [wa]s prevalent in England about the treatment of native races under European and American rule," suggests his support of his wife's expansion of her efforts to black women around the world.[20]

Though neither Booker nor Margaret Washington ever actually visited the continent, they gained insight on the needs of Africans through "experiments of Tuskegee students in Togo and other parts of Africa in cotton culture." Booker Washington approved hosting the meeting of the International Congress of the Negro at Tuskegee in 1912 and also sought to form an organization called the "International Council of the Friends of Africa." Aimed on building a permanent society in Africa, the council would "stand, in its relation to the civilized world, as a sort of guardian of the native people of Africa."[21]

Many nationalists like Marcus Garvey and Dusé Mohamed Ali publicly displayed and acknowledged a profound respect and debt to Booker Washington's writings and teachings. Prior to his pilgrimage to North America, Marcus Garvey, with Amy Ashwood, co-founded the UNIA in Jamaica in 1914. Garvey became intrigued by Booker Washington's approach and ideas on self-sufficiency and self-help after reading *Up from Slavery*. Garvey traveled to the United States in order to meet Washington. Unfortunately, he arrived after Washington's 1915 death. Nevertheless, he remained in North America, and polarized notions of Pan-Africanism and concepts of "race first."[22]

The Washingtons sought to extend their involvement beyond the boundaries of the United States at various points throughout their lives. Clubwoman Mary McCrorey recalled Margaret Washington's desire to establish the ICWDR years before plans were actually formulated. Cognizant of the brutality African American women were subjected to within America, the New Negro woman was also concerned about the colonization of her sisters abroad. Thus, Washington expanded notions of uplift to encompass educating women on all non-western cultures, "no matter whether those races [were] willing to be affiliated with [American blacks] or not."[23]

At the turn of the century, while both black and white women fought for suffrage and womanhood, and against sexism, black women were also fighting against racism and violence. In a letter to Terrell, Washington wrote: "But the white women of England and the United States have only one burden to bear, after all, the burden of sex. What would they do I wonder if they were double-crossed, so to speak, as the colored women of this country are?"[24] Ultimately, black women's clubs had a profound impact on black and white Americans. Washington had traveled abroad and stood at the forefront of the NFAAW, NACW, and the Southern Federation, making her an expert candidate for the international organization.[25] As with her other club endeavors, she wanted to use this organization to uplift black women. She felt that this would help their men and children, and ultimately the entire race. "We have a mission for our women the world over," she proclaimed.[26]

Many of the women who helped Washington form the ICWDR were middle and upper-class women. White women had already formulated international organizations on a large scale, like the International Council of Women (ICW), formed in 1888 through efforts of Susan B. Anthony and Elizabeth Cady Stanton. Washington modeled her club in some fashion after theirs. Although groups affiliated with the ICW were historically white, the NACW had worked with the organization in some form since the turn of the century. This may have been the reason for internal similarities between the ICWDR and ICW. Washington also used the models set forth by the Tuskegee Machine. The initial members of the ICWDR were among the leading African American women, many of whom had become dissatisfied with the limited outreach of their present organizations. Their positions within the international council formed by Washington were as follows:[27]

Mrs. Booker T. Washington, Tuskegee Institute, President
Mrs. Mary Church Terrell, Washington, D.C. 1st Vice-President
Mrs. Addie W. Hunton, Brooklyn, N. Y. 2nd Vice-President
Mrs. Elizabeth C. Carter, New Bedford, Massachusetts,
    Recording Secretary
Mrs. Mary S. Josenberger, Ft. Smith, Arkansas, Treasurer

Miss. Nannie Burroughs, Washington, D.C., Executive Chairman

Mrs. John Hope [Lugenia Burns Hope], Atlanta, Georgia, Social Committee Chairman

Mrs. Addie W. Dickerson, Philadelphia, Foreign Relations Committee Chairman

Mrs. Emily Williams, Hampton, Virginia, Education Committee Chairman

Mrs. Mary B. Talbert, South Africa, Associate Member of Education Committee

Mrs. Nettie Langston Napier, Associate Member of Education Committee

Mrs. Mary McCloud Bethune, Daytona, Florida, Member.[28]

Margaret Washington's social reform efforts helped to solidify her position. Perhaps being the widow of the late Booker T. Washington and her career as Lady Principal of Tuskegee gave Margaret Washington the upper hand in leadership. Addie W. Hunton of Brooklyn, New York, and second vice-president of the ICWDR, stated a few years before the organization's creation that women were wise in selecting the leadership of Margaret Washington. As a seasoned clubwoman her expertise brought the cause of black women to the forefront of public agendas for social and legal change.[29]

Still, some women felt that Margaret Washington should resign her other responsibilities in order to work for the International Council. In early 1925, Lugenia Burns Hope of Atlanta, Georgia, wrote to Washington, "you can find half a dozen persons who could do what you are doing [at Tuskegee] . . . But no one can do for this Council what you can—The world will listen to you."[30] Washington must have shared the sentiments of Hope, and the earlier disapproval of Wells-Barnett when in 1922 she relinquished her position indefinitely as editor of the *National Notes*, stating: "I did not feel that I could do the work the way the women wanted it done."[31]

While there were many incidents that led to the formation of the ICWDR, racism, rejection from white organizations and a lack of race consciousness were the leading forces. Washington created an organization that black women could use as a network for communication and community betterment. At their first meeting in Richmond, Virginia, which took place in August 1922 after the NACW meeting that year, Washington, along with Council board members, devised an agenda and plan for the international organization.[32]

In addition to the women who were in attendance at the Richmond meeting, a few days later on August 14 "representatives from Africa, Haiti, West Indies, Ceylon," in conjunction with women heading national organizations in the United States, met in Washington D.C. and officially formed the International Council of Women of the Darker Races of the World. Women representing foreign countries read communications and listed the degree of their involvement in the ICWDR. The main objective of the organization was the "economic, social and political welfare of the women of all the dark races," but more importantly "the dissemination of the knowledge of the history and literature of the darker races of the world."[33]

The constitution was drafted at the first meeting; within it, Washington listed the greatest goal of the council to be education. Although she believed that colored women around the world should have a working knowledge of each other, she was equally if not more concerned about the education of women and children within the United States regarding black history. It was her continued desire to have black history in every school. Much of the reform work she participated in was geared towards increasing the knowledge base of African Americans.

The organization's goals included: "The dissemination of knowledge of people of color the world over in order that there may be a larger appreciation of their history and accomplishments, and so that they themselves may have a greater degree of respect for their own accomplishments and a greater pride in themselves."[34]

The Council represented a continuation of Margaret Washington's involvement with Carter G. Woodson, who she considered "one of our strongest and best writers." Because she understood the importance of race vindication and its significance in shaping the way blacks actually saw themselves, she worked diligently to incorporate positive black images everywhere possible. "We are not fighting any race, we are simply looking out for our own . . . the first law of nature is self-preservation," she noted. Margaret Washington relied on many of the works of Woodson, Lothrop Stoddard, Steven Brown and Booker T. Washington among others, to assist in all of her efforts to introduce a curriculum of African American history into schools.[35]

Along with finalizing the organization's preamble at the first meeting, the Council discussed membership issues. The ICWDR could not exceed 100 members and "it shall be composed of women residing in countries where people of the darker races live." This included all non-Caucasian women. There was also a membership entry fee of twenty-five dollars, which was reduced to twenty dollars the second year. They established three primary objectives of the Council: education, political affairs, and social uplift. During Washington's presidency, however, most initiatives were focused on education. "The first thing we are doing, is trying to get into every school private, public or otherwise Negro Literature and History," wrote Washington.[36] In fact, after the formation of the ICWDR, Washington wrote Woodson explaining their educational goals and describing the role that she wanted him to play within the organization. She asked that he "make out a course of study in negro history and literature."[37]

Margaret Washington's focus on education had a lot to do with her training at Fisk and work at Tuskegee. She had been a teacher since the age of fourteen and viewed education as a feasible vehicle for racial uplift. As Fredrick Douglass stated, and which the Washingtons strongly believed: "the trouble with us as a people has been to work without a knowledge of the theory of work . . . It used to be said, if you want to keep a secret from the Negro, put it in a book or a newspaper."[38] Furthermore, by the early 1920s, Margaret Washington was disturbed to find "how few of our children even know of our own great leaders," such as Fredrick Douglass or Sojourner Truth. She diligently extended her efforts so that this injustice would no longer prevail.[39]

Like Washington, the women of the ICWDR were educators in their various communities. Mary McLeod Bethune founded the Normal and Industrial Institute for black girls in Daytona Beach, Florida—the Daytona Educational and Industrial Training School which later became Bethune-Cookman University. Bethune would be the first black woman involved with the White House, as she assisted four different presidents. "From 1935 to 1942 [she] served as the director of the Division of Negro Affairs of the National Youth Administration." In addition, Bethune was a close friend of Washington throughout her life.[40] Mary Jackson McCrorey served as the principal of the Negro School in Athens for four years and for twenty-one years, from 1895–1916, served as associate principal at Haines Institute in Augusta, Georgia. McCrorey also taught at Johnson C. Smith University. Lugenia Burns Hope taught at the all-male Atlanta Baptist College while extending her efforts into the community. Adelaide Casely Hayford taught at a Girls Vocational School and Teachers Training Centre in Sierra Leone, West Africa.[41]

At the ICWDR's 1922 meeting, Washington asked the group to develop a course of study that the women of the organization could use to become knowledgeable about colored women around the world. The women also created committees within their own communities so they could educate the general public on women of the darker races. This exchange of knowledge became a common practice within many women's clubs associated with the ICWDR.⁴²

While Washington saw a great opportunity for women throughout the Diaspora to join together in the uplifting of the race, she did not anticipate the impact physical distances would have on the members of the organization. Distance made it very difficult to transmit information and communicate on a regular basis. In October 1922, only a few months after the formation of the organization, Washington wrote Terrell stating, "I have sent out at least fifty letters since I saw you. It takes a good deal of time in a work of this kind when you are so far separated from each other . . . Every woman when I have written about the date wants a different date."⁴³ This frustration was also expressed to other members within the ICWDR. Most committees consisted of women from various states. Addie Dickerson wrote a letter to Terrell discussing the agenda that they were to devise with Nannie Burroughs, declaring, "I wish it were possible for the three of us to get together personally, for somehow when suggestions are talked out, it means so much."⁴⁴

After the 1922 meeting Washington managed a very strenuous schedule. She concurrently held high positions in the NACW, the Southern Federation of Colored Women and the TWC while also maintaining her position as Lady Principal at Tuskegee Institute. These duties, combined with a history of fragile health, may have placed more on her than she had anticipated. During early correspondences with Council members, Washington stressed the need to "make hay while the sun is shining," yet in later letters she adopted the quote of a fellow train passenger who advised, "Brother if you want to go far go slow." Nevertheless, whether fast or slow, she continued to labor in the trenches of global racial uplift.⁴⁵

During the 1920s many black Americans expressed discontent with America's occupation of Haiti. Although the United States sent Marines to Haiti in the summer of 1915, it was not until after the First World War that African Americans began to place Haiti on their national political agendas. In 1922 the State Department informally solicited the president of Tuskegee Robert Moton for an independent trip to Haiti to study the state of their educational system. When Moton could not go due to his responsibilities at Tuskegee, William T. B.

Williams, an educator at the school, was chosen to go in his place. Because Washington promoted many of the ICWDR reforms throughout the school, she enlisted the support of Williams to promote the ICWDR's educational agenda. "We can secure help from men like Mr. Williams," she wrote to Terrell, "and others who are constantly traveling and visiting schools."[46]

Shortly after this collaboration Washington was notified that Williams's wife Emily, also Washington's colleague, was scheduled to travel to Haiti. Upon hearing this news Washington sent a letter to Council members asking that they contribute $100 of the treasury's $170 in support of ICWDR's efforts in Haiti. "I know a woman who is going near this place. She will go on there if we will help." However, Washington failed to mention Emily Williams's name. In this regard, she created a wave of suspicion among Council members who were very particular about the competency of this unknown woman.[47] The letters that Washington received from the ICWDR's members evidenced their distrust of the situation. Mary Church Terrell, who was rather outspoken, declared: "I am unwilling to vote to take the funds out of our treasury to send anybody to Haiti to represent us without knowing who the person is . . . Even our president should not ask us to vote to send a woman whose identity nobody knows but herself." Mary McCrorey and Marion Wilkerson sent similar letters expressing their concerns. Although blunt, these responses were not unusual among clubwomen, who were leaders within their various communities, and had worked together on numerous initiatives. Washington was not sensitive to this type of correspondence, indicating when she conveyed to Terrell: "I hope you will write me freely about anything. I am not thin-skinned at all when it comes to something that I want to see put over."[48] Nannie Burroughs wrote Washington, declaring: "I do not know the person and, like in many other things, we will have to trust your judgment. On the surface, it doesn't appeal to me as a very wise thing to do. If you were going, I would say O.K., but a hundred dollars is too much to put into an investigation unless we get an unusual person and are sure that they are going to bring back a hundred dollars' worth. If the women do not get their money's worth, they will be very slow in Okay-ing anything else."[49] Washington immediately sent a letter to the ICWDR members with Williams's name, and received the approval she needed to release the funds on behalf of the organization.

As a civilian, Washington actively participated in the fight against

America's occupation of Haiti. Prior to Williams's trip, she sent a letter to Haiti's president, Louis Borno, expressing the aims and goals of the ICWDR and explaining the purpose of Williams's visit. When Emily Williams returned from Haiti, she gave a brief report to Washington detailing her trip. Washington later learned from Williams that President Brono "was much impressed with your letter." Williams also declared her trip to be a great success, emphasizing the fact that women of Haiti were in desperate need of assistance. This investigation stressed the need for the ICWDR presence in Haiti, and the need to establish learning centers for its women.[50]

Following Williams's trip to Haiti, Washington extended an invitation to Theodora Holly of Port-au-Prince. Williams had briefed Holly about the ICWDR on her visit. Holly was no stranger to political activism. Her father James Theodore Holly, was a black emigrationist who petitioned for the presence of missionaries in Haiti during the nineteenth century. When Holly came to America she agitated for Haiti's independence and even joined with other Pan-Africanists to increase global awareness surrounding the nation of Haiti.[51]

The ICWDR was scheduled to have its second annual meeting in August of 1923, at Nannie Burroughs's National Training school in Washington, D.C. Prior to this however, Washington learned from Holly that "Our haytian girls are splendid so far as talents and social culture are concerned, but are not alive to the world-wide progress of Women in general and of their Colored American sisters in Particular."[52] With this in mind, Washington extended membership of the ICWDR to Holly so that she might incorporate studies of all black women across the Diaspora. Washington invited Holly to the ICWDR's meeting in 1923, but Holly declined because "I am utterly unprepared financially." Nevertheless, through assistance from the ICWDR members, she was in attendance and became the organization's vice president for Haiti.[53]

At the Council's second meeting, the constitution was finally approved and distributed. The members also called for a review of Emily Williams's findings on the women and children of Haiti and created a committee solely responsible for publishing "the results of our study of the conditions . . . of Haiti." The French government was applauded for their efforts to change race relations and discrimination in Haiti. At this meeting, the organization discussed opening up membership to "women who have an international outlook and not necessarily clubwomen," while also adding new clubs that shared similar ideals and function.[54]

Washington had a very difficult time scheduling a date for the second meeting that would be conducive to everyone's schedule. As a result, some members were unable to attend. This came as no surprise since prior to the meeting Washington wrote to Terrell expressing that: "Every woman whom I have written about the date wants a different date, all the way from October through January. Women are mighty hard things to please. I know no time is going to suit any large majority of them unless it is in the summer and I hate to think of waiting that long."[55] Some women, like Mary Talbert who did not attend, sent in letters of recommendation for women to be elected to positions they may have occupied the previous year.[56]

Although the purpose of the ICWDR was to disseminate information about women of color to the African American public, particularly to women and children, the internal strife that existed within the organization cannot be ignored. Washington wanted the goals and objectives of the ICWDR to remain private until the organization had formalized much of their constitution which, to many in the group, had not yet been accomplished. What is more, the women who made up the organization were powerful and successful through their own efforts. Nevertheless, Washington went public to the *Washington Post* after the second meeting. In doing so she disclosed what many, like Mary Church Terrell, proclaimed to be inaccuracies. Terrell wrote to Washington shortly after the news release, inquiring about the article:

> I was very much surprised to see an account of our new League in the *Washington Post* a few days after we came from Richmond—I thought you wished the matter to be kept from the public for a while—Then there was an account in the *New York Age*—In each statement Mrs. Hunton was represented to be the first Vice President and myself the second—Please send a correct report to the papers—I am first Vice President and Mrs. Hunton is second Vice President, as you know—It seems queer that the same mistake should be made in both papers, unless it was made deliberately by someone who did it intentionally—For ways that are dark and tricks that are various.[57]

Tensions within the Black Women's Club Movement were certainly not new. According to Deborah Gray White, Terrell, in particular, "shot out stinging five-and six- page letters to fellow clubwomen over minor disagreements or incidents."[58] The inconsistency in the passage that Terrell referred to was the result of the second meeting. The ICWDR met in 1923 and Terrell was unable to attend because of her husband's hospitalization. And so, in response to Terrell's misunderstanding of the events that transpired which left her as second-vice-president instead of first-vice-president, Washington responded, stating: "We elected you as second Vice President instead of first. It is not the custom to elect anyone to any office in her absence but we thought we could have done this better than we could have done the other and so we put it through."[59] In that same meeting, Washington was named the president of the organization for another year. They went ahead with their educational campaign.

In 1924, after the organization held its third annual meeting, Washington devised a plan that eventually transformed the ICWDR. She instructed the women to formalize efforts they had conducted since the heyday of the organization. ICWDR leaders officially formed study groups in their communities. In a 1924 letter to ICWDR members Washington stated: "There is one thing I want to ask you to do, and that is to form in your own community a study club, say of seven women, whose business it will be, or whose pleasure it will be to study any question or all questions in a systematic way, relative to the darker races, no matter whether those races are races willing to be affiliated with us or not."[60]

By urging the women to be active participants in their community, Washington emphasized many of the techniques she had practiced with the TWC. "I am not asking you to do what I have not already done . . . in my own community."[61]

On many occasions, she would go into the community and instruct the women on proper ways to act and behave. However, she never failed to take it further by participating in the various activities that she expected them to execute. She explained that there should be no division within the race, and that middle and elite-class women should not attempt to separate themselves from the masses. She espoused these views and ideologies as she sent the clubwomen out into the communities even into the twentieth century. Elite women like Washington saw themselves as a part of the larger black community; however, class remained a significant factor for admission into the club. For example, although Amy Jacques Garvey, second wife of Marcus Garvey, was a Pan-Africanist, she did not hold a college degree, and as a result was not invited to join the International Council. According to historian Ula Taylor, "Although the council had similar intellectual goals, the unquestionable elite pedigree of its [ICWDR] members placed women like Garvey" on the outside of their programs. This shortcoming ran through the fabric of all Washington's club efforts. While she espoused views of cohesive collaborations, she herself remained exclusively separate. Although all of her initiatives sought to advance the less fortunate of the race, they were still excluded from membership. This reflected the hierarchical mindset associated with racial uplift and her belief that "we are a great fine race, even though we do have many who do not come up to the standard."[62]

Still, Washington remained closely connected to the community and saw herself as an active participant of club work initiatives. "For during the past year or two in my own community we have had a committee of seven, whose business it has been to study in a systematic way once a week any question pertaining to any person of color anywhere in the world, and we have had a great success with it."[63] According to clubwoman Jennie Moton, Washington had used the knowledge she obtained from her involvement with the ICWDR to influence the study of the African Diaspora among Tuskegee Students: "Washington organized the International Council of Women of the Darker Races of the World and inspired a course of study at Tuskegee on conditions of women in foreign lands. She thought and spoke of them as her sisters, and it was her hope that this Council would bring together the women of the darker races in a close and more sympathetic contact."[64]

The women of the ICWDR were excited about the study-club promoted by Washington. Some women wrote to her discussing their own committees. Christine Smith lauded Washington, saying: "Your suggestion about studying the darker races is a splendid one."[65]

After the establishment of the "Committees of Seven" the women requested that Margaret Washington send them the model that she used at Tuskegee. Janie Porter Barrett, clubwoman and founder of the Virginia Industrial School for Colored Girls (a rehabilitation center for African American delinquents) later wrote describing the progress of her committee. She sought to study the conditions of women around the world. Starting in March and spanning until May, the women of her club were to learn about the women of color in China, India, Africa and Japan.

Barrett explained: "The plan is to have each one dress in native costume and carry out their customs and manners in refreshments as well as dress. While two ladies conduct the program, each woman has to tell something authentic about the people under discussion."[66] Barrett later reported that different women within her committee would be traveling abroad, and upon their return they would put together pamphlets that described their experiences and, most importantly, the women that they encountered.[67]

Members of the ICWDR were educating themselves so that they could be better equipped to educate other African Americans. Council members used the organization to become vital participants in the political activities of Africans around the world. The ICWDR served as a cohesive network of black women's commitment to fight against the spread of white supremacy. Educating themselves on the conditions of black women across the African Diaspora, then all women of other non-Caucasian races, positioned them to be informed agents of American foreign policy and to disseminate knowledge about the progress and achievements of blacks outside as well as inside American borders.

Washington's vision of uplift by way of education was not a new phenomenon. However, what she did placed her agenda on a local stage with the TWC, then on a national scale with the NACWC, and finally on an international platform with the ICWDR. Washington was instrumental in advancing the study of black life, especially the achievements of black women. She commonly asserted that: "we are not trying to displace any other literature or history, but trying to get all children [and women] of [this] country acquainted with the Negro."[68]

The ICWDR made an impression on society in only a short time. The organization contributed to a school in West Africa and helped alleviate impoverished conditions in Cuba as well as Haiti. Through Washington and other board members the organization promoted the inclusion of African American history and literature in schools like Tuskegee Institute, revealing that Washington and the ICWDR were pioneers in teaching African American culture and women's history.[69]

Washington's work was devoted to improving the quality of life for black women and children. Until her death, she worked to uplift the race through various social outlets. She collaborated with Carter G. Woodson to introduce black history into black schools. This project was very dear to her and carried over into her work with the ICWDR. Whether working within clubs, serving as Lady Principal at Tuskegee, or in the community spreading a philosophy of racial uplift, Washington was constantly working for her race.

Washington devoted her life to bettering the black community and saw many improvements. After her husband's death in 1915, she continued their struggle, but nearly a decade later she became very ill. On June 4, 1925, with her adopted daughter Laura by her side, Margaret "Maggie" James Murray Washington died at her home in Tuskegee, Alabama. Shortly after her death, Mrs. R. R. Moton wrote in the *Tuskegee Messenger*: "Mrs. Washington is asleep—not dead. 'Can a woman die whose ideals live?' Tuskegee and our country have lost a great character in her passing, but her memory and influence will live always." Margaret Washington was buried at Tuskegee Institute next to her husband, Booker T. Washington.[70]

Margaret Washington's organizational skills, along with her vision of improvement, were refined before her death. Club work and education were truly the foundation of her life career, and she reveled in the work. Her attempts to apply the Tuskegee model of education, her formation of clubs and leadership roles within them, her pivotal role in creating educational outlets as a means of uplift, and her shortcomings in club work are all triumphs of a woman who helped to lay important groundwork for civil and social movements of the twenty-first century.

Conclusion

> Let us realize that we are two separate races living in a country side by side, each equally responsible for the good citizenship of the country, and therefore each equally deserving of a fair chance and fair play in every way.
> —Margaret Murray Washington
> (*The Negro Home*, 1920)[1]

It is difficult to conceptualize the complete life and club work of an activist like Margaret Murray Washington. At first glance, she is remembered as the third wife of race leader Booker T. Washington. Upon further investigation, we understand how she served her community as Tuskegee's Lady Principal, founder and president of the Tuskegee Woman's Club, the National Federation of Afro-American Women, the National Association of Colored Women, the Alabama Federation of Colored Women, the Southern Federation of Colored Women, and the International Council of Women of the Darker Races of the World. Yet, beyond her marital status and extensive club work, Margaret Washington was a prolific educator and international humanitarian.

Margaret Washington became a leader during a period many scholars termed Booker T. Washington's era of accommodation. However, throughout her life she successfully helped to transform the way black female education in the post-Reconstruction South was professionalized and modernized. Her life reveals the extent to which Southern black female reformers were pioneers in the betterment of the community and the race and represents the efforts of one of the most influential clubwomen of the Progressive Era. Most of her social reforms fit into the Tuskegee model of uplift, and she used this approach to leadership to extend the efforts and agendas of Booker T. Washington onto the females of the race.

Margaret Washington's transition to uplift leadership began during her early childhood which gave her a unique perspective on the great race problem. Born in the rural town of Macon, Mississippi to a black mother and an absentee father, Washington used her childhood experiences to understand the changing tides of race relations in America and as a tool for connecting with the larger public. Unlike old elite black women of her era, Washington shared an upbringing more similar to that of impoverished blacks during the mid to late nineteenth and early twentieth centuries. Her early years served as a testament of the possibilities that blacks could achieve through education and perseverance. Washington could attest to many of the injustices black men and women endured during the post-Reconstruction South. She often retold the story of how poverty had impacted her and how she vaguely remembered her father, but grew up with her mother and siblings in a one-room shack. Because of these experiences, Washington recognized that all people were not necessarily born to privilege but nonetheless could become model citizens. She spent her life trying to prove this ideology. She was a living testament to the fact that blacks in the South could overcome poverty, illiteracy, disfranchisement, and white supremacy. Washington used her personal trials not simply as a testimonial for individuals, but as a model that could be applied to all black people. In essence, if given a fair chance, despite their beginnings, blacks were no different from any other race.[2]

Once Margaret Washington arrived at the steps of Tuskegee Institute, she affirmed her commitment to the larger black community. As the new Lady Principal and wife of race leader Booker T. Washington, Margaret Washington's duties multiplied in scope. Their partnership placed her among many of the premier black leaders of the 20th century during an era when the role of women was usually defined by their domestic responsibilities. Her status allowed her to fight for things she believed rightfully belonged to all American citizens—suffrage, the equal right to access public facilities and transportation, and an end to racial and sexual discrimination. Eventually, Washington's efforts had a significant impact on the state of black society in particular and the South in general.

New standards of elitism offered the Washingtons a course to advance their agendas of racial uplift. It also gave them an avenue to influence decisions of the masses and elite blacks through the concept of racial uplift, despite the problematic structural impediments to progress among poor blacks. These uplift initiatives helped Washington and other clubwomen combat white supremacy by creating a presumably non-threatening approach to deal with the great "Negro Problem."

Washington used her position as Lady Principal to revolutionize the way black women were educated in the South. She integrated ideas of respectability into the daily lives of Tuskegee's female students. Although contested, she used the professionalization and modernization of home economics, believing in the validity and usefulness females gained when they became more proficient in the art of domesticity. She also encouraged women to buy land and to own their homes. Washington used the resources at Tuskegee Institute to reform the way black female education was approached and disseminated, she argued that education helped black women to be more effective leaders and more knowledgeable in every aspect of home life.

Throughout her years at Tuskegee, Washington believed that concepts of racial pride could hinder the spread of bigotry while also improving the way blacks saw themselves within American society. She recognized that black women could use both head and hands, both domesticity and femininity, both culture and performance to change their personal situations and to shift perceptions of the race as a whole. Her success as Lady Principal at Tuskegee, although taxing, positioned Washington to demonstrate how educating women benefited the race as a whole. With heightened emphasis on scientific domesticity, she proved that although generations of black women had engaged in some form of domestic work, they were also capable of understanding the scientific components of their labor, further proving that blacks were no different from any other race.[3]

As a result of her work with women at Tuskegee Institute, Washington believed that the greater Tuskegee community was also in desperate need of uplifting. Her transition into club work happened at a time when women's clubs were identified as the new power to influence public sentiments. Clubwomen also saw their organizations as forums for addressing and changing the ailments that were affecting blacks in America. She began her uplift efforts in Tuskegee with her Mothers' Meetings and the Tuskegee Woman's Club, which she considered her greatest work until the end. The day-to-day interactions she shared with local women and children drew her closer to the organization. Throughout her presidency of the TWC she guided and instructed women of Tuskegee on concepts of self-help, self-sufficiency, and social reforms, during a time of heightened hostility towards blacks. While she imposed many middle-class values onto Tuskegee's local residents, she believed that through this imposition race relations could be improved. According to Jennie Moton, clubwoman and wife of Robert R. Moton, Margaret Washington's TWC was "one of the best-known groups in the South, and has done a magnificent work, first in bringing the women of the Institute in close touch with one another, together with helping the poor and dependent high ideas and Ideals in Negro women." Washington placed added pressures on the TWC because she saw it as a way to solidify her position at the top of the black elite. Furthermore, her success within the TWC was imperative to the achievement of women at the school because it proved that a life of service to your race was a life worth aspiring to.

Washington was one of the most influential of Alabama's female reformers at the turn of the century. Her conviction that Southern women, on a large scale, did not receive equal representation in their advancement as did other black women of other regions, drove her to form the Alabama Federation of Colored Women's Clubs in 1898. Washington's efforts with Alabama's youth proved revolutionary. Because the South was notorious for charging black adolescences with petty crimes and sending them to adult facilities, Washington and other southern reformers formed the Mt. Meigs Reformatory for Juvenile Negro Law-Breakers. Clubwomen believed that children could be rehabilitated if given the proper supervision and environment. Her efforts with Mt. Meigs, which became a state institution in 1911, were an example of how she and other clubwomen used their organizations to foster state support and funding for black youth in the South.

At the height of her career, Washington ceased to see herself as an individual, but rather as an ambassador for her race. She used her success with local clubs to better position herself to head the National Association of Colored Women from 1912 to 1916. Under her leadership improvements were made in rural conditions, female education, health and hygiene, and more attention was placed on the equality of public facilities designated for blacks. Furthermore, as president, Washington successfully joined the NACW with the traditionally all-white National Council of Women. Her presidency of the NACW positioned her to not only bring awareness to southern black women, but it also represented her rise of leadership in the black elite.[4]

Conclusion

In 1922 Washington moved to the international level of her career. She formed the International Council of Women of the Darker Races of the World, becoming, in her own way, a Pan-Africanist. The council represented the height of African American women's international activism. Throughout her years of involvement, education was paramount; she placed it above all other initiatives. Within the ICWDR Washington was a leading proponent of black women's history. She was convinced that the history of African American women was not unlike the history of other women of color the world over. She implemented courses to study the state of black women around the world. This initiative took the ICWDR to Haiti, Brazil, and parts of Africa, among other places. However, the fruits of this endeavor were short-lived as Washington died only three years after its inception.

Perhaps Washington's biggest flaw was her unwillingness to approach the "Negro Problem" from a bottom-up perspective and her view of placing class over race. As stated in chapter four, the inferior condition of the race was in part due to their economic status. Washington viewed that economic difference as a consequence of white supremacy and the legacy of slavery, rather than traits innate to African Americans; she still believed that race women had a duty to elevate the lives of the poor. However, once Washington shed the layers of her past, she adopted elitist ideas and imposed Victorian concepts concerning appropriate behavior, dress, and culture onto the masses. Her club initiatives were open only to educated middle-class and elite black women. The infrastructure of these black women's clubs paralleled the social reform efforts of the era. Washington subscribed to these norms while often trying to defend her position by continuously applying hands-on training efforts to the women of her community.

Margaret Washington's efforts at keeping blacks exclusively in the South despite disfranchisement and southern brutality also represented a flaw in leadership. It was in the best political interest of Margaret Washington and her husband to convince blacks of their place in the southern economy. In a letter to clubwoman Lugenia Hope, Washington declared " . . . there are certain stipulations with reference to these funds that cannot be overstepped . . . Mr. Rosenwald is very cranky on certain subjects; that is, he doesn't wish to give his money to city work at all, but to country work." In this capacity, such stipulations limited the type of outreach programs Margaret Washington could obtain funding for. In hindsight, this provides a greater understanding of why the Washingtons focused a great deal of their initiatives toward the southern agenda. Although most black people lived in the South, focusing on southern needs garnered ample support from white philanthropists, a crucial component to implementing change.[5]

Margaret Washington was not simply an emissary of the Tuskegee Machine. Her work in the community was, at times, in conflict with the Tuskegee model, but she made sure Booker T. Washington's legacy and ideals survived him. Until her death in 1925, Margaret Washington worked to improve conditions for African Americans in the South and the world over. She had such a profound influence that, after her death on June 4, 1925, a flood of letters of condolence and sympathy poured into Tuskegee from friends and acquaintances. Her life had ended, but the events she set in motion lived on. Mrs. R. R. Moton, wife of Washington's successor Robert Moton, declared in the *Tuskegee Messenger* that Mrs. Booker T. Washington was simply asleep and not dead: "Tuskegee and our country have lost a great character in her passing, but her memory and influence will live always."[6]

Margaret Washington's lifelong commitment to the uplift struggle within the black community gained momentum during the Progressive Era as middle class women rushed to the streets in the name of reform. Margaret Washington extended the Tuskegee model onto the women and children of the race, but more importantly she did so at a time when the women's sphere was confined to their domestic responsibilities. She was a builder, a founder, and a devoted humanitarian in every sense of the term. She was a visionary leader and an advocate for the rights of men and women.

Margaret Washington worked beside her husband to change the way women were educated, how they tended to their home life and how they expanded their realms of influence to the public sphere. Before her death, Washington was inducted into Delta Sigma Theta Sorority, Incorporated. She then spearheaded initiatives to charter the Zeta Beta chapter of Delta Sigma Theta at Tuskegee University in December 1922. The following year she conducted a Race Relations speaking tour of southern cities where she addressed crowds of white women. She was a tireless worker until the end. Following Washington's death, her legacy can still be felt at Tuskegee University and throughout the world. Clubwomen and public officials across the nation banded together and formed day-camps for girls, vocational schools, and reformatories to honor the fallen revolutionary. While there is no longer a Girls' Industrial Department at the University, students, faculty, and patrons alike can visit the historic Dorothy Hall which, since 1998, joined with the Kellogg Hotel and Conference Center. Upon entering campus through the Lincoln Gate, one can see the multi-complex admissions building that bears her name. Inasmuch, Margaret Washington welcomes students, staff, faculty, and visitors to the educational grounds that she once called home.[7]

Into the twenty-first century, women of Tuskegee and the South shifted their outreach to fit liberation movements of the time. The Civil Rights Movement of the 1950s and 1960s did much to aid integration of the races. By 1964 the Civil Rights Act was passed and a year later in 1965 the Voting Rights Act was signed into law by President Lyndon B. Johnson. However, in March of 1965 the United States Department of Labor released the Moynihan Report titled "The Negro Family: The Case for National Action." Written by Assistant Secretary of Labor Daniel Patrick Moynihan, the study attempted to blame blacks for their second-class citizenship. Just as life was, at the time Margaret Washington made the Negro Home the center of her outreach initiatives, nearly fifty years later black families still remained under attack. Black intellectuals and activists were outraged. Grassroots organizations took to the streets. This time with tightened fists, dashikis, natural hair, and the armor of Black Power. Black men and women have continued to fight for black liberation and economic freedom! A struggle that continues!

NOTES

Introduction

1. Margaret Murray Washington, "The Negro Home," Speech, Memphis Women's Inter-Racial Conference, Memphis, Tennessee, October 1920, Doc.20, NACW, in Papers of Margaret Murray Washington [MMWP], Frissell Library, Tuskegee University Archives [TUA], (Tuskegee AL, Tuskegee University) reel 6: 47–52.

2. The Alabama Women's Hall of Fame, located in Marion, Alabama, began in 1970 and sought "to honor the lives of outstanding women from the state of Alabama." Induction Ceremonies, Alabama Women's Hall of Fame, Judson College, October 4, 1972, MMWP, TUA.

3. "Mrs. M. L. Gaston to Dr. L. H. Foster," February 29, 1972 (TUA); *Tuskegee Alumni Bulletin*, 1925, TUA; Excerpt from The *Atlanta Dependent*, in *Tuskegee Alumni Bulletin* 1925, TUA; Luther Hilton Foster, Jr. served from 1953 to 1981 as the fourth president of the Tuskegee Institute, a private, historically black University in Tuskegee, Alabama, now known as Tuskegee University. He served as the president at the time of Margaret Washington's induction and read from her biography during the ceremony; Sheena Harris, "Margaret Murray Washington: A Southern Reformer and the Black Women's Club Movement," in *Alabama Women: Their Lives and Times* (Athens, Georgia: University of Georgia Press, 2017) edited by Susan Youngblood Ashmore and Linquist Dorr, 129.

4. Paula Giddings, *When and Where I Enter: The impact of Black Women on Race and Sex in America* (New York: HarperCollins, 1984), vi; Jacqueline M. Moore, "Anna Julia Cooper: Educator, Clubwoman, and Feminist," in Nina Mjagkij, *Portraits of African American Life Since 1865* (Wilmington, Delaware: Scholarly Resources Inc. Imprint, 2003), 73.

5. Joan Quigley, *Just Another Southern Town: Mary Church Terrell and the Struggle for Racial Justice* (Oxford University Press, 2015); Ashley Robertson, *Mary McLeod Bethune in Florida: Bringing Social Justice to the Sunshine State*, (The History Press, 2015).

6. Jacqueline Anne Rouse, "Out of the Shadow of Tuskegee: Margaret Murray Washington, Social Activism, and Race Vindication," *Journal of Negro History*, Vol. 81, No. 1/4 (Winter-Autumn, 1996): 31.

7. Patricia Hill Collins, *Black Feminist Thought: Knowledge, Consciousness, and the Politics of Empowerment* (Routledge, 2008).

8. Nell Irvin Painter, *Sojourner Truth: A Life, A Symbol* (W.W. Norton & Company, 1997); Ula Yvette Taylor, *The Veiled Garvey: The Life and Times of Amy Jacques Garvey*, (Chapel Hill: University of North Carolina Press, 2002); Gerald Horne, *Race Woman: The Lives of Shirley Graham DuBois* (NYU Press, 2002).

9. White, *Ar'n't I A Woman*; Dorothy Sterling; *We Are Your Sisters: Black Women in Nineteenth Century History* (W. W. Norton and Company, 1997); N. F. Mossell, *The Work of the African American Woman* (Oxford University Press, 1988).

10. James T. Currie, "From Slavery to Freedom in Mississippi's Legal System," *The Journal of Negro History*, vol. 65, No. 2 (Spring, 1980), pp 112–25; The actual year of Margaret's birth has been a controversy for scholars. The years that have been used are 1861, 1864 and 1865. She is listed in both the 1870 and 1880 census as being born in 1861. The 1870 census records also mention four other siblings: Laura who was 10; Willis who was seven; Thomas who was four, and Joseph who was 9 months old and who, unlike Margaret and her other siblings was listed as black. Margaret remembers that her father died when she was nearly seven years old. Also, Fisk published her birth year as 1864 and Margaret commonly used the year 1865, which is the year on her tombstone, even though it is not supported by the 1870 and 1880 census records in U.S. Bureau of the Census, *Census of Population and Housing, 1870, 1880*; See Noralee Frankel, *Freedom's Women: Black Women and Families in Civil War Era Mississippi* (Bloomington: Indiana University Press, 1999),16; Rouse, "Out of the Shadow," 31; Scott, "Mrs. Booker T. Washington's," in Harlan and Smock, *Booker T. Washington Papers*, 9:289; Pruitt, "Margaret Murray Washington," 855; Clement Richardson, *The National Cyclopedia of the Negro Race*, (Montgomery: National Publishing Company, 1919), 63; Henry Kletzing and William Henry Crogman, *Progress of a Race*, (Atlanta: Gilder Lehrman, 1901), 446; Hartshorn W. Newton, *An Era of Progress and Promise, 1863–1910*, (Boston: Priscilla Publishing Company, 1910), 423; Frank Lincoln Mather, *Who's Who of the Colored Race: A*

General Biographical Dictionary of Men and Women of African Descent, vol. 1, (Chicago, Ill: [sn] 1910, 278.

11. Adelaide M. Cromwell, *The Other Brahmins: Boston's Black Upper Class 1750–1950* (University of Arkansas Press, 2004), passim; Joel Williamson, *New People: Miscegenation and Mulattoes in the United States* (New York: The Free Press, 1980), passim; Intersectionality is a feminist theory introduced by Kimberlé Crenshaw; Respectability Politics was first introduced by Evelyn Brooks Higginbotham in "African American Women's History and the Metalanguage of Race." *Signs*, Winter 1992,17(2): ; Brittney Cooper, *Beyond Respectability: The Intellectual Thought of Race Women, (Women, Gender, and Sexuality in American History)*, (Illinois: University of Illinois Press, 2017), passim.

12. Henry Lewis Morehouse "The Talented Tenth," *The Independent*, vol. 48 (23 April 1896); W. E. B. Du Bois, "The Talented Tenth," 31–75 in *The Negro Problem: A Series of Articles by Representative American Negroes of To-Day* (New York: James Pott & Co., 1903).

13. Audrey Thomas McCluskey, *A Forgotten Sisterhood: Pioneering Black Women Educators and Activists in the Jim Crow South* (Lanham, Maryland: Rowman & Littlefield Publishing Inc., 2014) 1; James Anderson, *The Education of Blacks in the South, 1862–1935* (Chapel Hill: University of North Carolina Press, 2010), passim; Sharon Gay Pierson, *Laboratory of Learning: HBCU Laboratory Schools and Alabama State College Lab in the Era of Jim Crow* (2013).

14. Paula Giddings, *When and Where I Enter: The Impact of Black Women on Race and Sex in America*, (New York: HarperCollins, 1984), vi; Jacqueline M. Moore, "Anna Julia Cooper: Educator, Clubwoman, and Feminist," in Nina Mjagkij, *Portraits of African American Life Since 1865* (Wilmington, Delaware: Scholarly Resources Inc. Imprint, 2003), 15

15. Addie Waits Hunton, "The Southern Federation of Colored Women," in *The Voice of the Negro*, Vol. 2, 80–85 (1905).

Chapter One

1. Margaret Murray Washington, *The Negro Home*, 6.
2. Currie, "From Slavery to Freedom in Mississippi's Legal System," 112–125; Isaac Steer, ex slave, Lauderdale County, Mississippi, *Born in Slavery: Slave Narratives from the Federal Writer's Project, 1936–1938*, Mississippi Narratives, IX, LOC; U.S Bureau of the Census, *Census of Population and Housing, 1870, 1880*; See Noralee Frankel, *Freedom's Women: Black Women and Families in Civil War Era Mississippi* (Bloomington: Indiana University

Press, 1999),16; Rouse, "Out of the Shadow," 31; Scott, "Mrs. Booker T. Washington's," in Harlan and Smock, *BTWP*, 9:289; Pruitt, "Margaret Murray Washington," 855; Richardson, *National Cyclopedia*, 63; Kletzing and Crogman, *The Remarkable Advancement*, 446; Newton, *An Era of Progress*, 423; Mather, *Who's Who*, 278.

    3. Dora Franks, ex slave, Monroe County, Mississippi, *Born in Slavery: Slave Narratives from the Federal Writer's Project,1936–1938*, Mississippi Narratives, IX, LOC; Jones, *Labor of Love, Labor of Sorrow*.

    4. David H. Jackson Jr., *Booker T. Washington and the Struggle Against White Supremacy*; David M. Oshinsky, *"Worse Than Slavery:" Parchman Farm and the Ordeal of Jim Crow Justice* (Free press Paperback, 1996); Rayford Logan, *The Negro in American Life and Thought: The Nadir 1877–1901* (Dial Press, 1954); Gatewood, *Aristocrats of Color*, passim; Mary Frances Berry, *My Face is Black is True*, passim; Leon Litwack, *How Free Is Free*, passim.

    5. Unknown author, "Margaret Murray Washington," MMWP located in TUA; U.S. Bureau of the Census, *Census of Population and Housing, Macon, Noxubee County, 1870 and 1880*; Based on the 1870s Census, there was a white James Murray in a neighboring township with a wife and kids.

    6. Peter Wallenstein, "Reconstruction, Segregation, and Miscegenation: Interracial Marriage and the law in the South, 1865–1900," *American Nineteenth Century History*, 6, No 1 (March 2005).

    7. Stephan Talty, *Mulatto America at the Crossroads of Black and White Culture: A Social History* (New York: HarperCollins Publishers, 2003), 54.

    8. Christian G. Samito, *Becoming American Under Fire: Irish Americans, African Americans, and the Politics of Citizenship During the Civil War Era* (Cornell University Press, 2009), 6–8.

    9. Margaret Murray Washington, "We Must Have a Cleaner Social Morality," in *Charleston News and Courier*, September 13, 1898; It is unclear whether Margaret Murray was actually born with a "master." There is speculation that her mother was born a slave; however, no sources support either claim. Therefore, if Margaret Murray's mother escaped slavery at the beginning of war efforts Margaret Murray was in all actuality legally born enslaved.

    10. Jones, *Labor of Love, Labor of Sorrow*, 157.

    11. Jones, *Labor of Love, Labor of Sorrow*, 157. Although this quote list the daily pay at $.75 to $1.00, these figures are somewhat high, and in many cases, does not represent the daily pay of black women in Mississippi's early post-slavery years.

    12. Frankel, *Freedom's Women*, 56; Job security was so scarce in the aftermath of slavery that many former slaves returned back to their master's plantation. According to ex slave Jane Sutton "us was jus' turnt loose to

scratch for us ownse'ves. Us was glad to stay on wid de white folks" in Jane Sutton, ex slave, Monroe County, Mississippi, *Born in Slavery: Slave Narratives from the Federal Writer's Project*, 1936–1938, Mississippi Narratives, IX, LOC; Rouse, "Out of the Shadow," 31; Pruitt, "Margaret Murray Washington," 855; Jones, *Labor of Love, Labor of Sorrow*, 52–57; Richardson, *National Cyclopedia*, 63; Mather, *Who's Who*, 278.

13. Scott, "Mrs. Booker T. Washington's," in Harlan and Smock, BTWP, 9:290; Mrs. R. R. Moton, *The Tuskegee Messenger*, June 1925.

14. The first three of Lucy Murray's children are listed as Mulatto. The last two, however, are listed as black in the census records. The reasoning behind this is unclear. However, it does suggest that they possibly had different fathers or that the census enumerators simply guessed their race based on the color of their skin. U.S. Bureau of the Census, *Census of Population and Housing, Macon, Noxubee County*, 1880; Margaret Murray Washington, "We Must Have a Cleaner Social Morality," in *Charleston News and Courier*, September 13, 1898.

15. Within the same district as Margaret and her family—District 15—there lived a man by the name of Joseph Cotton who was fifty years old. He was married to Sarah Cotton and they had four children. There is no claim to this speculation outside of the fact that Margaret Washington's youngest brother bore his name and not that of her father, James Murray; U.S. Bureau of the Census, *Census of Population and Housing, Macon, Noxubee County*, 1880.

16. Jones, *Labor of Love, Labor of Sorrow*, 92.

17. *The United States Census*, 1880 Macon Noxubee County Mississippi District 31.

18. The Quaker family was a brother and sister duo by the name of Saunders. Hugh Barbour and J. W. Frost, *The Quakers* (New York: Greenwood Press, 1988), 8–9; "Training Dusky Griseldas: Mrs. Booker T. Washington's Missionary work among Negro House-Wives," *San Francisco Bulletin*, August 2, 1903, in Harlan and Smock, BTWP, 7:248; Pruitt, "Margaret Murray Washington," 855.

19. Pruitt, "Margaret Murray Washington," 855; Barbour and Frost, *The Quakers*, 8–9; "Training Dusky Griseldas," in Harlan and Smock, BTWP, 7:248.

20. Scott, "Mrs. Booker T. Washington's," in Harlan and Smock, BTWP, 9:290; It is important to note that an exclusive reliance on *U.S. Census* can also be problematic. In many cases the enumerators were whites who frequently generalized the age, proper spelling, and birth year of the various black residents. This was also particularly true in the years following slavery, when many formerly enslaved blacks did not know their exact birth year.

21. Scott, "Mrs. Booker T. Washington's," in Harlan and Smock, *BTWP*, 9:289; City Hall, *Visitor's Guide History of City of Macon & Noxubee County*.

22. Chana Kai Lee, *For Freedom's Sake: The Life of Fannie Lou Hamer* (The University of Illinois Press) 1999, 5.

23. If Maggie actually "ran away" after the death of her father, this emphasizes the extent of poverty that she and her family endured. This rendition of events also portrays her father as living in the household. Either way, it was unlikely that he actually resided in her household. Still, at an early age Margaret left her home.

24. Rouse, "Out of the Shadow," 31–33; "Training Dusky Griseldas," in Harlan and Smock, *BTWP*, 7:248.

25. Mary Frances Berry, *My Face is Black is True*, 18.

26. Crigler, Jr., and Sledge, eds., *History of the First Baptist Church*, 23; Jackson, *A Chief Lieutenant*, 16–17; See John Hope Franklin, *From Slavery to Freedom: A History of Negro Americans* (New York: Knopf, 1988), 220; Wharton, *The Negro In Mississippi*, 106, 191–92; W. E. B. Du Bois, *Black Reconstruction in America, 1860–1880* (New York: Athenaeum, 1992), 431–51; Mary Frances Berry, *My Face is Black is True*, 18; Wesley, *History of the National Association*, 21. Although Margaret Murray moved to Nashville in 1875, she would not enroll into Fisk until 1881.

27. While it was illegal to teach slaves to read and write in most southern states, there were some slave owners who taught their slaves to read. According to former slave Isaac Steer, "my mistis was Miss Sarah Stowers an' she teached me how to read. She teach me how to be mannerly, too." Isaac Steer, ex slave, Lauderdale County, Mississippi, *Born in Slavery: Slave Narratives from the Federal Writer's Project, 1936–1938*, Mississippi Narratives, IX, LOC; Bobby L. Lovett, *The African American History of Nashville, Tennessee, 1780–1930* (Fayetteville: The University of Arkansas Press, 1999), 57; Jackson, *Booker T. Washington and the Struggle against White Supremacy*, 18, 123.

28. Scott, "Mrs. Booker T. Washington's," in Harlan and Smock, *BTWP*, 9:290.

29. George R. Bently, *A History of the Freedmen's Bureau* (New York: Reprinted Octagon Books, 1974), vii; Eric Foner, *A Short History of Reconstruction,1863–1877* (New York: Harper and Row, 1990), 96; White, *Ar'n't I a Woman*, 170–71; Jackson, *A Chief Lieutenant*, 7.

30. Titus Brown, *Faithful, Firm, & True: African American Education in the South* (Macon, Georgia: Mercer University Press, 2002), 1–2; U.S. Bureau of the Census, *Census of Population and Housing, Macon, Noxubee County, 1880*, lists Lucy Murray as literate; Jackson, *A Chief Lieutenant*, 7;

White, *Ar'n't I a Woman*, 170–71; Robert J. Franciosi, *The Rise and Fall of American Public Schools: The Political Economy of Public Education in the Twentieth Century* (Westport, Ct: Praeger Publishers, 2004), 101; Don H. Doyle, *New Men, New City New South, Atlanta, Nashville, Charleston, Mobile, 1860–1910* (University of North Carolina Press: Chapel Hill, 1990), 30.

31. It can be gathered that Margaret did not teach past the basic elementary level considering the fact that prior to this new wave of black schools and facilities of learning, education was restricted on a large scale; Scott, "Mrs. Booker T. Washington's,'" in Harlan and Smock, *BTWP*, 9:289; Thompson, "Margaret Murray Washington (1865–1925)," in Darlene Clark Hine, Elsa Barkley Brown, Rosalyn Terborg-Penn, *Black Women in America: An Historical Encyclopedia*, Vol. 2 (Bloomington: Indiana University Press, 1993), 1233–34.

32. *The Fisk Herald*, "The History of Fisk," June 1888 located the Fisk University's Archives (hereafter FUA); Richardson, *A History of Fisk*, 2.

33. *The Fisk Herald*, "The History of Fisk," June 1888, located in FUA; *The Fisk Herald*, May 1888, located in FUA; Richardson, *A History of Fisk*, 2.

34. Richardson, *A History of Fisk*, 3.

35. Richardson, *A History of Fisk*, 3; U.S. Bureau of the Census, *Census of Population and Housing, Nashville. Davidson County Tennessee*, 1860; Foner, *A Short History of Reconstruction*, 129; *The Fisk Herald*, "History of Fisk," June 1888; Harris, *Margaret Murray Washington*, 132.

36. Richardson, *A History of Fisk*, 6; *The Fisk Herald*, "History of Fisk," June 1888.

37. *The Fisk Herald*, "Fisk University and Industrial education," February 6, 1889, located in FUA.

38. *The Fisk Herald*, "The History of Fisk," June 1888, located in FUA; *The Fisk Herald*, "Fisk University and Industrial education," February 6, 1889, located in FUA; Saundra Jean Graham, "The Fisk Jubilee Singers and the Concert Spiritual: The Beginning of an American Tradition" (Ph.D. Dissertation, 2001) Located in Special Collections at the University of Memphis; Richardson, *A History of Fisk*, 6; Joe Richardson, *Christian Reconstruction: The American Missionary Association and Southern Blacks, 1861–1890* (Athens: The University of Georgia Press, 1986), 134–35; Paula J. Giddings, *Ida A Sward Among Lions: Ida B. Wells and the Campaign Against Lynching*, 23–24.

39. *The Fisk Herald*, "The History of Fisk," June 1888, located in FUA; Richardson, *A History of Fisk*, 6, 25; *New York Times*, January 5, 1880; Lovett, *African American History*, 160; Lynn Abbott and Doug Seroff, *Out of Sight: The Rise of African American Popular Music, 1889–1895* (University Press of Mississippi, 2002), 3; Harris, *Margaret Murray Washington*, 132.

40. W. E. B. Du Bois, *Dusk of Dawn: An Essay Towards an Autobiography of a Race Concept* (New York: Schocken Books, 1968), 30–31; Rouse, "Out of the Shadow," 32; Gibson, *The New Progress of a Race*, 179; Clement Richardson, *The National Cyclopedia of the Colored Race* (Montgomery: National Publishing, 1919), 63; Mather, *Who's Who*, 278.

41. Mather, *Who's Who*, 278; James T. Hotchkin, *A History of the Purchase and Settlement of Western New York* (New York: M.W. Didd1948), 420–22; Du Bois, *Dusk of Dawn*, 30–31; Rouse, "Out of the Shadow," 32; Gibson, *The New Progress of a Race*, 179; Richardson, *National Cyclopedia*, 63.

42. The *Fisk Herald*, June 1886; Austin R. Merry earned his bachelors and masters degrees from Fisk University. He was the first black person in Madison county with a college degree and became the first black educator and principal hired at South Jackson School for Coloreds.

43. *The Fisk Herald*, Letter from Margaret J. Murray to the *Fisk Herald*, August 1887, located in FUA.

44. Mary Church Terrell, *A Colored Woman in a White World*, 65–66.

45. Richardson, *A History of Fisk*, 17.

46. Jon W. Gibson and William H. Crogman, *The Colored American from Slavery to Honorable Citizenship* (Naperville, Illinois: 1897), 527; Richardson, *A History of Fisk*, 19, 46; Washington, *Up from Slavery*, 100.

47. Richardson, *A History of Fisk*, 19, 46; Washington, *Up from Slavery*, 100.

48. Du Bois, *Dusk of Dawn*, 31–32; *New York Times*, January 5, 1887; Richardson, *A History of Fisk*, 48

49. Du Bois was born in Great Barrington, Massachusetts, in 1868. After receiving his bachelor's degree from Fisk, he earned a doctorate from Harvard in history. He would become an American civil-rights activist, Pan-Africanist, sociologist, educator, historian, novelist, essayist, and editor; Du Bois, *Dusk of Dawn*, 31–32; *New York Times*, January 5, 1887; Richardson, *A History of Fisk*, 48; Lane, *A Documentary*, 99.

50. Richardson, *A History of Fisk*, 48; Lane, *A Documentary*, 99.; *The Fisk Herald*, May 1884; Harris, *Margaret Murray Washington*, 133.

51. Lee, *For Freedom's Sake*, 9.

52. Richardson, *A History of Fisk*, 48; Du Bois, *Dusk of Dawn*, 31–32; *New York Times*, January 5, 1887; *The Fisk Herald*, "The New South," January 1889, located in FUA; Hine, Hine and Harrold, *The African American Odyssey*, 401.

53. Richardson, *A History of Fisk*, 48–49; Letter from William Edward Burghardt Du Bois to Booker T. Washington Gt. Barrington, Mass, July 27, 1894, in Harlan and Smock, *BTWP*, 3:459.

54. Paula J. Giddings, *Ida: A Sword Among Lions: Ida B. Wells and the Campaign Against Lynchings* (HarperCollins, 2008), 75; Lane, *A Documentary*, 95–96.

55. Fisk University commencement program for 1889 is located in the Fisk University Archives (FUA), Nashville, TN; *The Fisk Herald*, July 1889.

56. *The Fisk Herald*, "On Visitors" July 1889, located in FUA; Richardson, *A History of Fisk*, 48; Letter from William Jenkins to Booker T. Washington, Nashville Tn., March 3, 1889 in Louis and Harlan *BTWP* 2:514; Letter from Margaret James Murray to Booker T. Washington, Fisk University Nashville, Tennessee, May 5, 1889 in Harlan and Smock, *BTWP*, 3:3.

57. *The Southern Letter*, May, 1889; Rouse, "Out of the Shadow," 31; Scott, "Mrs. Booker T. Washington's," in Harlan and Smock, *BTWP*, 9:290; Gibson and Crogman, *The Colored American*, 527; Gibson, *The New Progress of a Race*, 179; Giddings, *When and Where I Enter*, 111; Harris, *Margaret Murray Washington*, 132.

Chapter Two

1. Margaret Murray Washington, *The Negro Home*, 6.

2. Moore, *Leading the Race*, 33; Booker T. Washington, *Up from Slavery: An Autobiography* (New York: Doubleday Publishing, 1901); Margaret frequently expressed love for the south, her home of Mississippi in particular, although she visited infrequently. "For the first time in six years I find myself in the state of Mississippi, my old home. I cannot make you understand what the emotions were which stirred my heart as I crossed the line and heard the name Corinth called out by the conductor, and all along the lines the names sound strangely sweet to my ear." Located in *The Fisk Herald* "Margaret J. Murray to the *Fisk Herald*,' August 1887, located in FUA; Jackson, *A Chief Lieutenant*, 13; Gatewood, *Aristocrats of Color*, 347.

3. L. Albert Scipio II, *The Building of Tuskegee*, Roman Publications, 1987, 34.

4. Scipio II, *The Building of Tuskegee*, 34.

5. Leon Litwack, *How Free is Free*, 13; Norrell, *Up from History*, 39–40; Giddings, *Ida*, 165; Margaret Murray Washington, "The Gain in the Life of Negro Women," located in *Outlook Magazine*, 1904.

6. Scipio II, *The Building of Tuskegee*, 38.

7. Washington, *Up from Slavery*, 4; Norrell, *Up from History*, 21.

8. Booker T. Washington, *Up from Slavery: An Autobiography* (New York: Doubleday Publishing, 1901) 1–2, 19; Jackson, Jr., *Booker T. Washington and the Struggle against White Supremacy*, 1–2, 15–18; Louis R Harlan, *Booker T.*

Washington. *Wizard of Tuskegee, 1901–1915* (Oxford, New York: Oxford University Press, 1983) 19–21; Robert J. Norrell, *Up From History: The Life of Booker T. Washington* (Cambridge: The Belknap Press of Harvard University Press, 2009) 26–27, 30–31, 39–40, 209; Harlan, *Making of a Black Leader*, vii; John Edger Wideman, *My Soul Has Grown Deep: Classics of Early African American Literature* (Philadelphia and London: Running Press, 2001) 632–33; Robert Francis Engs, *Freedom's First Generation: Black Hampton, Virginia, 1861–1890* (Philadelphia, 1979)142–144; Robert Francis Engs, *Educating the Disfranchised and Disinherited: Samuel Chapman Armstrong and Hampton Institute, 1839–1893* (Knoxville, 1899) 78.

    9. Richardson, *A History of Fisk*, 56; Norrell, *Up from History*, 30–31; Engs, *Freedom's First Generation*, 142–144; Robert F. Engs, *Educating the Disfranchised and Disinherited: Samuel Chapman Armstrong and Hampton Institute, 1839–1893* (Knoxville, 1899), 78.

    10. Margaret Murray Washington, "The Negro Home," 4–5.

    11. While the *Fisk Herald* editors adamantly professed that "Fisk University, since its first days, has steadfastly had as its chief aim the higher education of the colored people. From this end, it has not deviated in its purpose by the breath of a hair." They still acknowledged that "it enters upon industrial work only so far as may be in harmony with higher education. The college work is first, the industries second." Located in *The Fisk Herald*, "Fisk University and Industrial Education," February 1889 at FUA; Joe Richardson, *Christian Reconstruction: The American Missionary Association and Southern Blacks, 1861–1890* (Athens: The University of Georgia Press, 1986), 134–35; Margaret Murray Washington, "The Negro Home," 6.

    12. Kimberlé Crenshaw, "Demarginalizing the Intersection of Race and Sex: A Black Feminist Critique of Antidiscrimination Doctrine, Feminists Theory and Anti-Racist Politics," *University of Chicago Legal Forum*, volume 1989, issue 1.

    13. Jackson, Jr., *A Chief Lieutenant of the Tuskegee Machine*, 16; W. E. B. Du Bois, *The Philadelphia Negro: A Social History* (University of Pennsylvania Press, 1996), 7; Adolph L. Reed Jr., *W. E. B. Du Bois and American Political Thought: Fabianism and the Color Line* (Oxford University Press, 1999), 37.

    14. Margaret Washington's mixed parentage may have influenced her transition into a higher class. Booker Washington, the son of an absentee white father, only married women of mixed parentage. Willard Gatewood termed this fascination with light skin the "blue-vein syndrome," as an individual's status was determined by the ability to see their veins. This philosophy went beyond ideas of mixed parentage and

connected class to the ability to pass as white. No evidence suggests, however, that Margaret Washington subscribed to the idea of passing. Still, due to societies prevailing notions of beauty, it may have positively impacted the larger community's acceptance of her leadership abilities; Gatewood, *Aristocrats of Color*, 14–15; Norrell, *Up from History*, 64–5; Williamson, *New People*; Frank Büchmann-Møller, *You Just Fight for Your Life: The Story of Lester Young* (New York: Praeger Publishers, 1990), 1–2.

15. "An Excerpt from the Journal of Florence Ledyard Cross Kitchelt," located in Harlan and Smock, *BTWP*, 6:84.

16. Many of Margaret's club affiliations were headed by "fair" skinned black women who preferred the term colored over black or Afro-American, as many believed it spoke more to their identity in American culture. In spite of these debates, and according to Gatewood, issues of color prevented Josephine Bruce (who could pass as white) from obtaining the NACW Presidency in 1906; Gatewood, *Aristocrats of Color*, 70; Moore, *Leading the Race*, 2–8; Frazier, *Black Bourgeoisie*, 224–25; Giddings, *Ida*, 364, 374.

17. Leon Litwack, *How Free is Free*, 13; Norrell, *Up from History*, 39–40; Giddings, *Ida*, 165; MargaretMurray Washington, "The Gain in the Life of Negro Women," located in *Outlook Magazine*, 1904.

18. Harlan and Smock, *BTWP* 3:243, 246; Lane, *A Documentary*, 25; Hallie Quinn Brown, *Homespun Heroines and other Women of Distinction*, (Xenia, Ohio: Aldine Publishing Co., 1926), 225.

19. Giddings, *When and Where I Enter*, 98–100; Margaret, "The Negro Home," 6. It was common during this time for educated women to focus their energies on the maintenance of the home. Clubwoman Mrs. Nellie F. Francis, of Minnesota said this of the home, "for the home is the central idea of civilization itself – the true microcosm the nucleus around which other worlds may grow," in *National Association Notes*, "Women's Influence," 1912.

20. Lane, *A Documentary*, 32 Giddings, *Ida*, 98, 100.

21. *The Southern Letter*, May, 1889; *Southern Workman*, June 1889, located in the TUA; *Tuskegee News*, January 12, 1954; Washington, *Up from Slavery*, 329; Lane, *A Documentary*, 33; Gibson, Progress of a Race, 179; Kletzing and Crogman, The Remarkable Advancement, 446; Benjamin Brawley, Negro Builders and Heroes (Chapel Hill: University of North Carolina Press, 1937), 157; Rouse, "Out of the Shadow," 32; Norrell, Up from History, 63–65, 74–75; Harris, *Margaret Murray Washington*, 133.

22. Margaret James Murray to Booker T. Washington, October 1891, in Harlan and Smock, *BTWP*, 3:174–75; Lane, *A Documentary*, 33; Norrell, *Up from History*, 100–101.

23. Margaret Murray Washington letter to Booker T. Washington July

1892 in Linda Lane, *A Documentary*, 32; Booker T. Washington also married his second wife, Olivia Davidson at her sister's home, Mary A. Elliott. "The Announcement of the wedding of BTW and Olivia A. Davidson," Athens, Ohio, August 11, 1886," located in Harlan and Smock, *BTWP*, 2:306.

24. Margaret Murray Washington letter to Booker T. Washington July 1892 in Linda Lane, *A Documentary*, 32; Booker T. Washington also married his second wife, Olivia Davidson at her sister's home, Mary A. Elliott. "The Announcement of the wedding of BTW and Olivia A. Davidson," Athens, Ohio, August 11, 1886," located in Harlan and Smock, *BTWP*, 2:306.

25. "The Certificate of Marriage of Washington and Margaret James Murray," Tuskegee, Alabama, October 12, 1892, located in Harlan and Smock, *BTWP* 3:268.

26. Margaret James Murray to Booker T. Washington, October 1891, in *BTWP*, 3:174–75 located in LOC; Harlan, *Wizard*, 108–9.

27. Margaret Murray Washington, "We Must Have a Cleaner Social Morality," in *Charleston News and Courier*, September 13, 1898.

28. Harlan, *BTWP*, 2:361 located in LOC; Giddings, *Ida*, 37; Shaw, *What a Woman Ought to Be and to Do*, 45.

29. Gibson and Crogman, *The Colored American*, 527; Letter from Margaret to Booker T. Washington located in Lane, *A Documentary*, 28; Giddings, *When and Where I Enter*, 99, 112; Margaret Murray Washington, *The Negro Home*, 6; Letter from former student to Margaret Murray Washington, n.d., in Lane, *A Documentary*, 25–26, 33; Gibson, *Progress of a Race*, 179; Kletzing and Crogman, *The Remarkable Advancement*, 446; Norrell, *Up From History*, 119; Margaret Murray Washington, "We Must Have a Cleaner Social Morality," in *Charleston News and Courier*, September 13, 1898. Louis Harlen, ed., *BTWP*, vol. 2 (Urbana, Chicago, and London: University of Illinois Press, 1972), 305.

30. Gibson and Crogman, *The Colored American*, 527; Letter from Margaret to Booker T. Washington, Lane, *A Documentary*, 28; Giddings, *When and Where I Enter*, 99, 112; Margaret Murray Washington, *The Negro Home*, 6; Letter from former student to Margaret Murray Washington, n.d., in Lane, *A Documentary*, 25–26, 33; Gibson, *Progress of a Race*, 179; Kletzing and Crogman, *The Remarkable Advancement*, 446; Norrell, *Up From History*, 119; Margaret Murray Washington, "We Must Have a Cleaner Social Morality," in *Charleston News and Courier*, September 13, 1898. Louis Harlen, ed., *BTWP*, vol. 2 (Urbana, Chicago, and London: University of Illinois Press, 1972), 305.

31. Josephine Bruce father was a prominent dentist and her mother

worked as a singer and musician. Graham, *The Senator and the Socialite*, 26; Joseph Willson, *Sketches of the Higher Class of Colored Society in Philadelphia* (Merrihew and Thompson Printers, 1841); Willard B. Gatewood, "Josephine Beall Wilson Bruce," in *Black Women in America: An Historical Encyclopedia*, edited by Darlene Clark Hine, Elsa Barkley Brown, and Rosalyn Terborg-Penn, vol. I, 187–188; Bruce A Glassrudi, "Josephine Beall (Wilson) Bruce," in *African American Women: A Biographical Dictionary*, edited by Dorothy Salem (New York Publishing, 1993), 75–77.

32. Washington, *Up from Slavery*, 19; Norrell, *Up from History*, 26–27; Jackson, *Booker T. Washington and the Struggle against White Supremacy*, 1–2.

33. Norrell, *Up from History*, 26.

34. Annjennette Sophie McFarlin, "Hallie Quinn Brown, Black Woman Elocutionist: 1845(?)–1949" (Ph.D. diss., Washington State University, 1975), 14–26; Michelle M. Rief, "Banded Close Together": An Afrocentric Study of African American Women's International Activism, 1850–1940, and the International Council of Women of the Darker Races (Ph.D. diss., Temple University, 2002), 91.

35. Margaret James Murray to Booker T. Washington, October 1891, in *BTWP*, 3:174–175; Margaret James Murray letter to Booker T. Washington, July 10, 1892 in Harlan, *BTWP* 3:246; Margaret Murray Washington, "The Negro Home," 4–5.

36. Jackson, *Booker T. Washington and the Struggle Against White Supremacy*; Logan, *The Negro in American Life and Thought, passim*.

37. *New York Times*, "Mr. Roosevelt explains the Dinner Incident," October 19, 1901.

38. Ibid.; The 1901 publication of Booker T. Washington's *Up from Slavery* sealed their position as leading figures during the Progressive Era; Washington, *Up from Slavery*, passim; Jackson, *Booker T. Washington and the Struggle Against White Supremacy*, 3; Logan, *The Negro in American Life and Thought*; Norrell, *Up from History*, 5–6; Harlan, *The Wizard of Tuskegee*, vii-viii; Giddings, *Ida*, 436.

39. Josephine Willson's father, Joseph Willson a Philadelphia dentist, published a book *Sketches of the Higher Classes Among the Colored Society in Philadelphia*. Published in 1841, when most blacks were still enslaved, Willson's book gave a rigid analysis of the well-educated, upper class American black society. The book even detailed how wealthy blacks maintained their status and culture. Joseph Willson, *Sketches of the Higher Class of Colored Society in Philadelphia* (Merrihew and Thompson Printers, 1841), 4–12; Graham, *The Senator and the Socialite*, 25–28, 264.

40. Due to the implications of this large sum, Booker changed the stipulations of the endowment so that his salary would come from the endowment rather than Tuskegee. Carnegie to Baldwin, April 17, 1903, in Harlan and Smock, *BTWP* 7:120; Booker T. Washington to Carnegie, April 19, 1903, Andrew Carnegie Papers, LOC; Jackson, *Booker T. Washington and the Struggle Against White Supremacy*; Harlan, *Wizard*, 136; Giddings, *Ida*, 440–41.

41. Margaret Murray Washington, "The Gain in the Life of Negro Women," *Outlook* Magazine, 1904.

42. Harlan, *The Wizard of Tuskegee*, 169, 170; Neverdon-Morton, *Afro-American Women of the South*, 122.

43. Harlan, *The Wizard of Tuskegee*, 169–70.

44. Williamson, *New People*, 4; Terrell, *Black Woman in a White World*, passim.

45. Margaret and Booker visited many of Europe's elites including Queen Victoria, Mark Twain, Lord James Bryce, Sir Henry Stanly amongst a slew of others. Margaret James Murray Washington to Francis Jackson Garrison, New York City, August 7, 1899, in Harlan and Smock, *BTWP*; Frazier, *Black Bourgeoisie*, 203–4; Norrell, *Up from History*, 177–79; Terrell, *A Colored Woman in a White World*, 130–32.

46. Harlan, *Wizard of Tuskegee*, 108; *Tuskegee Student*, XIII (Sept. 28, 1901), 3.

46. *Boston Globe*, Oct. 20, 1901, clipping; Booker T. Washington to Jane E. Clark, June 5, 1905; Harlan, *Wizard of Tuskegee*, 112–13; Giddings, *Ida*, 437.

48. Harlan, *Wizard of Tuskegee*, 109, 112–13, 123.

49. *Boston Globe*, October 20, 1901, clipping.

50. Letter from Isabel Hayes Chapin Barrows to Booker T. Washington, Feb. 4, 1899 located in Harlan and Smock, *BTWP*, 5:26.

51. Harlan and Smock, *BTWP*, 5:27.

52. *Tuskegee Student* May 5, 1900, located in the TU; Information on the plays can be found in issues of the *Tuskegee Student* and Lane, *A Documentary*, 252–62.

53. "An Account of the Wedding of Portia Marshall Washington and William Sidney Pittman, November 2, 1907, in *BTWP* 9:392 LOC; Interestingly, the wedding of Josephine and Blanche Bruce was also held at the residence of the bride's father, "in a neat two-story frame house… giving evidence of the good taste and enlightened ideas of the occupants." "The Marriage of Senator Bruce To Miss Josephine Willson," June 26, 1878, in The *Cleveland Gazette*; William Falk, *Rooted in Place: Family and Belonging in a Southern Black Community* (Rutgers University Press, 2004), 147; Jessie

Bernard, *Marriage and Family Among Negroes* (Prentice Hall Publishers, 1966), passim; Mary Frances Berry and John Blassingame, *Long Memory: The Black Experience in America* (Oxford University Press, 1982), 8; *The Tuskegee Student*, 13 May 1916, TUA.

54. Norrell, *Up from History*, passim.

55. Washington, *Up From Slavery*, 189.

56. Ibid.

57. Lane, *A Documentary*, 235.

58. *BTWP*, 4:103n1 located in the LOC; Booker T. Washington to Portia Marshall Washington, January 9, 1906 in *BTWP* located in the LOC.

59. Giddings, *When and Where I Enter*, 93; Many notions of specialization could be entertained with this move by Northern black elite women, some may say that it was Margaret's marriage to Booker T. Washington that afforded her the honor amongst other elite black women; but, to the contrary I argue that it was Margaret's entrance into the new black elite, and her different (while still elitist) approach to solving the race problem. I would also argue that the thinking of elitist women was so exclusive that they would not allow a woman who was not of elite status to represent them at the head of their first National organization of black women; Sarah Deutsch, Women and the City: Gender, Space, and Power in Boston, 1870–1940 (Oxford University Press, 2000), 24; Crumwell, *The Other Brahmins*, 4.

60. Wesley, *The History*, 279; Feldman, *A Sense of Place*, 273n54.

61. What should not be lost in this point is the fact that the new black elite understood the laws of the land. They knew they would need the support and contributions of white philanthropists in order to provide for the needs of the masses; Moore, *Leading the Race*, 5; After Reconstruction, the new black elites came to the realization that they had more in common with the black masses than they had with elite whites. This decreased their desire to abandon the masses in a hopeless attempt to join with whites.

62. Jones, "Mary Church Terrell and the National Association of Colored Women, 1896 to 1901," 22; Hine, *Black Women in United States History*, 320; Nancy Woloch, *Women and the American Experience* (New York: McGraw-Hill, 2006), 290; Lane, *A Documentary*, 164; Goings traces the different stereotypes of African American men and women from the 1880s up until the seventies. See Goings, *Mammy and Uncle Mose*, passim; Lerner, "Early Community Work of Black Women," 159; Shaw, *What a Woman Ought to Be and to Do*, 54; Gatewood, *Aristocrats of Color*, 112.

63. Margaret Murray Washington, "We Must Have a Cleaner Social Morality," at Old Bethel A.M.E. Church, 1898 in *Charleston News and Courier* (September 13, 1898). This was one of many all-white functions

Margaret and Booker attended in order to secure favors. The black community was outraged with them both and the community felt they had "place[d] the white people first." *Cleveland Gazette*, July 20, 1901, in *BTWP*, 6:178 located in the LOC; Giddings, *Ida*, 434.

64. Moore, *Leading the Race*, 1.

Chapter Three

1. Margaret Murray Washington, *The Negro Home*, 5. Chapter 3 notes start here
2. *The Tuskegee Student*, 1 April 1905 located in TUA.
3. Scipio II, *The Building of Tuskegee*, 37.
4. Scipio II, *The Building of Tuskegee*, 37.
5. Booker T. Washington, *Up from Slavery*, Doubleday, 1901, 128.
6. Washington, *Up from Slavery*, 1–2; Jackson, Jr., *Booker T. Washington and the Struggle against White Supremacy*; Norrell, *Up from History*; Harlan, *The Wizard of Tuskegee*, 19–21.
7. Jackson, *Booker T. Washington and the Struggle Against White Supremacy*, 33.
8. The term Metalanguage of race was coined by Evelyn Brooks Higginbotham and is a discussion of race as a liberatory discourse and a discourse of violence and repression. Evelyn Brooks Higginbotham, "African-American Women's History and the Metalanguage of Race," *Signs* Vol. 17, No. 2 (Winter, 1992), pp. 251–74.
9. Richardson, *The History of Fisk*, 56.
10. Du Bois, *The Souls of Black Folk*, 38; Terrell, *A Colored Woman*, 231.
11. Du Bois, *The Souls of Black Folk*, 47.
12. James L. Leloudis, *Schooling the New South: Pedagogy, Self, and Society in North Carolina, 1880–1920* (The University of North Carolina Press: Chapel Hill & London, 1996), 147–48; Margaret Murray Washington letter to Dr. Robert R. Moton, September 23, 1921, Moton Papers located in TUA; Jackson, *A Chief Lieutenant*; Rouse, *Lugenia Burns Hope*.
13. Margaret Murray Washington, "Training Our Girls for the Responsibility of Life," The *Fisk Herald*, June 1890.
14. Margaret Murray Washington letter to Dr. Robert R. Moton, September 23, 1921, Robert Moton Papers located in TUA; Jackson, *A Chief Lieutenant of the Tuskegee Machine*, passim; Rouse, *Lugenia Burns Hope*, passim.
15. Gibson and Crogman, *The Colored American from Slavery to Honorable Citizenship*, 527; Elizabeth Lindsay Davis, *Lifting as we Climb* (Washington, D.C.: National Association of Colored Women, 1933), 171. Giddings,

When and Where I Enter, 112; Emmett Scott letter to Margaret Murray Washington, April 15, 1916, located in TUA.

16. Emmett Scott letter to Margaret Murray Washington, October 19, 1916, located in TUA.

17. Margaret Murray Washington letter to Emmett Scott, September 19, 1916, MMWP located in TUA.

18. Margaret James Murray letter to Booker T. Washington, February 27, 1892, in Harlan and Smock, *BTWP* 3:221.

19. *The Southern Letter*, September 1907; Wells, *Crusade*, 36; Paula Giddings, *Ida*, 55–56; Tim Wise, *White like Me: Reflections on Race from a Privileged Son* (Berkeley, California: Soft Skull Press, 2008).

20. Margaret Murray Washington letter to Robert R. Moton, February 11, 1916, MMWP, located in TUA.

21. Ibid; Louis Harlan, *Booker T. Washington: The Wizard of Tuskegee*, 144–45.

22. Jacqueline Goggin, *Carter G. Woodson: A Life in Black History* (Baton Rouge and London: Louisiana State University Press, 1993) 42; Caroline Gebhard, "Bess Bolden Walcott: A Legacy of Women's Leadership at Tuskegee Institute," in *Alabama Women: Their Lives and Times* (Athens, Georgia: University of Georgia Press, 2017) edited by Susan Youngblood Ashmore and Linquist Dorr, 225–28.

23. Jacqueline Goggin, *Carter G. Woodson: A Life in Black History* (Baton Rouge and London: Louisiana State University Press, 1993) 42, 56.

24. Ibid.

25. Booker T. Washington letter to Margaret James Murray, May 3, 1890 in Harlan and Smock, *BTWP* 3:54; Mary Church Terrell, *A Colored Woman in a White Would*, 275–76; Margaret Murray Washington to Booker T. Washington, July 1892, in Harlan and Smock, *BTWP* 3:253; Harlan and Smock, *BTWP*, 156–58.

26. Senator Blanche K. Bruce died only months before Washington made the offer to his widower Josephine Bruce. Booker T. Washington to Josephine Bruce, Harlan and Smock, *BTWP*; Booker T. Washington letter to Margaret James Murray, May 3, 1890, in Harlan and Smock, *BTWP* 3:54; Booker T. Washington letter to Hallie Quinn Brown, August 10, 1892, in Harlan and Smock, *BTWP* 3:255.

27. Graham, *The Senator and the Socialite*, 210.

28. Ibid.

29. Graham, *The Senator and the Socialite*, 209–11.

30. Margaret Murray Washington, *The Negro Home*, 5; Margaret Murray Washington letter to Robert R. Moton, May 17, 1921, located in

TUA; Lane, *A Documentary*, 131; Neverdon-Morton, *Afro-American Women of the South*, 36–37; Margaret Murray Washington, "We Must Have a Cleaner Social Morality," in *Charleston News and Courier*, (September 13, 1898).

31. Margaret Murray Washington letter to Robert R. Moton, May 17, 1921, located in TUA; Lane, *A Documentary*, 131; Neverdon-Morton, *Afro-American Women of the South*, 36–37; Margaret Murray Washington, "We Must Have a Cleaner Social Morality," in *Charleston News and Courier*, (September 13, 1898).

32. Margaret Murray Washington letter to Robert R. Moton, May 17, 1921, located in TUA.

33. Margaret Murray Washington letter to Robert R. Moton, May 17, 1921, located in TUA; Margaret advocated the mastery of reading and writing in the midst of her learning to master them.

34. Emmett Scott letter to Margaret Murray Washington February 23, 1916, located in TUA; Harlan, *Wizard of Tuskegee*, 107–8; Letter from former student to Margaret Murray Washington, n.d., in Lane, *A Documentary*, 25–26.

35. *The Southern Letter*, October 1907.

36. Rouse, "Out of the Shadow," 32; Mather, *Who's Who*, 278; Margaret Murray Washington letter to Mr. Palmer December 14, 1916, located in TUA.

37. Margaret Murray Washington, *The Negro Home*, 6; Giddings, *When and Where I Enter*, 47.

38. Margaret Murray Washington letter to Robert R. Moton, May 17, 1921, located in TUA.

39. Margaret Murray Washington letter to Warren Logan, June 1922, located in, TUA.

40. How the dispute was handled by law officials and her parents is unclear. They more than likely had to pay a minor fine. Margaret Murray Washington letter to the Executive Council, December 14, 1916, TUA; Elizabeth Benson, OHP, July 7, 1974 located in Lane, *A Documentary*, 25.

41. Margaret Murray Washington letter to the Executive Council, December 14, 1916, located in TUA.

42. Emmett Scott letter to Margaret Murray Washington, October 12, 1916, located in TUA.

43. Hine, *Black Women in United States History*, 320

44. Margaret Murray Washington letter to Mr. Taylor, December 26, 1916, located in TUA.

45. Margaret Murray Washington letter to Emmett Scott, October 28, 1916, located in TUA.

46. Wideman, *My Soul has grown Deep*, 633; Rouse, "Out of the Shadow," 32; Richardson, *The History of Fisk*, 56.

47. Richardson, *A History of Fisk*, 67.

48. Madame C.J. Walker letter to Margaret Murray Washington, November 15, 1915 in *BTWP*, 13:449–51; *The Tuskegee Student*, 28 October 1916.

49. Harlan, *The Wizard of Tuskegee*, 152; undated salary list, 1903; memorandum from the auditing department, May 31, 1908.

50. Harlan, *The Wizard of Tuskegee*, 152; undated salary list, 1903; memorandum from the auditing department, May 31, 1908; "Rosenwald Remembers Teachers," Cleveland *Gazette*, July 3, 2015.

51. Wiseman, *My Soul has Grown Deep*, passim; Harlan, *The Wizard of Tuskegee*, 152; undated salary list, 1903; memorandum from the auditing department, May 31, 1908, "Rosenwald Remembers Teachers," Cleveland *Gazette*, July 3, 2015.

52. *The Southern Letter*, March 1901.

53. Emmett Scott letter to Margaret Murray Washington February 23, 1916, located in TUA, *Cleveland Gazette*, July 24, 2015

54. Meier and Rudwick, *Along the Color Line*, 56.

55. *Baltimore Afro-American Ledger*, 17 January 1903; Wiseman, *My Soul has Grown Deep*; Giddings, *Ida*, 440.

Chapter Four

1. Margaret Murray Washington, *The Negro Home*, 5.

2. Harlan and Smock, *BTWP* 4:238.

3. Howard Thurman, *The Luminous Darkness: A Personal Interpretation of the Anatomy of Segregation and the Ground of Hope* (Richmond, Indiana: Friends United Press) 1956, pp. 5–6.

4. Harlan and Smock, *BTWP* 1:135; Litwack, *Trouble in Mind*, xv; Ritterhouse, *Growing up Jim Crow*, passim; William H. Chafe, Raymond Gavins, and Robert Korstad eds., *Remembering Jim Crow: African Americans Tell About Life in the Segregated South* (The New York Press, 2001) 1.

5. Wesley, *History of the National Association*, 21–23; Rouse, "Out of the Shadow," 33; Scott, "Mrs. Booker T. Washington's," in Harlan and Smock, *BTWP*, 9:291–92; Milton C. Sernett, *Bound for the Promised Land: African American Religion and the Great Migration*, 31; Norrell, *Up from History*, 106–7.

6. "Mrs. Booker T. Washington's," in Harlan and Smock, *BTWP*, 9:291.

7. "Mrs. Booker T. Washington's," in Harlan and Smock, *BTWP*, 9:291; Neverdon-Morton, *Afro-American Women of the South*, 36.

8. Ritterhouse, *Growing up Jim Crow*, 5.

9. *The Tuskegee Student*, December 5, 1908; Scott, "Mrs. Booker T. Washington's," in Harlan and Smock *BTWP*, 9:291.

10. Washington, *Tuskegee and Its People*, IX; The *Tuskegee Student*, December 5, 1908.

11. Florence L. Lattimore, "The Palace of Delight at Hampton," In *the Southern Workman* vol. 44. Hampton Normal and Agricultural Institute (Hampton, Virginia, 1916).

12. Lattimore, "The Palace of Delight at Hampton," In *the Southern Workman* vol. 44.

13. Margaret James Murray letter to Booker T. Washington, July 10, 1892 in Harlan and Smock, *BTWP* 3:246.

14. *The Tenth Annual Report of the Tuskegee Woman's Club*, in Harlan and Smock, *BTWP*, 8:475.

15. Gibson & Crogman, *The Colored American*, 527; Rouse, *Lugenia Burns Hope*, 89; Neverdon- Morton, *Afro-American Women of the South*, 1, 133; Smith, *Sick and Tired of Being Sick and Tired*, passim; Thomas, *The New Woman in Alabama*, 1.

16. Gatewood, "Aristocrat of Color: South and North Black Elite, 1880–1920," *The Journal of Southern History*, 54, no. 1 (February 1988), 6; Lerner, "Early Community Work of Black Club Women," 160.

17. "An Account of Addresses by Washington and Mrs. Washington delivered at Charleston" in Harlan and Smock, *BTWP*, 4:464; Jackson, *A Chief Lieutenant*, 22; Lerner, "Early Community Work," 167.

18. Mary Church Terrell, *"What Role Is the Educated Negro Woman to Play in the Uplifting of Her Race?"* in Twentieth Century Negro Literature, ed. Daniel W. Culp (Naperville, Ill.: J. L. Nichols, 1902), 175.

19. Smith, *Sick and Tired of Being Sick and Tired*, 18, 25.

20. Wesley, *History of the National Association*, 21–23; Rouse, "Out of the Shadow," 33; Scott, "Mrs. Booker T. Washington's," in Harlan and Smock, *BTWP*, 9:290; Lane, *A Documentary*, 245.

21. Rouse, *Lugenia Burns Hope*, 66–67.

22. Rouse, "Out of the Shadow," 33; Scott, "Mrs. Booker T. Washington's," in Harlan and Smock, *BTWP*, 9:293; Smith, *Sick and Tired of Being Sick and Tired*, 27–28; Oshinsky, *Worse than Slavery*, 80.

23. *Tuskegee Student*, 18 March 1916, located in TUA; Rouse, "Out of the Shadow," 33.

24. Scott, "Mrs. Booker T. Washington's," in Harlan and Smock, *BTWP*, 9:292; Rouse, *Lugenia Burns Hope*, 8.

25. Rouse, *Lugenia Burns Hope*, 3; Scott, "Mrs. Booker T. Washington's," in Harlan and Smock, *BTWP*, 9:292.

26. Rouse, "Out of the Shadow," 33; Scott, "Mrs. Booker T. Washington's," in Harlan and Smock, *BTWP*, 9:293; "The Tenth Annual Report of the Tuskegee Woman's Club," Tuskegee, Alabama, 1905, in Harlan and Smock, *BTWP*, 8:475; Smith, *Sick and Tired of Being Sick and Tired*, 27.

27. The Bowen Plantation later served as the grounds of Tuskegee Institute. Josiah Henson, *Truth Stranger Than Fiction: Father Henson's Story of His Own Life*, (originally published in 1858. Barnes & Noble, Inc 2008) 9.

28. Washington, *Tuskegee and its People*, IX; Scipio II, *The Building of Tuskegee*, Roman Publications, 38.

29. Washington, *Tuskegee and its People*, IX.

30. *New York World*, 1895, Neverdon-Morton, *Afro-American Women of the South*, 137; Smock, *Booker T. Washington*, 93–98; *New York World*, 1895, Neverdon-Morton, *Afro-American Women of the South*, 137; Smock, *Booker T. Washington*, 93–98; Lane, *A Documentary*, 216, 218, 223; Jackson, *A Chief Lieutenant*, 23–24.

31. Scott, "Mrs. Booker T. Washington's," in Harlan and Smock, *BTWP*, 9:293.

32. Hine and Thompson, *A Shining Thread of Hope*, 169.

33. Rouse, "Out of the Shadow," 33; Jones, *Labor of Love*, 63.

34. Scott, "Mrs. Booker T. Washington's," in Harlan and Smock, *BTWP*, 9:292.

35. Harlan and Smock, *BTWP*.

36. Ibid.

37. "The Tenth Annual Report," in Harlan and Smock, *BTWP*, 8:475; Rouse, *Lugenia Burns Hope*, 9.

38. Ibid; Oshinski, *Worse Than Slavery*, 80.

39. "The Tenth Annual Report," in Harlan and Smock, *BTWP*, 8:475.

40. "The Tenth Annual Report," in Harlan and Smock, *BTWP*, 8:476–77.

41. "The Tenth Annual Report," in Harlan and Smock, *BTWP*, 8:475, 477–78; Hine and Thompson, *A Shining Thread of Hope*, 184.

42. "The Tenth Annual Report," in Harlan and Smock, *BTWP*, 8:476–77, 478.

43. "The Tenth Annual Report," in Harlan and Smock, *BTWP*, 8:476–77, 479; Rouse, *Lugenia Burns Hope*, 59.

44. "The Tenth Annual Report," in Harlan and Smock, *BTWP*, 8:479; *The Tuskegee Student*, 1 April 1916.

45. "The Tenth Annual Report," in Harlan and Smock, *BTWP*, 8:479; *The Southern Letter*, March 1901; Neverdon-Morton, *Afro-American Women of the South*, 206–7.

46. Rouse, *Lugenia Burns Hope*, 9.

47. "The Tenth Annual Report," in Harlan and Smock, *BTWP*, 8:480; Rouse, *Lugenia Burns Hope*, 9; Mrs. Nellie F. Francis, "Women's Influence," *National Association Notes 1913* located in TUA.

48. "The Tenth Annual Report," in Harlan and Smock, *BTWP*, 8:479; *The Southern Letter*, March 1901; "The Tenth Annual Report," in Harlan and Smock, *BTWP*, 8:479; A Letter from Margaret Murray Washington to Mrs. Ednah Dow Cheney, in Harlan and Smock, *BTWP*, 6:11.

49. "The Tenth Annual Report," in Harlan and Smock, *BTWP*, 8:479; Gregory Eiselein and Anne K. Phillips eds., *The Louisa May Alcott Encyclopedia* (Westport, Connecticut: Greenwood Press, 2001), 48–49.

50. "The Tenth Annual Report," in Harlan and Smock, *BTWP*, 8:479.

51. Pruitt, "Margaret Murray Washington," 856.

Chapter Five

1. Margaret Murray Washington, *The Negro Home*, 4.

2. Poem quoted by Margaret Murray Washington during a speech to the National Association of Colored Women's Clubs, in Lane, *A Documentary*, 204. Actual poem written by Ralph Waldo Emerson, *The Works of Ralph Waldo Emerson*, vol. 8 (Letters and Social Aims) [1908].

3. Woloch, *Women and the American Experience*, 286–88; Lane, *A Documentary*, 163.

4. Woloch, *Women and the American Experience*, 286–88; Margaret Murray Washington, "The Organizing of Women's Clubs, June 22, 1910 located in Lane, *A Documentary*, 163, 236–38.

5. Lane, *A Documentary*, 163, 288.

6. Woloch, *Women and the American Experience*, 289.

7. Ibid.

8. Woloch, *Women and the American Experience*, 290; Jones, "Mary Church Terrell," 23. Shaw asserts that some elite blacks felt that they were judged by the best of their race and not the worse. See Shaw, *What a Woman Ought to Be and to Do*, 167; Gatewood, *Aristocrats of Color*, 111–12, 246–47; Cromwell, *The Other Brahmins*, passim; It should be noted that while most of the women who joined historically white organizations where of mixed parentage, Josephine Ruffin, was considered an exception. She was of a darker hue and is noted as refusing to be an outcaste because of her color;

Bert James Loewenberg and Ruth Bogin, eds., *Black Women in Nineteenth-Century American Life: Their Words, Their Thoughts, Their Feelings* (The Pennsylvania State University Press, 1976), 25.

9. Jones, "Mary Church Terrell," 20–21; Goings shows the progress of different stereotypes that persisted in American History. See Goings, *Mammy and Uncle Mose*; Shaw, *What a Woman Ought to Be and to Do*, 73; Moore, "Anna Julia Cooper: Educator, Clubwoman, and Feminist," 76–77.

10. "How to Keep Women at Home," *Colored American Magazine*, Vol. 14, No. 1 (January, 1908): 8.

11. Ibid.

12. Ibid.

13. Jones, "Mary Church Terrell," 21; Giddings, *When and Where I Enter*, 96, 115; Smith, *Sick and Tired of being Sick and Tired*, 17–18; Martha H. Patterson, *Beyond the Gibson Girl: Reimagining the American New Woman 1895–1915* (Chicago: University of Illinois Press, 2005), 23; *The Tuskegee Student*, 18 March 1916; Lane, *A Documentary*, 245–46.

14. Lerner, "Early Community Work of Black Women," 161 Jones, "Mary Church Terrell," 20–22; Gatewood, *Aristocrats of Color*, 249.

15. Jones, "Mary Church Terrell," 22; Hine, *Black Women in United States History*, 320; Woloch, *Women and the American Experience*, 290; Lane, *A Documentary*, 164; Goings traces the different stereotypes of African American men and women from the 1880s up until the seventies. See Goings, *Mammy and Uncle Mose*, passim; Lerner, "Early Community Work of Black Women," 159; Shaw, *What a Woman Ought to Be and to Do*, 54; Gatewood, *Aristocrats of Color*, 112.

16. Harlan, *Wizard of Tuskegee*, 379–82, 19, 98.

17. Lerner, "Early Community Work of Black Women," 161; Jones, "Mary Church Terrell," 20–22; Gatewood, *Aristocrats of Color*, 249; Shaw, *What a Woman Ought to Be and to Do*, 54; Lerner "Early Community Work of Black Women," 159; Smith, *Sick and Tired*, 28; Giddings, *When and Where I Enter*, 95–97.

18. Terrell, *A Colored Woman in a White World*, 185; Mary Church Terrell, "Colored Woman's League," p. 2, Mary Church Terrell Collection, Box 102–3, Manuscript Division, LOC, MSRC.

19. Hine, *Black Women in United States History*, 315–18; Rita B. Dandridge, *Black Women's Activism: Reading African American Women's Historical Romances*, (New York: Peter Lang Publishing, Inc, 2004), 7; Logan, "We Are Coming," 133–34; Wesley, *History of the National Association of Colored Women's Clubs*, 4–5; Harlan, *Wizard*, 98; Giddings, *Ida*, 362–64; Dorothy Salem, *To Better Our World*, 18.

20. Although Helen Cook, president of the national Colored Women's League, attended the 1895 convention in Boston, her club did not join the NFAAW. In part due to the fact that she did not have the voting power as president to absorb her club into another club without first getting a vote from the League members. In later correspondence Terrell asserts that the women of the League were willing to join forces. "Minutes of the first National Conference of Colored Women," 1896," Part 1, Minutes of the National Publications and Presidential notes, located in NRML National Association of Colored Women, Reel, 1. p. 1, 35; Hine, *Black Women in United States History*, 315–18, 105; Lane, *A Documentary*, 165; Lerner "Early Community Work of Black Women," 161; Jones, "Mary Church Terrell," 20–21; Woloch, *Women and the American Experience*, 290; Jackson, *A Chief Lieutenant*, 42; Rouse, "Out of the Shadow," 36; Gatewood, *Aristocrats of Color*, 112; Cromwell, *The Other Brahmins*, 1–3; Logan, "We Are Coming:," 133–34.

21. "Minutes of the first National Conference of Colored Women," 1896," Part 1, Minutes of the National Publications and Presidential notes, located in NRML National Association of Colored Women, Reel, 1; Davis, *Lifting as we Climb*, 18; Giddings, *When and Where I Enter*, 98.

22. "Minutes of the first National Conference of Colored Women," 1896," Part 1, Minutes of the National Publications and Presidential notes, located in NRML National Association of Colored Women, Reel, 1; Giddings, *When and Where I Enter*, 98, 105; Lane, *A Documentary*, 165; Lerner, "Early Community Work of Black Women," 161; Jones, "Mary Church Terrell," 20–21; Woloch, *Women and the American Experience*, 290; Hine, *Black Women in United States History*, 320–21; Emma Lou Thornbrough, *T. Thomas Fortune: Militant Journalist*, (Chicago and London: The University Press of Chicago, 1972) 126–27.

23. Lane, *A Documentary*, 165; Jackson, *Booker T. Washington and the Struggle Against White Supremacy*.

24. Harlan, *Wizard of Tuskegee*, 89; Lane, *A Documentary*, 165–66; Rosalyn Terborg-Penn, *African American Women in the Struggle for the Vote, 1850–1920*, 88.

25. Minutes of the first National Conference of Colored Women," 1896," Part 2, Minutes of the National Publications and Presidential notes, located in NRML, NACW, Reel, 1.

26. "Minutes of the first National Conference of Colored Women," 1896," Part 2, Minutes of the National Publications and Presidential notes, located in NRML, NACW, Reel, 1 p. 13; Hine, *Black Women in United States History*, 323; Lane, *A Documentary*, 165–66; Linda O. McMurray, *To Keep the Waters Troubled: The Life of Ida B. Wells* (Oxford University Press, 1998),

347–48; A speech given by Margaret Murray Washington titled "National Association of Colored Women's Clubs delivered in 1913," *Nashville Globe*, June 20, 1913.

27. Minutes of the first National Conference of Colored Women," 1896, Part 1, Minutes of the National Publications and Presidential notes, located in NRML, NACW, Reel, 1.

28. "Minutes of the first National Conference of Colored Women," 1896, Part 1, Minutes of the National Publications and Presidential notes, located in NRML, NACW, Reel, 1; Many of the women present that day felt that the name "colored" had no meaning for black folk as a race; Lane, *A Documentary*, 165–66; Giddings, *When and Where I Enter*, 95; Shaw, *What a Woman Ought to Be and to Do*, 78; Gatewood, *Aristocrats of Color*, 43–44, 249; Jones, "Mary Church Terrell," 23; Wesley, *History of the National Association of Colored Women's Clubs*, 43; Giddings; *Ida*, 374.

29. Terrell, *A Colored Woman In a White World*, 151; *Women's Era*, July 1896, 8; Giddings, *Ida*, 374.

30. Terrell, *A Colored Woman in a White World*, Passim; Lane, *A Documentary*, 165–166; Giddings, *When and Where I Enter*, 95; Shaw, *What a Woman Ought to Be and to Do*, 78; Gatewood, *Aristocrats of Color*, 43–44, 249; Jones, "Mary Church Terrell," 23; Wesley, *History of the National Association of Colored Women's Clubs*, 43; Hine, *Black Women in United States History*, 324.

31. Moore, "Anna Julia Cooper: Educator, Clubwoman, and Feminist," 72–73; Lester C. Lamon, *Black Tennesseans 1900–1930* (Knoxville: The University of Tennessee Press, 1977), 188; Hine, Hine and Harrold, *The African American Odyssey*, 406; Terrell, *A Colored Woman in a White World*, 32, 62.

32. Hine, Hine and Harrold, *The African American Odyssey*, 406; Lamon, *Black Tennesseans 1900–1930*, 188, 183–84; Jones, "Mary Church Terrell," 21; Gilbert Jonas, *Freedom's Sword: The NAACP and the Struggle Against Racism in America, 1909–1969* (New York: Routledge, 2004), 401.

33. Jones, "Mary Church Terrell," 21; Giddings, *When and Where I Enter*, 96–97; Wesley, *History of the National Association of Colored Women's Clubs*, 43; Terrell, *A Colored Woman in a White World*; Bess B. Walcott, "Cornelia Bowen: An Artist in Courageous Living," *The Tuskegee Messenger*, August 1934.

34. Wesley, *History of the National Association of Colored Women*, 3–4; Lane, *A Documentary*, 171; NACW Constitution, located in MMWP at TUA.

35. Terrell, *A Colored Woman in A White World*, 192; Giddings, *When and Where I Enter*, 101; Daphne Spain, *How Women Saved the City*, (University of Minnesota Press, 2001), 98. Lane, *A Documentary*, 5, 178; Jones, "Mary Church Terrell," 20–21.

36. Terrell, *A Colored Woman in A White World*, 231; Giddings, *When and Where I Enter*, 101; Lane, *A Documentary*, 177.

37. Lane, *A Documentary*, 177, 179–80; Giddings, *When and Where I Enter*, 98–99, 101.

38. Giddings, *When and Where I Enter*, 98–99, 101, 115; Lerner, "Early Community Work of Black Women," 161; Jones, "Mary Church Terrell," 24; Rouse "Out of the Shadow," 36.

39. Wesley, *History of the National Association of Colored Women's Clubs*, 50; Christine Lutz, "Addie W. Hunton: Crusader for Pan-Africanism and Peace," in Nina Mjagkij, *Portraits of African American Life*, 111–12; Mrs. Nellie F. Francis, "Women's Influence," in *National Association Notes* located in TUA; It should be noted that Josephine Ruffin's *Women's Era* was the first newspaper published for and by African American women in the United States.

40. Raymond W. Smock, *Booker T. Washington: Black Leadership in the Age of Jim Crow*, 151–52.

41. Margaret Murray Washington letter to Robert R. Moton, September 2, 1919, Moton Paper, TUA; McMurray, *To Keep the Waters Troubled*, 347–48; Duster, ed., *Crusade for Justice: The Autobiography of Ida B. Wells-Barnett*, 328–29; Thomas Holt, "The Lonely Warrior: Ida B. Wells-Barnett and the Struggle for Black Leadership," in John Hope Franklin and August Meier, eds., *Black Leaders of the Twentieth Century* (Urbana: University of Illinois Press, 1982), 48–60; Norrell, *Up from History*, 176–77; Rouse, "Out of the Shadow of Tuskegee;" Giddings, *Ida*, 493.

42. McMurray, *To Keep the Waters Troubled*, 347–48; Duster, ed., *Crusade for Justice: The Autobiography of Ida B. Wells-Barnett*, 328–29; Thomas Holt, "The Lonely Warrior: Ida B. Wells- Barnett and the Struggle for Black Leadership," in John Hope Franklin and August Meier, eds., *Black Leaders of the Twentieth Century* (Urbana: University of Illinois Press, 1982), 48–60; Norrell, *Up from History*, 176–77; Rouse, "Out of the Shadow of Tuskegee;" Giddings, *Ida*. 493.

43. Christine Lutz, "Addie W. Hunton: Crusader for Pan-Africanism and Peace," in Nina Mjagkij, *Portraits of African American Life*, 111–12.

44. Lane, *A Documentary*, 216, 218, 223; Jackson, *A Chief Lieutenant*, 23–24.

45. *National Association Notes*, 1904; Harris, *Margaret Murray Washington*, 134–37.

46. *New York World*, 1895, Nerverdon-Morton, *Afro-American Women*, 137; Smock, *Booker T. Washington*, 93–98.

47. Hunton, "The Southern Federation," 850.

48. Nerverdon-Morton, *Afro-American Women*, 137; Lane, *A Documentary*, 263.

49. Hunton, "The Southern Federation," 850.

50. Hunton, "The Southern Federation," 850–51.

51. Hunter, "The Southern Federation," 850–51; Rouse, "Out of the Shadow of Tuskegee," 31–46; Oshinsky, *Worse Than Slavery*, 79.

52. Washington, "National Association of Colored Women's Clubs" 1913; Neverdon-Morton, *Afro-American Women*, 137–38; *Minutes of the Ninth Annual session of the Alabama Federation of Colored Women's Clubs*, Salem, Alabama, July 3–6, 1907; Michelle Alexander, *The New Jim Crow: Mass Incarceration in the Age of Colorblindness* (New York: The New Press, 2010), passim.

53. Reverend R. C. Bedford, "Mt. Meigs Institute, Alabama," in *Southern Workman* (April 1894), 87; Nerverdon-Morton, *Afro-American Women in the South*, 137–38; *Minutes of the Ninth Annual session of the Alabama Federation of Colored Women's Clubs*, Salem, Alabama, July 3–6, 1907; Leon F. Litwack, *Trouble in Mind: Black Southerners in the Age of Jim Crow*, 271–72; Margaret Murray Washington's speech, "National Association of Colored Women's Clubs" is located in *Notes*, June 1913.

54. Washington, "National Association of Colored Women's Clubs," 1913. Khalil Gibran Muhammad, *The Condemnation of Blackness: Race, Crime, and the Making of Modern Urban America* (Harvard University Press, 2010), 60–64.

55. Nerverdon-Morton, *Afro-American Women*, 137–38; *Minutes of the fifteenth Annual session of the Alabama Federation of Colored Women's Clubs*, Mobile, Alabama, July 2–4, 1913 in MMWP located in TUA.

56. Nerverdon-Morton, *Afro-American Women*, 137–38; Lane, *A Documentary*, 281.

57. Reverend R. C. Bedford, "Mt. Meigs Institute, Alabama," in *Southern Workman* (April 1894), 87; Nerverdon-Morton, *Afro-American Women in the South*, 137–38; *Minutes of the Ninth Annual session of the Alabama Federation of Colored Women's Clubs*, Salem, Alabama, July 3–6, 1907; Leon F. Litwack, *Trouble in Mind: Black Southerners in the Age of Jim Crow*, 271–72; Donald Spivey, *"If You Were Only White:" The Life of Leroy "Satchel Paige"* (Columbia and London: University of Missouri Press) 2012, 18–22.

58. Ibid.

59. Washington, "National Association of Colored Women's Clubs," 1913.

60. Ibid.

61. Wesley, *History of the National Association of Colored Women's clubs*, 59; Jackson, *A Chief Lieutenant*, 226n139.

62. Nerverdon-Morton, *Afro-American Women*, 137–38; Wesley, *History of the National Association of Colored Women's Clubs*, 70; Twenty-fourth conference minutes June 6–8, 1922 in MMWP located in TUA.

63. Wesley, *History of the National Association of Colored Women's Clubs*, 70, 467; Lane, *A Documentary*, 169–71; Rouse, "Out of the Shadow," 34; Davis, *Lifting as We Climb*, 171; Hine, Brown, and Terborg-Penn, *Black Women in America*, 1234; Pruitt, "Margaret Murray Washington," 856; Richardson, *National Cyclopedia*, 63.

64. Giddings, *When and Where I Enter*, 113.

65. Ibid.

66. Ibid.

67. Washington, "Clubwork," in Lane, *A Documentary*, 179.

68. Lane, *A Documentary*, 5, 178, 181; Giddings, *When and Where I Enter*, 79; Woloch, *Women and the American Experience*, 453; Jackson, "Booker T. Washington and the Struggle against White Supremacy," 184; Harlan, *Wizard of Tuskegee*, 379–82; Dray, *At the Hands of Persons Unknown*, 179–82; Barnett Dodson, "An Account of the Assault on Washington," in Harlan and Smock, *BTWP*, 11: 27–30; Nell Irvin Painter, *Creating Black Americans: African American History and Its Meanings, 1619 To The Present* (New York: Oxford University Press, 2007), 180–81; The following book paints a vivid picture of the brutality that persisted at the end of the nineteenth century through the beginning of the twentieth-century. Orlando Patterson, *Rituals of Blood: Consequences of Slavery in Two American Centuries* (New York: Basic Civities Inc, 1998), passim.

69. "Monroe Work" in *Encyclopedia of the World Biography*, 2nd ed. 17 vols (Detroit: Gale Research, 1998); "Monroe Work" in Rayford W. Logan and Michael R. Winston, eds., *Dictionary of American Negro Biography* (New York: WW Norton, 1982).

70. Dodson, "An Account," located in Harlan and Smock, *BTWP*, 11:27–30; Patterson, *Rituals of Blood*; Washington, "Clubwork," located in Lane, *A Documentary*, 5, 178, 181; Giddings, *When and Where I Enter*, 79; Woloch, *Women and the American Experience*, 453; Jackson, *Booker T. Washington and the Struggle against White Supremacy*, 184; Harlan, *Wizard of Tuskegee*, 379–82; Dray, *At the Hands*, 179–82; Painter, *Creating Black Americans*, 180–81; Patterson, *Rituals of Blood*, passim.

71. Washington, "National Association of Colored Women's Clubs," 1913.

72. The following is an author who credits Margaret for coining the Term "New Negro Women." See Patterson, *Beyond the Gibson Girl*, 50–51, 58; A speech given by Margaret Murray Washington titled "National

Association of Colored Women's Clubs delivered in 1913," *Nashville Globe*, June 20, 1913.

73. Washington, "National Association of Colored Women's Clubs," 1913; Lane, *A Documentary*, 199, 201.

74. *Outlook Magazine*, May 1904.

75. Washington, "National Association of Colored Women's Clubs," 1913.

76. Giddings, *When and Where I Enter*, 23; *The Memphis Daily Appeal*, December 1884, as cited in Giddings, *When and Where I Enter*; Holt, *The Lonely Warrior*, 41–42.

77. *The Afro-American*, August 4, 1916 in Lane, *A Documentary*, 71.

78. Washington, "National Association of Colored Women's Clubs," 1913.

79. Lane, *A Documentary*, 15, 201.

80. Hine, Brown and Terborg-Penn, *African American Women*, 104–5.

81. Adella Hunt Logan, "A Woman's Suffrage Symposium," in *The Crisis* (1912): 242–43.

82. Washington, "National Association of Colored Women's Clubs," 1913.

83. Ibid; Smock, *Booker T. Washington*, 94.

84. Oral Histories of Harriette Booth, OHP, June 1979, located in Lane, *A Documentary*, 67.

85. Margaret Murray Washington, "We Must Have a Cleaner Social Morality," at Old Bethel A.M.E. Church, 1898 in *Charleston News and Courier* (September 13, 1898); *Cleveland Gazette*, July 20, 1901, in Harlan and Smock, *BTWP*, 6:178.

86. *Cleveland Gazette*, July 20, 1901, in Harlan and Smock, *BTWP*, 6:178.

87. Harlan, *Wizard of Tuskegee*, 128, 133–36, 140–42; Jackson, *A Chief Lieutenant*, 113–14; Rouse, "Out of the Shadow," 37.

88. Rouse, "Out of the Shadow," 37; Lane, *A Documentary*, 5.

89. Rouse, "Out of the Shadow," 37; Lane, *A Documentary*, 5, 178; *Lifting as We Climb*, 4.

90. Gatewood, *Aristocrats of Color*, 4, 290; Lane, *A Documentary*, 207–8; Jackson, *A Chief Lieutenant*, 3; Beverly Greene Bond, "Roberta Church: Race and the Republican Party in the 1950s," in Mjagkij, *Portraits of African American*, 183.

91. *National Association Notes*, June 1913, 4.

92. Bond, "Roberta Church," 203; Goings, *Mammy and Uncle Mose*, 21–25.

93. Rouse, "Out of the Shadow," 39.

94. *National Association Notes*, 1914

95. *National Association Notes*, June 1913; Rouse, "Out of the Shadow," 39; Lane, *A Documentary*, 203.

96. Lane, *A Documentary*, 203.

97. David H. Jackson, Jr., "Booker T. Washington's Tour of the Sunshine State, March 1912," in *Go Sound the Trumpet!: Selections in Florida's African American History*, David H. Jackson, Jr. and Canter Brown, Jr. Eds., (University of Tampa Press, 2005), 194.

98. Harlan, *Wizard of Tuskegee*, 452–54; Jackson, *A Chief Lieutenant*, 187; Norrell, *Up from History*; 417.

99. BTW to Emmett Jay Scott, January 16, 1914 in *BTWP*, 13:417; Harlan, *Wizard*, 451–52; Norrell, *Up From History*, 418–20.

100. Jackson, *A Chief Lieutenant*, 187; Harlan, *Wizard of Tuskegee*, 452–54; Norrell, *Up from History*, 418–19.

101. U.S. Bureau of the Census, 1920.

102. U.S. Bureau of the Census, 1920.

103. Even Louis Harlan who has written extensively on Washington does not add much on the NACW. He only dedicates one page to it in his two-volume work on Washington; Harlan, *Making of a Black Leader*, and Harlan, *Wizard of Tuskegee*, 108.

Chapter Six

1. Margaret Murray Washington, *The Negro Home*, 6.

2. Hine, Hine and Harrold, *The Afro-American Odyssey*, 406–7.

3. "Race Man is Whipped by Ku Klux Klan in South" [1918] The Tuskegee Institute News Clippings File, 1899–1919, NRML, Reel 8.

4. "Ku Klux Klan again busy in South, paying attention to slackers," [1918], The Tuskegee Institute News Clippings File, 1899–1819, NRML, Reel 8.

5. Chad Williams, *Torchbearers of Democracy: African American Soldiers in the World War I Era* (University of North Carolina Press, 2010); Adriane Lentz-Smith, *Freedom Struggles: African Americans and World War I* (Harvard University Press, 2009), 2–7; Philip Dray, *At The Hands of Persons Unknown: Lynchings of Black America* (New York: Random House, 2002), viii.

6. Williams, *Torchbearers of Democracy*; Lentz-Smith, *Freedom Struggles*, 1.

7. *Tuskegee Student*, 1 March 1919.

8. *Tuskegee Student*, 1 March 1919; Nell Irvin Painter, *Creating Black Americans: African American History and Its Meaning, 1619 To the Present*

(New York: Oxford University Press, 2007), 189; Lane, A Documentary, 54, Ohio Union, January 28, 1919.

9. Le'Trice D. Donaldson, Duty Beyond the Battlefield: African American Soldiers Fight for Radical Uplift, Citizenship, and Manhood, 1870–1920 (Illinois: Southern Illinois University Press, 2020), 75; Theodore Kornweibel, Jr., Investigate Everything: Federal Efforts to Ensure Black Loyalty during World War I (Bloomington: Indiana University Press, 2002), 235.

10. Steven Watson, The Harlem Renaissance: Hub of African American Culture, 1920–1930 (New York: Pantheon, 1995), 4; Nathan Irvin Huggins, Harlem Renaissance (Oxford University Press, 1971, 2007), 5–7; Giddings, When and Where I Enter, 171, 183–87; Hine, Hine and Harrold, The Afro-American Odyssey, 406–7.

11. Margaret Murray Washington, "We Must Have a Cleaner Social Morality," at Old Bethel A.M.E. Church, 1898 in Charleston News and Courier (September 13, 1898); Dray, At the Hands of Persons Unknown; "Constitution," n.d., MCTP, LOC, Reel 14; "National Organization of Colored Women Formed," [1922] The Tuskegee Institute News Clippings File, 1899–1919, NRML, Reel 17; The organization was formed in 1922 after the NACW's meeting in Richmond, Virginia.

12. P. Olisanwuche Esedebe Pan-Africanism: The Idea and Movement, 1776–1991 (Howard University Press: Washington, D.C., 1994), 42.

13. Niagara's Declaration of Principles, 1905; As early as 1897 Margaret Washington had been engaged in international activities. As part of a speaking tour she addressed an international audience in Toronto, Canada. She also traveled with her husband to Europe in 1899. These activities opened her mind to the possibilities of the race and limitations that existed across the globe.

14. Terrell, A Colored Woman in a White World, 237–44; Olisanwuche Esedebe, Pan-African Connection: From Slavery to Garvey and Beyond (Dover: Majority Press, 1984); Esedebe, Pan-Africanism, 42; Niagara's Declaration of Principles, 1905; Rief "'Banded Close Together," 141.

15. Terrell, A Colored Woman in a White World, 243–44; Harris, Margaret Murray Washington, 138–39.

16. National Association Notes, June 1905; Susan B. Anthony to Mr. and Mrs. Booker T. Washington, BTWP, 4:540–41; Wesley, The History, 59–61.

17. Hakim Adi and Marika Sherwood, Pan African History: Political Figures from Africa and the Diaspora Since 1787 (Routledge, New York, 2003), 6; Tony Martin, The Pan-African Connection: From Slavery to Garvey and Beyond (Dover: Majority Press, 1984), vii; Esedebe, Pan-Africanism, 42–45.

18. "National Organization of Colored Women Formed," [1922] The Tuskegee Institute News Clippings File, 1899–1919, NRML, Reel 17; "Constitution," n.d., Moorland-Springarn Research Center, Howard University, Washington D.C. (hereafter referred to as MSRC), Box 102–12, Folder 420.

19. Mary Jackson McCrorey to Margaret Murray Washington, May 16, 1924, MCTP, MSRC, Box 102–12, Folder 420.

20. "How To Keep Women At Home," *Colored American Magazine*, Vol. 14, No. 1 (January, 1908): 8; Letter to the editor of the *Indianapolis Freeman*, London, July 15, 1899, BTWP 5:154.

21. "Industrial Education in Africa," *The Independent* March 15, 1906.

22. Harlan and Smock, BTWP, 10: 512; Milfred C. Fierce, *The Pan-African Idea in the United States 1900–1919* (New York: Garland Publishing, 1993), 175–176; Robert A. Hill, ed., *Pan-African Biography* (Las Angeles: Crossroads Press, 1987), 23; Colin Grant, *Negro with a Hat*, 2; Ula Yvette Taylor, *The Veiled Garvey*, 25–26.

23. Margaret Murray Washington to Mary Church Terrell, October 4, 1924, LOC, Reel 5.

24. Neverdon-Morton, *Afro-American Women of the South*, 1.

25. Neverdon-Morton, *Afro-American Women of the South*, 1; Giddings, *When and Where I Enter*, passim.

26. Margaret Murray Washington to Mary Church Terrell, April 28, 1924, MCTP, LOC, Reel 14.

27. Deborah Gray White, *Too Heavy A Load*, 133–34; Michelle Rief, "Thinking Locally, Acting Globally: The International Agenda of African American Clubwomen, 1880–1940," *Journal of African American History*, 89 no. 3 (Summer 2004), 203.

28. "International Council of Women of the Darker Races of the World," [1922], MCTP, LOC, Reel 14.

29. Addie Waits Hunton, "The Southern Federation of Colored Women," *The Voice of the Negro*, Vol. 4 (June 1905): 850–51.

30. Lugenia Barns Hope to Margaret Murray Washington, January 5, 1925, MCTP, MSRC, Box 102–12, Folder 240.

31. Margaret Murray Washington to Mary Church Terrell, October 16, 1922, MCTP, LOC, Reel 5.

32. "International Council of Women of the Darker Races of the World," MCTP, NRML, Reel 14.

33. "National Organization of Colored Women Formed," [1922] The Tuskegee Institute News Clippings File, 1899–1919, NRML, Reel 17; "Constitution," n.d., MCTP, LOC, Reel 14.

34. "Constitution," n.d., MCTP, LOC, Reel 14.

35. Margaret Murray Washington letter to Mary Church Terrell, September 6, 1922, MCTP, LOC, Reel 5; *National Association Notes*, June 1913; Lane, *A Documentary*, 203; Rouse, "Out of the Shadow," 39.

36. Margaret Murray Washington letter to Mary Church Terrell, September 20, 1922, MCTP, LOC, Reel 5.

37. Julie Des Jardins, "Reclaiming the Past: Women, Gender, Race and the Construction of Historical Memory in America, 1880–1940" (Ph.D. diss., Brown University, 2000), 265–70.

38. Bobby Lovett, *The African American History of Nashville, Tennessee* (University of Arkansas Press, 1999), 211.

39. "International Council of Women of the Darker Races of the World," MCTP, NRML, Reel 14.

40. White, *Too Heavy a Load*, 147–49.

41. "International Council of Women of the Darker Races of the World," [1922], MCTP, NRML, Reel 14; Mary Jackson McCrorey, "Funeral Service Bulletin," January 16, 1944, Johnson C. Smith University Archives, Digitalsmith; "Minutes on the Death of Mrs. H. L. McCrorey," January 16, 1944, Johnson C. Smith University Archives, Digitalsmith, Vol. 10, No. 4.

42. Margaret Murray Washington letter to Mary Church Terrell, October 4, 1924, MCTP, LOC, Reel 5.

43. Margaret Murray Washington to Mary Church Terrell, October 16, 1924, MCTP, LOC, Reel 5.

44. Margaret Murray Washington letter to Mary Church Terrell, August 20, 1923, MCTP, LOC, Reel 5.

45. Margaret Murray Washington letter to Mary Church Terrell, October 16, 1922, MCTP, LOC, Reel 5.

46. Addie Dickerson letter to Mary Church Terrell, September 20, 1922, MCTP, LOC, Reel 5.

47. Margaret Murray Washington letter to My Dear Co-Worker, September 6, 1922, MCTP, LOC, Reel 5; Margaret Murray Washington letter to Mary Church Terrell, September 20, 1922, MCTP, LOC, Reel 5.

48. Margaret Murray Washington letter to Mary Church Terrell, September 20, 1922, MCTP, LOC, Reel 5.

49. Margaret Murray Washington letter to Dear Friend, November 9, 1922, MCTP, LOC, Reel 5.

50. Margaret Murray Washington letter to Dear Friend, November 9, 1922, MCTP, LOC, Reel 5; Addie Hunton letter to Margaret Murray Washington, November 20, 1922, MCTP, MSRC, Box 102-12, Folder 239; Margaret Murray Washington letter to Mary Church Terrell, October 16, 1922, MCTP, LOC, Reel 14.

51. Nannie Burroughs letter to Margaret Murray Washington, November 18, 1922, MCTP, MSRC, Box 102–12, Folder 239.

52. Emily H. Williams letter to Margaret Murray Washington, December 12, 1922, MCTP, MSRC, Box 102–12, Folder 240.

53. Theodore Holly letter to Margaret Murray Washington, December 12, 1922, MCTP, MSRC, Box 102–12, Folder 239; *Negro World*, April 28, 1923, 1; Brenda Gayle Plummer, "The Afro-American Response to the occupation in Haiti, 1915–1934, *Phylon*, 43, no. 2 (2nd Quarter, 1982).

54. Theodore Holly letter to Margaret Murray Washington, December 12, 1922, MCTP, MSRC, Box 102–12, Folder 239.

55. "Constitution," n.d., MCTP, LOC, Reel 14; "Washington, D.C.," Press Release, [1923], MCTP, MSRC, Box 102–12, Folder 239.

56. Margaret Murray Washington letter to Mary Church Terrell, October 16, 1922, MCTP, LOC, Reel 5.

57. Mary Church Terrell letter to Margaret Murray Washington, September 3, 1922, MCTP, MSRC, Box 102–12, folder 239; *The New York Age*, August 18, 1923. Because the article in which Terrell refers to is dated in 1923, it can be assumed that the date on the letter is incorrect.

58. White, *Too Heavy A Load*, 106–7.

59. Margaret Murray Washington to Mary Church Terrell, August 20, 1923, MCTP, LOC, Reel 5.

60. Margaret Murray Washington letter to Mary Church Terrell, October 4, 1924, MCTP, LOC, Reel 5.

61. Margaret Murray Washington letter to Mary Church Terrell, October 4, 1924, MCTP, LOC, Reel 5.

62. "An Account of Addresses by Washington and Mrs. Washington delivered at Charleston," *BTWP*, 4:464; Margaret Murray Washington letter to My Dear Co-Worker, September 6, 1922, MCTP, LOC, Reel 5; Jackson, *A Chief Lieutenant*, 22; Lerner, "Early Community Work," 167; Ula Yvette Taylor, *The Veiled Garvey*, 69–71.

63. Margaret Murray Washington letter to Mary Church Terrell, October 4, 1924, MCTP, LOC, Reel 5.

64. *The Tuskegee Messenger*, "Mrs. Booker T. Washington," 1925.

65. Margaret Murray Washington letter to Mary Church Terrell, October 4, 1924, MCTP, LOC, Reel 5; Christine Smith letter to Margaret Murray Washington, December 3, 1924, MCTP, MSRC, Box 102–12, Folder 240.

66. Janie Porter Barrett letter to Margaret Murray Washington, December 3, 1924, MCTP, MSRC, Box 102–12, Folder 239.

67. Janie Porter Barrett letter to Margaret Murray Washington, December 3, 1924, MCTP, MSRC, Box 102–12, Folder 239.

68. Margaret Murray Washington letter to Mary Church Terrell, September 6, 1922, MCTP, LOC, Reel 5.

69. Alice Carter Simmons letter to Mary Church Terrell, June 26, 1925, MCTP, LOC, Reel 5.

70. Brown, Homespun Heroines, 1233; Lane, A Documentary, 7, 293–294; Wesley, History of the National Association of Colored Women's Clubs, 90–91; Rouse, "Out of The Shadow," 31; Hine and Thompson, A Shining Thread, 226.

Conclusion

1. Margaret Murray Washington, The Negro Home, 6.

2. Frankel, Freedom's Women, 16; Rouse, "Out of the Shadow," 31; Scott, "Mrs. Booker T. Washington's," BTWP, 9:289; Pruitt, "Margaret Murray Washington," 855; Richardson, National Cyclopedia, 63; Kletzing, and Crogman, The Remarkable Advancement, 446.

3. Lane, A Documentary, 7, 293–94; Wesley, History of the National Association, 90–91; Rouse, 'Out of The Shadow," 31; Brown, Homespun Heroines, 1233; Hine and Thompson, A Shining Thread, 226.

4. Giddings, When and Where I Enter, vi; Moore, "Anna Julia Cooper: Educator, Clubwoman, and Feminist," 73.

5. Mrs. Washington to Mrs. Hope, November 6, 1914, in Neverdon-Morton, Afro-American Women of the South, 129.

6. Mrs. R. R. Moton, The Tuskegee Messenger, June 1925; Brown, Homespun Heroines, 1233; Lane, A Documentary, 7, 293–94; Wesley, History of the National Association of Colored Women's Clubs, 90–91; Rouse, "Out of The Shadow," 31; Hine and Thompson, A Shining Thread, 226.

7. "Form Charter of Delta Sigma Theta Sorority" New York Age, June 1922; Paula Giddings, In Search of Sisterhood: Delta Sigma Theta and the Challenge of the Black Sorority Movement (New York: HarperCollins, 1988), 27–29.

BIBLIOGRAPHY

Archival Sources

Washington, District of Columbia
    Manuscript Division, Library of Congress
        The Papers of Booker T. Washington
        The Papers of Andrew Carnegie
        National Association for the Advancement of
            Colored People Papers
        The Papers of Mary Church Terrell
    Howard University
    Moorland-Spingarn Research Center
    Mary Church Terrell Papers

Harlem, New York
    Schomburg Center for Research in Black Culture,
        New York Public Library
        The Papers of William Edward Burghardt Du Bois
        Andrew Carnegie collection
        The Papers of the National Council of Women
            of the United States

Oxford, Mississippi
    University of Mississippi Archives
    Macon Herald
    Macon Intelligencer

Memphis, Tennessee
    Memphis and Shelby County Room, Benjamin L. Hooks
        Public Library

The Mary Church Terrell Papers
The Papers of Booker T. Washington

Nashville, Tennessee
   Fisk University Archives
      Fisk Jubilee Singers Collection
      Margaret Murray Washington Collection
      The Fisk Herald
      The W.E.B. Du Bois Collection

Tuskegee, Alabama
   Tuskegee University Archives and Collections
      The Papers of Margaret Murray Washington
      Tuskegee Women's Club Organ
      The Papers of Robert R. Moton
      The Alabama Women's Hall of Fame, 1972
      The National Notes

Government

The Bureau of the Census; census forms; the census of 1860
The Bureau of the Census; census forms; the census of 1870
The Bureau of the Census; census forms; the census of 1880
The Bureau of the Census; census forms; the census of 1920
Born in Slavery: Slave Narratives from the Federal Writer's Project, 1936–1938.
Mississippi Narratives, Volume IX. Digitally reproduced by the Library of Congress. Available: memory.loc.gov. Accessed November 2011.
City Hall, Visitor's Guide History of City of Macon & Noxubee County

Periodicals

Boston Globe
Charleston News and Courier
Chicago Defender
Cleveland Gazette
Colored American Magazine
Harpers Weekly
Memphis Daily Appeal
Nashville Globe
National Association Notes
New York Age

New York Times
New York World
Outlook Magazine
The Baltimore Afro-American Ledger
The Crisis Magazine
The New Negro
The Southern Letter
The Southern Workman
Tuskegee Student
Voice of the Negro

Primary Sources

Brown, Hallie Quinn. *Homespun Heroines and Other Women of Distinction.* The Aldine Publishing Company, 1926.

Culp, Daniel W. Eds. *Twentieth Century Negro Literature.* Naperville, Illinois: J. L. Nichols Press, 1902.

Crogman, William H. & Jon W. Gibson. *The Colored American from Slavery to Honorable Citizenship.* Naperville, Illinois: 1897, reprinted in 1902.

Du Bois, W. E. B. *The Souls of Black Folk.* Chicago: A. C. McClurg & Company, 1903.

———. *Dusk of Dawn: An Essay Towards an Autobiography of a Race Concept.* New York: Schocken Books, 1968.

———. *The Philadelphia Negro: A Social History.* University of Pennsylvania Press, Reprinted 1996.

Duster, Alfreda M., Ed. *Crusade for Justice: The Autobiography of Ida B. Wells.* Chicago & London: The University of Chicago Press, 1970.

Garner, James W. *Reconstruction in Mississippi.* New York: The Macmillian Company, 1901.

Gibson, Jon W. *The New Progress of a Race.* Naperville, Illinois: J. L. Nichols & Company, 1925.

Gibson, Jon W., and William H. Crogman. *The Colored American from Slavery to Honorable Citizenship.* Naperville, Illinois, 1897.

Henson, Josiah. *Truth Stranger Than Fiction: Father Henson's Story of His Own Life.* Originally Published in 1858. Barnes and Noble Inc., 2008.

Kletzing, Henry, F. & William H. Crogman. *The Remarkable Advancement of the Afro-American.* Naperville, Illinois: J. L. Nichols & Company, 1897.

Lane, Linda R. *A Documentary of Mrs. Booker T. Washington.* Lewiston, New York: The Edwin Mellen Press Inc., 2001.

Mather, Frank L. *Who's Who of the Colored Race*. Vol. 1. Chicago, 1915.

Newton, William, Ed. *An Era of Progress and Promise 1863–1910*. Boston: Priscilla Publishing Company, 1910.

Richardson, Clement, Ed. *The National Cyclopedia of the Colored Race*. Montgomery: National Publishing, 1919.

Terrell, Mary Church. *A Colored Woman in a White World*. Amherst: Humanity Books, 1940, 2005.

"Training Dusky Griseldas: Mrs. Booker T. Washington's Missionary work among Negro House-Wives." *San Francisco Bulletin*, August 2, 1903. In Louis Harlan and Raymond Smock, Eds. *Booker T. Washington Papers*. 14 Vols. Urbana: University of Illinois Press, 1972–1989.

Washington, Booker T. *Up From Slavery: An Autobiography*. New York: Doubleday Publishing, 1901. Reprinted, Penguin, 1986.

———. *Tuskegee & Its People: Their Ideals and Achievements*. Massachusetts: D. Appleton and Company, 1905. Reprinted, Read Books Ltd. 2013.

Willson, Joseph. *Sketches of the Higher Class of Colored Society in Philadelphia*. Merrihew and Thompson Printers, 1841.

Secondary Books and Essays

Abbott, Lynn and Doug Seroff. *Out of Sight: The Rise of African American Popular Music, 1889–1895*. University Press of Mississippi, 2002.

Adi, Hakim and Marika Sherwood, *Pan African History: Political Figures from Africa and the Diaspora since 1787*. Routledge Press, 2003.

Anderson, James. *The Education of Blacks in the South, 1860–1935*. Chapel Hill: University of Northe Carolina Press, 2010.

Aptheker, Herbert. Eds. *A Documentary History of the Negro People in the United States, 1910–1932*. Citadel Press, 1973.

Barbour, Hugh & J. William Frost. *The Quakers*. New York: Greenwood Press, 1988.

Bently, George R. *A History of the Freedmen's Bureau*. New York: Reprinted Octagon Books, 1974.

Bernard, Jessie. *Marriage and Family Among Negroes*. Prentice Hall Publishers, 1966.

Berry, Mary F. *My Face is Black is True: Callie House and the Struggle for Ex-Slave Reparations*. New York: Alfred A. Knopf, 2005.

Blassingame, Berry and John *Long Memory: The Black Experience in America*. Oxford University Press, 1982.

Bond, Beverly Greene. "Roberta Church: Race and the Republican Party in the 1950s." In *Portraits of African American Life Since 1865*.

Ed. by Nina Mjagkij. Wilmington, Delaware: Scholarly Resources Inc., 2003.

Bond, Bradley G. *Mississippi: A Documentary History*. Oxford: University Press of Mississippi, 2003.

Boyle, Kevin. *Arc of Justice: A Saga of Race, Civil Rights, and Murder in the Jazz Age*. New York: Henry Holt and Company, 2004.

Branch, Muriel and Dorothy Rice, *Miss Maggie: A Biography of Maggie Lena Walker*. Marlborough House Publishers, 1984.

Brawley, Benjamin. *Negro Builders and Heroes*. Chapel Hill: University of North Carolina Press, 1937.

Brown, Hallie Quinn. *Homespun Heroines and other Women of Distinction*. Xenia, Ohio: Aldine Publishing Co. 1926.

Brown, Titus. *Faithful, Firm, & True: African American Education in the South*. Macon, Georgia: Mercer University Press, 2002.

Buchmann-Møller, Frank. *You Just Fight For Your Life: The Story of Lester Young*. Praeger Publishers, 1990.

Bundles, A'Lelia. *On Her Own Ground: Life and Times of Madam C. J. Walker*. NewYork: Scribbner, 2002.

Chafe, William H. and Raymond Gavins and Robert Korstad. Eds. *Remembering Jim Crow: African Americans Tell About Life in the Segregated South*. New York: The New York Press, 2001.

Clinton, Catherine. *Harriet Tubman: The Road to Freedom*. Boston, Massachusetts: Little, Brown & Company, 2004.

Collins, Patricia Hill. *Black Feminist Thought: Knowledge, Consciousness, and the Politics of Empowerment*. New York: Routledge, 2009.

Cooper, Brittney. *Beyond Respectability: The Intellectual Thought of Race Women. Women, Gender, Sexuality in American History*. Illinois: University of Illinois Press, 2017.

Cooper, William James and Thomas Terrill. *The American South: A History*. McGraw-Hill College Press, 1996.

Crenshaw, Kimberlé, Nell Gotanda, Gary Peller, Kendall Thomas. eds. *Critical Race Theory: The Key Writings That Formed the Movement*. New York: The New Press, 1996.

Crigler, T. W. Jr., and Broox Sledge. Eds. *History of the First Baptist Church 1835–1960, Macon Mississippi*. Montgomery, Alabama: The Paragon Press, 1960.

Cromwell, Adelaide M. *The Other Brahmans: Boston's Black Upper Class 1750–1950*. University of Arkansas Press, 2004.

Dabel, Jane E. *A Respectable Woman: The Public Roles of African American Women in 19th-Century New York*. New York University Press, 2008.

Bibliography

Dandridge, Rita B. *Black Women's Activism: Reading African American Women's Historical Romances.* New York: Peter Lang Publishing, Inc., 2004.

Davidson, James West. *'They Say': Ida B. Wells and the Reconstruction of Race.* Oxford, New York: Oxford University Press, 2009.

Davis, Elizabeth L. Ed. *Lifting as we Climb.* Washington, D.C.: National Association of Colored Women, 1933.

Deutsch, Sarah. *Women and the City: Gender, Space, and Power in Boston, 1870–1940.* Oxford University Press, 2000.

Donaldson, Le'Trice. *Beyond the Battlefield: African American Soldiers Fight for Radical Uplift, Citizenship, and Manhood, 1870–1920.* Illinois: Southern Illinois University, 2020.

Doyle, Don. H. *New Men, New City, New South Atlanta, Nashville Charleston, Mobile, 1860–1910.* University of Nashville Press, 1990.

Dray, Phillip. *At The Hands of Persons Unknown: The Lynching of Black America.* New York: Random House Inc., 2002.

Du Bois, W. E. B and David Levering Lewis. *Black Reconstruction in America, 1860–1880.* New York: Atheneum, 1992.

Eiselein, Gregory and Anne K. Phillips. Eds. *The Louisa May Alcott Encyclopedia.* Westport, Connecticut: Greenwood Press, 2001.

Engs, Robert Francis. *Freedom's First Generation: Black Hampton, Virginia, 1861–90.* University Press of Pennsylvania, 1979.

———. *Educating the Disfranchised and Disinherited: Samual Chapman Armstrong and Hampton Institute, 1839–1893.* University of Tennessee Press, 1999.

Esedebe, P. Olisanwuche. *Pan-Africanism: The Idea and Movement, 1776–1991.* Howard University Press, 1994.

———. *Pan-African Connection: From Slavery to Garvey and Beyond.* Dover: Majority Press, 1984.

Falk, William. *Rooted in Place: Family and Belonging in a Southern Black Community.* Rutgers University Press, 2004.

Feldman, Lynne. *A Sense of Place: Birmingham's Black Middle-Class Community, 1890–1930.* Tuscaloosa and London: The University of Alabama Press, 1999.

Fierce, Milfred C. *The Pan-African Idea in the United States 1900–1919.* New York: Garland Publishing, 1993.

Foner, Eric. *A Short History of Reconstruction: 1863–1877.* New York: Harper & Row Publishers, 1990.

Fradin, Dennis B. and Judith B. Fradin. *Ida B. Wells: Mother of the Civil Rights Movement.* Houghton Mifflin Harcourt, 2000.

Fraizer, E Franklin. *Black Bourgeoisie: The Rise of A New Middle Class in the United States.* New York: The Free Press, 1957.

Franciosi, Robert J. *The Rise and Fall of American Public Schools: The Political Economy of Public Education in the Twentieth Century.* Westport, Connecticut: Praeger Publishers, 2004.

Frankel, Noralee. *Freedom's Women: Black Women and Families in Civil War Era Mississippi.* Bloomington: Indiana University Press, 1999.

Franklin, John Hope. *From Slavery to Freedom: A History of Negro Americans.* New York: Knopf, 1988.

Gaines, Kevin. *Uplifting the Race: Black Leadership, Politics, and Culture in the Twentieth Century.* The University of North Carolina Press, 1996.

Gatewood, Willard B. *Aristocrats of Color: The Black Elite, 1880–1920.* Fayetteville, Arkansas: University of Arkansas Press, 2000.

Gebhard, Caroline. "Bess Bolden Walcott: A Legacy of Women's Leadership at Tuskegee Institute." In Susan Youngbood Ashmore and Linquist Dorr. *Alabama Women: Their Lives and Times.* Athens: University of Georgia Press, 2017.

Giddings, Paula. *When and Where I Enter: The Impact of Black Women on Race and Sex in America.* New York: HarperCollins, 1984.

———. *In Search of Sisterhood: Delta Sigma Theta and the Challenge of the Challenge of the Black Sorority Movement.* New York: HarperCollins, 1988.

———. *Ida: A Sword Among Lions: Ida B. Wells and the Campaign Against Lynching.* HarperCollins Publishers, 2008.

Goggin, Jacqueline. *A Life in Black History: Cater G. Woodson.* Baton Rouge and London: Louisiana State University Press, 1993.

Goings, Kenneth W. *Mammy and Uncle Mose: Black Collectables in American.* Bloomington: Indiana University Press, 1994.

Grant, Colin. *Negro With A Hat: The Rise and Fall of Marcus Garvey.* Oxford University Press, 2008.

Gutman, Herbert. *The Black Family in Slavery and Freedom, 1750–1925.* Random House, 1976.

Harlan, Louis R. *Booker T. Washington: Making of a Black Leader, 1856–1900.* Oxford, New York: Oxford University Press, 1980.

———. *Booker T. Washington Wizard of Tuskegee, 1901–1915.* Oxford, New York: Oxford University Press, 1983.

Harris, Sheena. "Margaret Murray Washington: A Southern Reformer and the Black Women's Club Movement." In Susan Youngbood Ashmore and Linquist Dorr. *Alabama Women: Their Lives and Times.* Athens: University of Georgia Press, 2017.

Hine, Darlene Clark, William C. Hine and Stanley Harrold. *The African American Odyssey: Since 1865*. Vol. 2. Upper Saddle River, New Jersey: Pearson Education Inc., 2006.

———, and Kathleen Thompson. *A Shining Thread of Hope: The History of Black Women in America*. New York: Broadway Books, 1998.

———. Elsa Barkley Brown, & Rosalyn Terborg-Penn. Eds. *Black Women In America: An Historical Encyclopedia*. 2 Vols. Bloomington: Indiana University Press, 1994.

———. et. al., *Black Women in United States History*. Vols. 1–16. Brooklyn, New York: Carlson Publishing Series, 1990.

Holt, Thomas. "The Lonely Warrior: Ida B. Wells-Barnett and The Struggle for Black Leadership." In *Black Leaders of the Twentieth Century*. Ed. by John H. Franklin & August Meier. Urbana: University of Illinois Press, 1982.

Horne, Gerald. *Race Woman: The Lives of Shirley Graham DuBois*. New York: New York University Press.

Huggins, Nathan Irvin. *Harlem Renaissance*. Oxford University Press, 1971, 2007.

Hunter, Tera W. *To 'Joy My Freedom: Southern Black Women's Lives and Labor after the Civil War*. Cambridge: Harvard University Press, 1997.

Jackson, David H. Jr. *A Chief Lieutenant of the Tuskegee Machine: Charles Banks of Mississippi*. Gainesville: University Press of Florida, 2002.

———. *Booker T. Washington and the Struggle Against White Supremacy: The Southern Educational Tours, 1908–1912*. Palgrave MacMillan, 2008.

———. "Booker T. Washington's Tour of the Sunshine State, March 1912." In *Go Sound the Trumpet!: Selections in Florida's African American History*. Ed. by David H. Jackson, Jr. and Canter Brown, Jr. Tampa: University of Tampa Press, 2005.

Jones, Jacqueline. *Labor of Love Labor of Sorrow: Black Women, Work and the Family, from Slavery to the Present*. New York: Basic Books, 1985.

Jones, Martha S. *"All Bound Up Together": The "Woman Question" in African American Public Culture, 1830–1900*. Chapel Hill: University of North Carolina Press, 2007.

King, Wilma. *The Essence of Liberty: Free Black Women during the Slave Era*. Columbia and London: The University of Missouri Press, 2006.

Kornweibel, Theodore Jr. "Investigate Everything: Federal Efforts to Ensure Black Loyalty during World War I. Bloomington: Indiana University Press, 2002.

Lamon, Lester C. *Black Tennesseans 1900–1930*. Knoxville: The University of Tennessee Press, 1977.

Lee, Chana Kai. *For Freedom's Sake: The Life of Fannie Lou Hamer*. Urban and Chicago: University of Illinois Press, 1999.

Leloudis, James L. *Schooling the New South: Pedagogy, Self and Society in North Carolina, 1880–1920*. The University of North Carolina Press: Chapel Hill & London, 1996.

Lentz-Smith, Adriane. *Freedom Struggles: African Americans and World War I*. Harvard University Press, 2010.

Lerner, Gerda. *Black Women in White America: A Documentary History*. Random House, 1972.

Lewis, David Levering. *W.E B. Du Bois: Biography of Race 1868–1919*. New York: Henry Holt and Company, 1993.

———. *W.E.B. Du Bois: The Fight For Equality And The American Century 1919–1963*. New York: Henry Holt And Company, 2000.

Litwak, Leon F. *Trouble in Mind: Black Southerners in the Age of Jim Crow*. New York: Vantage Books, 1999.

———. *Been in the Storm So Long: The Aftermath of Slavery*. New York: Alfred A Knopf, 1979.

Loewenberg, Bert James and Ruth Bogin. Eds. *Black Women in Nineteenth-Century American Life: Their Words, Their Thoughts, Their Feelings*. Pennsylvania State University Press, 1976.

Logan, Rayford. *The Negro in American Life and Thought: The Nadir 1877–1901*. Dial Press, 1954.

Logan, Shirley Wilson, *"We Are Coming:" The Persuasive Discourse of Nineteenth-Century Black Women*. Carbondale and Edwardsville: Southern Illinois University Press, 1999.

Lovett, Bobby L. *The African American History of Nashville, Tennessee, 1780–1930*. Fayetteville: The University of Arkansas Press, 1999.

Lutz, Christine. "Addie W. Hunton: Crusader for Pan-Africanism and Peace." In *Portraits of African American Life Since 1865*. Ed. by Nina Mjagkij. Wilmington, Delaware: A Scholarly Resources Inc., 2003.

Marable, Manning. *Malcolm X: A Life of Reinvention*. New York, Viking Penguin Publishing, 2011.

Marable, Manning and Leith Mullings. Eds. *Let Nobody Turn us Around: an African American anthology: Voices of Resistance, Reform, and Renewal*. Rownan & Littlefield Publishers, Inc., 2009.

McMillen, Neil R. *Dark Journey: Black Mississippians in the Age of Jim Crow*. Urbana: University of Illinois Press, 1989.

McMurray, Linda O. *To Keep the Waters Troubled: The Life of Ida B. Wells.* Oxford University Press, 1998.
Meir, August and Elliott Rudwick. *Along the Color Line: Exploration in the Black Experience.* University of Illinois Press, 1976.
Moore, Jacqueline M. "Anna Julia Cooper: Educator, Clubwoman, and Feminist." In *Portraits of African American Life Since 1865.* Ed. by Nina Mjagkij. Wilmington, Delaware: A Scholarly Resources Inc., 2003.
Mossell, N. F. *The Work of the African American Woman.* Oxford University Press, 1988.
Muhammad, Khalil Gibran. *The Condemnation of Blackness: Race, Crime, and the Making of Modern Urban America.* Harvard University Press, 2010.
Neverdon-Morton, Cynthia. *Afro-American Women of the South and the Advancement of the Race, 1895-1925.* Knoxville: University of Tennessee Press, 1989.
Norrell J., Robert. *Up From History: The Life of Booker T. Washington.* Cambridge: The Belknap Press of Harvard University Press, 2009.
Oshinsky, David M. *"Worse Than Slavery:" Parchman Farm and the Ordeal of Jim Crow Justice.* New York: The Free Press, 1996.
Painter, Nell I. *Creating Black Americans: African American History and its Meaning 1619 to the Present.* New York: Oxford University Press, 2007.
Painter, Nell Irvin. *Sojourner Truth: A Life, A Symbol.* New York and London: W. W. Norton and Company, 1996.
———. *Exodusters: Black Migration to Kansas after Reconstruction.* New York: W.W. Norton & Company, 1976, 1986, 1992.
Patterson, Orlando. *Rituals of Blood: Consequences of Slavery in Two American Centuries.* New York: Basic Civities Inc., 1998.
Patterson, Martha H. *Beyond the Gibson Girl: Reimagining the American New Women 1895–1915.* Chicago: University of Illinois Press, 2005.
Pruitt, Bernadette. "Margaret Murray Washington." In *African American Lives.* Ed. by Henry Louis Gates Jr., & Evelyn Brooks Higginbotham. New York: Oxford University Press, 2004.
Quigley, Joan. *Just Another Southern Town: Mary Church Terrell and the Stuggle for Racial Justice.* Oxford University Press, 2015.
Ransby, Barbara. *Ella Baker and the Black Freedom Movement: A Democratic Movement.* Chapel Hill & London: The University of North Carolina Press, 2003
Reed, Adolph L. *W. E. B. Du Bois and American Political Thought: Fabianism and the Color Line.* Oxford University Press, 1999.

Richardson, Joe M. *A History of Fisk University 1865–1946*. Tuscaloosa, Alabama: University of Alabama Press, 1980.

———. *Christian Reconstruction: The American Missionary Association and Southern Blacks, 1861–1890*. Athens: The University of Georgia Press, 1986.

Ritterhouse, Jennifer. *Growing up Jim Crow: How Black and White Southern Children Learned Race*. North Carolina: The University of North Carolina Press, 2006.

Robinson, Ashley. *Mary McLeod Bethune in Florida: Bringing Social Justice to the Sunshine State*. South Carolina: The History Press, 2015.

Rosen, Ruth. *The World Split Open: How Modern Women's Movement Changed America*. Viking / Peruiun Press, 2000.

Roth, Darlene R. "Matronage: Patterns in Women's Organizations, Atlanta, Georgia, 1890–1940.' In Gerda Lerner ed., *Scholarship in Women's History: Rediscovered and New*. Brooklyn, New York: Carlson Publishing Inc, 1994.

Rouse, Jacqueline Anne. *Lugenia Burns Hope: Black Southern Reformer*. Athens: The University of Georgia Press, 1989.

Samito, Christian G. *Becoming American Under Fire: Irish Americans, African Americans, and the Politics of Citizenship During the Civil War Era*. London: Cornell University Press, 2009.

Sernett, Milton C. *Bound for the Promised Land: African American Religion and the Great Migration*. Duke University Press, 1997.

Shaw, Stephanie, J. *What a Women Ought to Be and to Do: Black Professional Women Workers During the Jim Crow Era*. Chicago: The University of Chicago Press, 1996.

Smith, Susan L. *Sick and Tired of Being Sick and Tired: Black Women's Health Activism in America, 1890–1950*. Philadelphia: University of Pennsylvania Press, 1995.

Smock, Raymond W. *Booker T. Washington: Black Leadership in the Age of Jim Crow*. Ivan R. Dee Press, 2009.

Spain, Daphne. *How Women Saved the City*. University of Minnesota Press, 2002.

Sterling, Dorothy, *We Are Your Sisters: Black Women in the Nineteenth Century*. New York and London: W. W. Norton & Company, 1984.

Talty, Stephan. *Mulatto America at the Crossroads of Black and White Culture: A Social History*. New York: HarperCollins Publishers, 2003.

Taylor, Ula Yvette. *The Veiled Garvey: The Life and Times of Amy Jacques*

Garvey. Chapel Hill and London: The University of North Carolina Press, 2002.

Thomas, Audrey. *A Forgotten Sisterhood: Pioneering Black Women Educators and Activists in the Jim Crow South*. Lanham, Maryland: Rowman & Littlefield publishing Inc., 2015.

Thomas, Mary Martha. *The New Woman in Alabama: Social Reforms and Suffrag, 1890–1920*. The University of Alabama Press, 1992.

Thompson, Kathleen. "Margaret Murray Washington (1865-1925)." In *Black Women in America: An Historical Encyclopedia*. Ed. by Darlene Clark Hine, Elsa Barkley Brown, & Rosalyn Terborg-Penn. Vol. 2. Bloomington: Indiana University Press, 1993.

Watson, Steven. *The Harlem Renaissance: Hub of African American Culture, 1920–1930*. New York: Pantheon, 1995.

Wesley, Charles Harris. *The History of the National Association of Colored Women's Clubs: A Legacy of Service*. Washington, D.C.: Mercury Press, 1984.

Wharton, Vernon L. *The Negro in Mississippi, 1865–1890*. New York: Harper & Row Publishers, 1965.

White, Deborah G. *Ar'n't I a Woman: Female Slaves in The Plantation South*. New York & London: W. W. Norton & Company, 1985.

———. *Too Heavy a Load: Black Women in Defense of Themselves 1894–1994*. New York: W. W. Norton & Company, Inc., 1999.

Wideman, John E. *My Soul has Grown Deep: Classics of Early African American Literature*. Philadelphia, London: Running Press, 2001.

Williams, Chad. *Torchbearers of Democracy: African American Soldiers in the World War I Era*. North Carolina: University of North Carolina Press, 2010.

Williamson, Joel. *New People: Miscegenation and Mulattoes in the United States*. New York: The Free Press, 1980.

Wise, Tim. *White Like Me: Reflections on Race from a Privileged Son*. Berkeley, California: Soft Skull Press, 2008.

Woloch, Nancy. *Women and the American Experience*. New York: McGraw Hill Inc., 2006.

Woodson, Carter G. *The Education of the Negro prior to 1861*. Washington, D.C.: Associated Publishers, 1919. Reprint, New York: A&B Publishers, 1999.

Woodward, C. Vann. *The Strange Career of Jim Crow*. Oxford University Press, 2002.

Articles and Journal Entries

Currie, James T. "From Slavery to Freedom in Mississippi's Legal System." *The Journal of Negro History*. Vol. 65, No. 2 (Spring, 1980): 112–25.

Gatewood, Willard B. Jr. "Aristocrat of Color: South and North Black Elite, 1880–1920." *The Journal of Southern History*. Vol. 54, No. 1 (Feb., 1988): 3–20.

Jones, Beverly W. "Mary Church Terrell and the National Association of Colored Women, 1896 to 1901." *The Journal of Negro History*. Vol. 67, No. 1. (Spring, 1982): 20–33.

Lerner, Gerda. "Early Community Work of Black Women." *The Journal of Negro History*. Vol. 59, No. 2. (April, 1974): 158–67.

Plummer, Brenda Gayle. "The Afro-American Response to the occupation in Haiti, 1915–1934." *Phylon*, 43, no. 2 .2nd Quarter, 1982.

Rouse, A. Jacqueline. "Out of the Shadow of Tuskegee: Margaret Murray Washington, Social Activism, and Race Vindication." *Journal of Negro History*. Vol. 81, No. 1/4 (Winter-Autumn, 1996): 31–46.

Dissertations

Graham, Saundra Jean. "The Fisk Jubilee Singers and the Concert Spiritual: The Beginning of an American Tradition." Ph.D. dissertation. New York University, 2001.

Gray, Laura Lynn. "Women and the American Interracial Movement: A Rhetorical Analysis." Ph.D. dissertation. Texas Women's University, 2002.

Jardins, Julie Des. "Reclaiming the Past: Women, Gender, Race and the Construction of Historical Memory in America, 1880–1940." Ph.D. dissertation. Brown University, 2000.

Patterson, Martha Helen. "'Survival of the best fitted': The trope of the new woman in Margaret Murray Washington, Pauline Hopkins, Sui Sin Far, Edith Wharton and Mary Johnston, 1895–1914." Ph.D. dissertation. The University of Iowa, 1996.

Rief, Michelle M. "'Banded Close Together': An Afrocentric Study of African American Women's International Activism, 1850–1940, and the International Council of Women of the Darker Races." Ph.D. dissertation. Temple University, 2003.

Index

accommodationism, 55, 147
Adams, Charles P., 65
Adams, Lewis, 30
Addams, Jane, 82
Adi, Hakim, 133
African diaspora, 129, 133–34, 139, 141, 144–45
Alabama Federation of Colored Women's Clubs, 9, 100, 112–14, 116
Alabama Women's Hall of Fame, 1
Ali, Dusé Mohamed, 134
Amito, Christian G., 13
Anthony, Susan B., 46, 132
Armstrong, Samuel Chapman, 30, 31
Ashwood, Amy, 134
Atlanta Neighborhood of Hope, 88

Ballantine, Anna Thankful, 33
Banks, Charles, 57, 127
Banks, Trenna, 57
Barrett, Janie Porter, 84–85, 144–45
Barrows, Isabel, 47
Belgarnie, Florence, 103
Benson, Elizabeth, 67
Bentley, George, 18
Berry, Mary Frances, 17
Bethune, Mary McLeod, 3, 7, 48, 109, 136, 138

black elites, 6–7, 28, 31, 32–33, 39–40, 43, 45–51, 63, 81, 104, 112, 169n59, 169n61, 176n8; character building and, 66; in women's clubs, 86–87, 119, 143, 151. *See also* Talented Tenth
black women, stereotypes about, 67, 69, 84, 102–3
Black Women's Club Movement, 1, 2, 4, 8–9, 10, 29, 49–50, 81–82, 91, 99–101, 135; opposition to, 102; tensions within, 140–44. *See also specific organizations*
Blackwell, Henry Brown, 105
Booth, Harriette, 123
Borno, Louis, 141
Bowen, Cornelia, 3, 8, 84, 90–91, 109, 112–13, 115
Boyd, Gwendolyn, 3
Brown, Hallie Quinn, 41, 43, 60
Brown, Henry, 15
Brown, Steven, 137
Bruce, Blanche K., 12, 39–40, 63, 171n26
Bruce, Josephine Beall Willson, 39–40, 41, 57, 62–63, 104, 109; background of, 43, 166n31, 168n53; NACW and, 124–25, 132; skin color of, 165n16
Bruce, Roscoe Conkling, 63, 71

205

Burroughs, Irene, 68–69
Burroughs, Nannie, 136, 139, 140, 141

Campbell, George Washington, 30
Carnegie, Andrew, 44, 70
Carver, George Washington, 60
Cheney, Ednah, 97
Chicago Women's Club, 101
citizenship rights, 2, 5, 29, 54, 86, 97, 103; birthdays and, 92–93; World War I and, 129
civil rights movement, 3, 57, 153
Clarke, Georgina, 15
Clemmings, Rafe, 129
Clifford, Carrie, 132
Colored Women's League, 41, 61, 103–4, 105, 106–7, 125, 178n20
convict lease program, 88, 116
Cook, Coralie Franklin, 132
Cook, Helen A., 104, 178n20
Cooper, Anna Julia, 104, 118
Cotton, Joseph, 15, 159n15
Cotton States and International Exposition, 42, 85, 105–6
country women, 113
Cravath, Erastus M., 19–20, 21
Crenshaw, Kimberlé, 32, 157n11
Cunningham, Julia, 57

Davidson, Olivia America, 6, 27–28, 34–35, 38, 54
Davis, Anne, 90
Dickerson, Addie W., 136, 139
Dillon, Hallie Tanner, 35
Douglass, Frederick, 6, 42, 61, 114, 127, 138
Douglass, Rosetta, 107
Dred Scott case, 5
Du Bois, W. E. B., 5, 26, 43, 56, 92, 132; background of, 23–24, 162n49

Ednah Cheney Club, 97
education. *See* industrial education; *and under* Washington, Margaret Murray
Elizabeth Russell Plantation, 86, 87–93
Emerson, Ralph Waldo, quoted, 99
Esedebe, P. Olisanwuche, 131

First National Conference of the Colored Women of America, 104–5
Fisk University, 5–6, 11, 18, 19–27, 31–32, 33, 60, 69–70, 164n11
Fortune, T. Thomas, 105
Foster, Luther Hilton, Jr., 155n3
Francis, Nellie F., 96, 165n19
Franks, Dora, 12
Frazier, E. Franklin, 46
Freedmen's Bureau, 18, 19–20

Garrison, Francis Jackson and Theresa Holmes, 45–46
Garrison, William Lloyd, 46, 105
Garvey, Amy Jacques, 4, 143–44
Garvey, Marcus, 4, 131, 134
Gaston, Minnie L., 1–2
Gatewood, Willard B., 86, 164n14, 165n16
General Federation of Women's Clubs, 101, 124
Giddings, Paula J., 26
Graham, Lawrence Otis, 62
Great Migration, 130, 131
Greene, Devotion, 66, 69
Greener, Richard T., 106
Gregory, William, 54
Guzman, Jessie, 49

Haiti, 10, 139–41, 145
Hall, Mrs. George C., 48
Hamer, Fannie Lou, 16
Hampton Institute, 27, 31, 34, 54, 84
Harlan, Louis, 42, 44, 59–60, 184n103

Harlem Renaissance, 131
Harper, Frances, 95, 96
Hayford, Adelaide Casely, 138
Hine, Darlene Clarke, 7
Historically Black Colleges and Universities (HBCUs), 2, 7, 26, 30, 50, 70
Holly, Theodora, 141
home economics. See industrial education; Washington, Margaret Murray: home focus
Hope, Lugenia Burns, 56–57, 88, 136, 138
Howard, Oliver Otis, 18
Howard University, 18, 63
Hunton, Addie W., 9, 113, 114, 132, 135–36, 142

industrial education, 4, 21, 25–26, 31–32, 43, 46–47, 53–57, 60; Domestic Sciences, 64–65; Terrell on, 109–10
International Council of Women, 132, 135
International Council of Women of the Darker Races (ICWDR), 10, 131–45; officers of, 135–36
intersectionality, 2, 4, 8, 10, 32, 135, 157n11

Jacks, John W., 103, 104, 120
Jackson, David H., 55
Jenkins, William, 27
Jim Crow, 11–12, 24, 25, 39, 50–51, 55, 82, 85, 93, 101, 119
Journal of Negro History, 126

Kenney, John A., 93
King, Martin Luther, Jr., 128
Kitchelt, Florence Ledyard Cross, 33
Ku Klux Klan, 129, 131

Lane, Elizabeth E., 85
Lane, Linda Rochell, 3

Lattimore, Florence, 85
Locke, Alain, 130
Logan, Adella Hunt, 85, 97, 109, 122
Lynch, John R., 12
lynching, 55, 103, 118, 119, 130

Marshall, James Fowle Baldwin, 54
Martin, Tony, 133
Mason, Rosa, 34
Matthews, Victoria Earle, 104–5, 108
McClusky, Audrey Thomas, 7
McCrorey, Mary Jackson, 133, 134, 138, 140
McMillen, Neil, 25
Merry, Austin Raymond, 22, 162n42
metalanguage of race, 55, 170n8
Miller, Lucile U., 48
Moore, Mary, 35
Morehouse, Henry L., 24, 25
Morgan, Gertrude Wright, 132
Mothers' Meetings, 4, 8, 49, 81–85, 121, 122
Moton, Jennie B., 14, 57, 109, 144, 146, 150, 152
Moton, Robert Russa, 57, 58, 64, 111, 139
Moynihan Report, 153
Mt. Meigs Reformatory for Boys, 8, 90–91, 115–17
Mt. Zion School, 54
mulattoes, 33, 45, 159n14
Murray, James, 4, 11–13, 16, 25, 160n23
Murray, Laura, 14, 16, 37–38, 89, 146
Murray, Lucy, 4, 5, 6, 8, 11–16, 19, 37, 62, 158n9
Murray, Thomas, 16, 37, 89
Murray, Willis, 14

National Association for the Advancement of Colored People (NAACP), 24, 70, 109, 126

National Association of Colored Women (NACW), 9, 61, 98, 99–100, 109–12, 114–15, 117–18, 124–26, 128; departments of, 121–22, 125; founding of, 107–8; NACW and, 132; NCW and, 124–25
National Council of Negro Women, 1
National Council of Women (NCW), 124–25
National Federation of Afro-American Women (NFAAW), 50, 61, 105–7
National Federation of Colored Women's Clubs, 9, 128
National Negro Business League, 106, 111
National Notes, 9–10, 110, 111, 132
National Urban League, 126
"Negro problem," 24–25, 42, 148, 151
Neighborhood Union, 57
New England Women's Club, 101
New Era Club, 103, 110, 124
New Negro concept, 130
New Negro woman concept, 10, 130, 134–35, 182n72
New South concept, 25
Niagara Movement, 24, 132
Norrell, Robert, 40, 48

Ogden, John, 19–20
O'Neal, Emmett J., 116
Oshinsky, David, 88

Paige, Leroy "Satchel," 117
Palmer, Mrs. J. H., 95–96
Pan-Africanism, 4, 10, 23, 130, 131–35
Peabody, Geoge Foster, 126
Pittman, William Sidney, 48
Plessy v. Ferguson, 5, 92
Porter, Susan Helen, 85

"positive propaganda," 4, 5, 72
prison reform, 115, 118, 120
public transportation discrimination, 121–22

Quigley, Joan, 3

race pride, 60–61, 117
racial uplift, 7, 10, 19, 32, 36, 50, 64, 82, 145–46, 148; industrial training and, 56, 65; international scope of, 135; stress of, 84–85; Tuskegee and, 30, 69, 71, 72
racism, 5, 12–14, 17, 20–21, 103, 135; scientific racism, 101. *See also* Jim Crow
Randolph, A. Philip, 129
respectability politics, 5, 17, 33, 36, 39, 46, 53, 58–59, 65–67, 69, 89, 120–21; clothing and, 67, 82, 92, 126; farmers and, 83; source of, 157n11
Revels, Hiram, 12
Richardson, Joe M., 21, 23, 55, 70
Robertson, Ashley, 3
Roosevelt, Theodore, 42–43
Rosenwald, Julius, 71
Rouse, Jacqueline Anne, 3
Ruffin, Josephine St. Pierre, 29, 50, 101, 103, 104–5, 110; "Ruffin Incident," 124
Ruffner, Viola Knapp, 40, 48

Saunders family, 15–17
Scipio, L. Albert, II, 54
Scott, Emmett J., 14, 15–16, 23, 57, 69, 71–72, 127, 129
segregation, 12, 25, 42, 51, 55, 109; legalization of, 121
Shadd, Mary Ann, 40
Sherwood, Marika, 133
Simmons, Roscoe Conklin, 130
skin color bias, 32–33, 164n14, 165n16, 176n8

slavery, 4–5, 11–12, 17–18, 24, 39, 151, 158n12; literacy and, 160n27
Smith, Christine, 144
Smith, Edward P., 19–20
Smith, Fanny Norton, 6, 27, 34
Southern Federation of Colored Women's Clubs, 9, 100, 113–14
Starr, Ellen Gates, 82
Stoddard, Lothrop, 137
suffrage movement, 96–97, 106, 122–23; Nineteenth Amendment and, 131
superwoman myth, 84
Sutton, Jane, 159

Talbert, Mary B., 136, 142
Talented Tenth, 24, 25
Talty, Stephan, 13
Taylor, Ula Yvette, 4, 144
temperance movement, 95–96, 100–101
Terrell, Mary Church, 3, 22, 45, 46, 55, 61, 87, 104, 106, 109–10, 112, 132, 140; background of, 108–9; touchiness of, 142–43
Terry, Emma James, 26
Thurman, Howard, 82
toxic masculinity, 5, 13, 58, 101
Trotter, William Monroe, 132
Truth, Sojourner, 107, 112, 138
Tubman, Harriett, 107
Tuskegee Institute (now University): Carnegie donation to, 44; Executive Council at, 65–66, 68, 71; founding of, 30, 54, 175n27; gender relations at, 57–58; Girls Industry at, 64, 69, 70; Greenwood community at, 44–45; Josephine Bruce at, 62–63; negative press on, 71–72; teachers' wages at, 62, 70–71; Vesta club at, 97; Washington's legacy at, 152–53. See also under Washington, Booker T.; Washington, Margaret Murray
Tuskegee Machine, 8, 9, 72, 110, 118, 135, 152
Tuskegee Negro Conference, 82–83
Tuskegee Woman's Club (TWC), 8–9, 49–50, 57, 81, 85–98, 100, 101, 103, 110, 128, 143; departments of, 86, 122; Jail division of, 93–94; as model for other clubs, 113; Thompson's Quarters Department of, 94–95

Ulrich, Henry, 119
Universal Negro Improvement Association (UNIA), 131, 134

vocational training. See industrial education
Voice of the Negro, 112, 113

Walcott, Bess Bolden, 8, 60
Walker, Madam C. J., 70
Washington, Booker T., 6, 9, 40–43, 48–49, 50, 118, 123, 124; Atlanta Compromise speech of, 42, 85, 105–6, 112; background of, 31; beating of, 119; death of, 10, 70, 126–27; Du Bois and, 24; earlier wives of, 6, 27, 34–35, 164n14; Garvey and, 134; National Negro Business League and, 106, 111; negative press and, 71–72; Pan-Africanism and, 133–34; Tuskegee Institute and, 27–28, 30–31, 34, 43, 54, 62, 70–71, 127; Tuskegee Negro Conference and, 82–83; Woodson and, 61. See also Washington, Margaret Murray: married life
Washington, Booker T., Jr. (Baker), 34–35, 36, 38, 47
Washington, Ernest Davidson, 6, 34–35, 36, 38, 47

Index

Washington, Josephine, 8, 115
Washington, Margaret Murray:
  appearance, 33, 47, 67; birth
  and early life, 2, 4–5, 8, 11–19,
  37, 156n10; club work, 4, 8–9,
  49–50, 81–98, 99–128, 131–45,
  149–50; death of, 146; Delta
  Sigma Theta Sorority, 152;
  education and early teaching
  career, 5–6, 11, 17, 19–28, 31–32,
  138, 161n31; flaws, 151; health
  issues, 23, 61, 87, 126, 139; home
  focus, 6, 8, 11, 29, 34, 38, 44–45,
  47, 49, 56, 64, 89, 153; influence
  and legacy, 1–2, 10, 147–53;
  international outlook, 131, 132,
  134–35, 185n13; journalism,
  5–6, 9, 24–25, 53, 110, 111;
  literary interests, 48; loneliness,
  61–62; married life, 2–4, 6–7, 10,
  26–27, 35–41, 45–48, 61–62, 118,
  127–28, 134; Oaks residence,
  The, 47–49, 127; posthumous
  awards and honors, 1; Quaker
  background, 5, 6, 15–16, 18, 19,
  36, 39, 40, 124; scholarship on,
  3; silence and secrecy, 4; social
  work stress, 84, 85; South focus,
  148–50, 151–52, 163n2; suffrage
  issue, 122–23; travels, 36, 41,
  45–46, 62, 127, 132, 134, 168n45;
  Tuskegee career, 2, 4, 6, 9, 27–
  28, 31–34, 40, 43, 53–72, 89, 98,
  139, 149
Washington, Margaret Murray,
  speeches and writings: "Gain
  of the Life of a Negro Woman,
  The," 44; "Individual Work for
  Moral Elevation," 105; "National
  Association of Colored Women's
  Clubs," 119–20; "Negro Home,
  The," 11, 29, 53, 81, 99, 129, 147;
  "Training Our Girls for the Re-
  spectability of Life," 36, 49, 102;
"We Must Have a Cleaner Social
  Morality," 63–64
Washington, Mrs. James B., 85
Washington, Portia Marshall, 6, 27,
  34, 36, 38, 46–47; wedding of, 48
Wells-Barnett, Ida B., 9–10, 24, 38,
  50, 72, 103, 104; background
  of, 58–59; *National Notes* and,
  111–12, 136; railroad suit, 121
White, Deborah Gray, 142–43
White, George L., 21
white supremacy, 26, 82–83, 101,
  134, 145, 148–49, 151
Whittaker, John W., 89, 102
Wilkerson, Marion, 140
Williams, Emily, 136, 140–41
Williams, Fannie Barrier, 101,
  103, 110
Williams, William T. B., 139–40
Williamson, Joel, 45
Willson, Joseph, 166n31, 167n39
Wilson, Woodrow, 129
Woloch, Nancy, 100–101
Woman's Era, 104, 110, 180n39
Women's Christian Temperance
  Union (WCTU), 95, 96, 100
Woodson, Carter G., 60–61, 125,
  126, 137, 138, 145
Work, Monroe Nathan, 119
World War I, black soldiers and, 10,
  129–31

Yates, Josephine Silone, 104, 115, 132